D1483619

THE SPELLING CONNECTION

The Spelling Connection

Integrating Reading, Writing, and Spelling Instruction

Ronald L. Cramer

THE GUILFORD PRESS
New York   London

Printed in the United States of America

This book is printed on acid-free paper.

Last digit is print number: 9   8   7   6   5   4   3   2   1

Library of Congress Cataloging-in-Publication Data

Cramer, Ronald L.
    The spelling connection: integrating reading, writing, and
spelling instruction / Ronald L. Cramer.
        p. cm.
    Includes bibliographical references and index.
    ISBN 1-57230-328-X (hardcover : alk. paper). —ISBN
1-57230-329-8
    (pbk. : alk. paper)
    1. English language—Orthography and spelling—Study and teaching
(Elementary) 2. English language—Composition and exercises—Study
and teaching (Elementary) 3. Language arts (Elementary) I. Title.
    LB1574.C65   1998
372.63—dc21   97-47395
                                                               CIP

Photographs in the book courtesy of Gerry Palmer.

For Amy, Jen, Ben
and Karen;
my colleagues and students at
Oakland University;
and
Russell Stauffer,
Edmund H. Henderson, and
W. Dorsey Hammond

Preface

I'm finally ready to do what Winston Churchill said happens after you've gotten beyond the early euphoric stage of book writing. I'm ready to "kill the monster and fling [it] to the public." The public that interests me is teachers. I'm a teacher, although I'm sometimes described as an "Ivory Tower" teacher because I practice my profession in a university setting. But we have this in common: We aspire to be good teachers.

What does it mean to be a good teacher? Nearly anyone can inform students, but it takes a good teacher to transform them. This task requires moral strength, self-discipline, kindness—in short, character. It also requires knowledge of our subject and a keen interest in learning. It is our *duty* to enlarge the academic potential that our students possess; it is our *privilege* to nourish their less heralded potentials. It is also our privilege to console the lonely student, to accept the unconventional student, to summon the creative spirit from its cloisters. The teacher who accepts these challenges as a privilege rather than a duty has a gift to offer his or her students: the gift of character, a quality all but ignored in our relentless pursuit of more and more instructional strategies.

Good teachers are artists, working not with inert paint and clay but with human flesh and bone and the malleable fabric of the mind. Like all good artists, they dream of perfection even though they know that perfection is not possible. Robert Browning expressed the human desire to seek perfection in these words: "Ah, but a man's reach should exceed his grasp, / Or what's a heaven for?" Like Robert Browning, I believe our dreams should exceed the likelihood of their fulfillment. Like William Faulkner, I think such dreams are healthy. Faulkner spoke of the artist's failure to match his work to his dreams: "he believes each time that this time he will do it, bring it off. Of course, he won't, which is why the condition is healthy."

Good teachers are language mavens. They challenge their students to use their inherent language power. Teaching has its simple pleasures—mine has always been listening to the language of children, which is perfectly modulated to the strong emotions that drive their discourse. They can express their yearnings eloquently when encouraged to do so. However, some children do not fully use their language power in school settings; the challenge is to invite children's language out of the closet. Good teachers respect children's language; they do not fear its bite. They extol its virtues; they do not malign its imperfect manifestations. Good teachers entice language out of the crevices of the mind so that it may be expressed, spoken or written, in artistic and academic endeavors.

Good teachers are good models. Their task is much like that of adult eagles, who do not teach their fledglings how to fly, but instead provide models of flight and the nourishment needed to strengthen the fledgling's wings. Preparing themselves for flight, fledgling eagles flap their wings in mock flight inches above a secure nest. Once a fledgling takes that courageous first leap out of the aerie into the boundless space, it's on its own. The good teacher nourishes his or her charges, strengthening their wings for independent flight as readers, writers, and spellers.

I've been talking about good teachers and the challenge of good teaching, but I haven't said anything about spelling yet. As a youngster, I sat through my share of spelling bees, that is, literally *sat*, since I seldom survived more than a round or two before taking my seat in semi-disgrace. Even so, most of my classmates enjoyed spelling bees, even those of us who sat down early. I think I know why. Spelling bees are competitive, noisy, gamelike, and involve commotion and movement not normally tolerated in traditional classrooms. Most importantly, spelling bees are not nearly as boring as many other alternatives. Spelling bees are still practiced in schools today, for the same reasons, I suppose. While they are not harmful, they are only marginally related to learning to spell. Competent spelling comes from other sources: reading, writing, and systematic spelling instruction.

Spelling instruction is one part of a larger set of responsibilities that good teachers face. Spelling is important in the context of reading and writing. We learn to spell because we read; we learn to spell so we can write. It is axiomatic that spelling is useful, but not as important as reading and writing. However, the American public thinks spelling is very important, and they assign it far more importance than most educators, perhaps because spelling is such a highly visible expression of literacy. To many Americans, spelling symbolizes literacy. Make a spelling error in a public setting and your level of literacy, even your intelligence, will be called into question. A few years back, when a vice-president of the United

States misspelled *potato,* the inferences drawn were: "not very smart," "not very literate." This was unfair—the correlations are questionable; but the conclusions were drawn, nevertheless.

What is the status of spelling instruction in the United States? The public wants schools to take spelling instruction seriously. The educational community, however, has reservations, not so much about the practical value of spelling instructions, but rather, about how to teach spelling and about its strategic position in the language arts curriculum. This book deals with both issues, presenting the options for how to teach spelling and placing spelling within the matrix of reading and writing.

ABOUT THIS BOOK

Organization

The Spelling Connection has seven chapters:

Chapter 1 concentrates on the beginnings of spelling. It focuses on the foundations of spelling knowledge, including the influence of listening, oral, and written language experiences. The distinguishing features of five stages of spelling growth are described, and developmentally appropriate activities are presented for each stage.

Chapter 2 describes the beginnings of writing. This chapter argues that spelling instruction cannot and should not stand alone; spelling instruction must be accompanied by a vigorous writing program. The chapter begins with a literacy story, describes how to prepare children for independent writing, outlines four early writing stages, and presents seven principles of beginning writing. Strategies for teaching writing are suggested.

Chapter 3 examines issues pertinent to invented spelling. This chapter defines and defends invented spelling, suggests prerequisite knowledge needed to invent spellings, and describes the linguistic features that support it. It is argued that invented spelling influences growth in writing, reading, and spelling. The relationship of invented spelling to learning standard spelling is explored, and suggestions for explaining invented spelling to parents are presented.

Chapter 4 delineates the threads that link reading, writing, and spelling. The chapter argues that writing influences reading; reading influences writing; and reading and writing influence spelling.

Chapter 5 outlines a plan for systematic spelling instruction. Three approaches are described: personalized, cooperative, and textbooks. Spelling principles and conventions are described and criteria for selecting spelling words are presented. Plans for systematic review of words and spelling concepts are presented and strategies for learning to spell are suggested.

Chapter 6 presents ways of assessing spelling knowledge and growth. Case studies illustrate how to assess early spelling knowledge and growth. Procedures for placing children at their appropriate spelling achievement levels are described and illustrated with case study data.

Chapter 7 is organized in a question–answer format. Questions teachers often ask are briefly answered. These questions and answers explore issues that concern teachers as they perform their daily classroom routines.

The appendices in this book derive from spelling error research conducted from 1991 through 1995. The results were originally published by Scott, Foresman and Company in a monograph: *Spelling Research & Information: An Overview of Current Research and Practices*

Purpose and Audience

This book is for teachers and prospective teachers. It deals with instructional issues in practical and theoretical terms, with special emphasis on issues that arise in classrooms where teachers work to integrate reading and writing with spelling. This book provides teachers with a research-based, theoretical orientation for teaching spelling, and it provides the practical strategies needed to implement an effective spelling program within their classrooms or school.

Spelling is important, but it must be acknowledged that it is subordinate in importance to reading and writing. Spelling is the handmaiden of writing; its significance is directly related to its value as a tool of writing. It has no inherent value in and of itself. Spelling knowledge is derived in part from reading and in part from the direct study of words and spelling concepts. When the interrelationships among reading, writing, and spelling are understood and provisions made within classrooms for implementing an integrated approach, the possibilities for improving spelling instruction are present.

Premises

A major premise of this book is that reading, writing, and spelling are closely connected. Consequently, spelling knowledge grows best in an instructional atmosphere that integrates these three components of the language arts. Another major premise of this book is that spelling must be systematically taught. If spelling is not taught, in the vague hope that it will be acquired through reading and writing alone, disappointment is likely. I recognize that some children acquire sufficient spelling knowledge on their own, probably as a result of wide reading and writing experiences. It is obvious, however, that many children do not acquire such knowledge on their own. Extensive research is not needed to discover the truth of this statement. Read the compositions of high school and college students and you will discover that the spelling knowledge of presumptively well-educated students has sunk into the netherworld.

Many students graduate from high school, even college, without a basic spelling vocabulary. It is not merely that they cannot spell challenging multisyllabic words. Rather, it is that many students do not possess a solid core of common English words. Everyday words, such as the following, are misspelled with dismaying frequency: a lot, their, there, believe, friend, weird, favorite, beautiful, restaurant, college, different, too, I'm, maybe.

It may argued that poor spelling is not a new phenomenon, but that is no excuse to continue in this fashion. It is time to take on the spelling challenge. There is a wrong and a right way to teach spelling. The argument of this book is that the right way involves integrating reading, writing, and spelling instruction.

Acknowledgments

Three colleagues have influenced my academic life. I studied under Russell Stauffer and Edmund Henderson. They were consummate teachers, generous mentors, close friends. In their respective professional interests, they were far ahead of the times in which they lived. I conducted my dissertation under their direction in conjunction with Stauffer's First Grade Reading Research Project at the University of Delaware. My study, in 1966 and 1967, investigated the influence of invented spelling on spelling growth. It may surprise some readers to discover that invented spelling did not suddenly appear on the scene in the 1980s. Carol Chomsky and Charles Read gave invented spelling its name, visibility, and its linguistic rationale in the early 1970s with their excellent researches, but it had a presence in classrooms instruction prior to their invaluable contributions.

Edmund Henderson, director of the McGuffey Reading Clinic at the University of Virginia prior to his untimely death, supported and inspired my interest in spelling. Under Ed's leadership, spelling research has had a renaissance. His influence on spelling research continues today among his many students, including spelling scholars Mary Abouzeid, William Barnes, Donald Bear, James Beers, Richard Gentry, Jean Gillet, Tom Gill, Dorsey Hammond, Marcia Invernizzi, Francine Johnston, Darryl Morris, Robert Schlagal, Charlie Temple, Shane Templeton, and Jerry Zutell.

Dorsey Hammond has been my companion and colleague for over 3 decades. We first met in September 1963 in Russell Stauffer's doctoral seminar. We have worked together from that day to this. Our children grew up next door to one another. We have written and taught together, debated reading theories, shared misleading stock tips. His friendship and broad knowledge of reading have enriched my personal and professional life beyond measure.

I've spent most of my professional life at Oakland University. I've worked with colleagues who have been close friends, supporters, mentors. My doctoral students have been the joy of my professional life. I am thankful for these good friends.

George Coon, Gerry Palmer, and Barbara Wilson read portions of this manuscript. Like Sherwood Anderson's wife and mother-in-law, they probably had a good laugh or two as they ferreted one egregious error after another. Their patience, kindness, and eagle eye made this a better book than it otherwise would have been.

I've heard lots of horror stories about editors and knew one or two I could tell you about. But these were rare exceptions. I have had a succession of intelligent and wise editors during the years I've written spelling, reading, and language arts textbooks for Scott Foresman Addison Wesley. These wise editors have become friends and intellectual companions: Roxy McLean, Mary Ann Hiland, Judy Nyberg, Kathy Domky, and Chris Jennison.

Finally, I have three children who have inspired my love and affection. As they grew up, I reveled in their acquisition of language and literacy. My pleasure in life is to know that Amy, Jen, and Ben love to read, write well, and love their father. What more could a professor of literacy ask? What greater gift could a father be given?

Contents

Contents

THE SPELLING CONNECTION

Chapter 1

The Beginnings of Spelling

The White Rabbit put on his spectacles. "Where shall I begin, please your Majesty?" he asked.
  "Begin at the beginning," the King said very gravely,
"and go on til you come to the end: then stop."
                                          —LEWIS CARROLL

INTRODUCTION

The American public takes spelling seriously. Have you ever notised how
quickly people judge intelligence and educational qualifications on the
basis of a few inocent spelling errors? Suppose, for example, the author
of this book misspelled *noticed* and *innocent*—as I did in the previous
sentence. Did you make a snap judgment about my intelligence or knowledge of the subject on the basis of these two spelling errors? If so, it is
not surprising. Spelling has long been symbolic of achievement in literacy:
Good spellers are smart, poor spellers are dumb. Of course, there is no
evidence to support this notion; nevertheless, the belief abides in much of
our public discourse and in our secret suspicions.

All right, if spelling is not a satisfactory measuring rod for intelligence,
what value might we assign it? At the very least, it ought to signal a high
level of literacy. High school graduates, let alone college graduates, ought
to spell accurately enough that one might assume their attainment of a
reasonably high level of literacy. When their spelling is poor, the public,
not unreasonably, assumes that the literacy of these individuals is inadequate. Yes, it is possible to spell poorly and read well, and, it is even
possible to spell poorly and write well, as a casual examination of certain
well-known authors' manuscripts will attest. But if one can acquire these
complex skills, why not acquire the skill of accurate spelling as well?

Perhaps good spelling is like good manners. You can get along without them, but you risk being perceived as rude and boorish.

THE CRADLE OF SPELLING

Not too long ago, many folks, including some eminent psychologists, viewed infants as incapable of thought—cute little blobs of protoplasm. Recent research has knocked this foolish idea into a cocked hat. While no one has suggested that $e = mc^2$ is the stuff of infant contemplation, it is quite clear that infants have much more on their minds than food and a dry diaper. We routinely underestimate children's capabilities. Literacy emerges from the day of birth, if not earlier. Children are capable of thought, probably much more complex thought than we are capable of measuring, although I can see no pressing need to measure it, since humans have a far greater propensity to mismeasure than to measure accurately, as Gould (1981) has illustrated in his excellent book *The Mismeasure of Man.*

Beginnings are hard, and they are important. Beginnings help determine the future course of literacy. Good beginnings make the acquisition of literacy more likely, while poor beginnings make it more difficult and less likely. Three foundational experiences will help put children on the road to reading, writing, and spelling success: (1) listening language experiences, (2) oral language experiences, and (3) written language experiences.

Listening Language Experiences

Reading Aloud

Unanimous agreement among reading researchers is rare, but one thing they agree on is the fundamental importance of reading aloud to children. I suppose you could find an attention-seeking heretic here and there who might wish to argue the point. But I speak here of researchers, not attention seekers.

Reading aloud accomplishes much of what is needed during these early years. Additionally, children must have materials with which to write and draw—pencils, paper, crayons, and paint. Books should be available to even the youngest child. These are the tangible necessities for entrance into the literary life. There are also intangible necessities. There must be encouragement to partake of the pleasures of the literate life; there must be an appreciation of early literacy efforts; there must be a welcoming attitude for risk taking, an understanding that success is seldom achieved without failure. These are the intangible and invaluable gifts that caring parents, mentors, and teachers can add to the literacy matrix.

Sounds and Letters

Knowledge of letter names and sounds is related to success and ease of learning to read, write, and spell. Fluency and familiarity with letters and sounds eases the way to beginning reading success. Adams (1990b) states, "A child who can recognize most letters with thorough confidence will have an easier time learning about letter sounds and word spellings than a child who still has to work at remembering what is what" (p. 12).

Knowledge of letter names and sounds has a compounding effect. Knowing letter names makes it easier to learn letter sounds; knowing letter names and sounds makes it possible to begin writing with invented spelling; writing with invented spelling strengthens fluency and familiarity with letters, sounds, and words. As knowledge builds, each piece of the puzzle strengthens pieces already in place. The result is a more successful introduction to reading, writing, and spelling. Learning to write the letters of the alphabet should begin early. Instruction in writing the letters and learning their names is needed. Handwriting instruction can be given in brief, informal sessions that emphasize legibility.

Phonemic Awareness

Phonemic awareness, the ability to distinguish one speech sound from another, is also essential. Children must learn to consciously distinguish one word from another and one sound within a word from another sound within a word. Once children can do this, they must also learn that speech sounds are represented in writing by letters or combinations of letters. This last step, matching letters to sounds, is prerequisite to writing with invented spelling, which in turn, has a positive effect on the development of phonemic awareness. Writing is one of the best ways to increase children's functional knowledge of letters and sounds (R. Cramer, 1968; B. Cramer, 1985; Stanovich, Cunningham, & Cramer, 1984).

Oral Language Experiences

Years ago, Carroll (1966) wrote a classic article on the relationships between oral and written language. Good ideas do not go out of style, though they may be supplemented with additional insights. The following discussion of oral language learning and its relationship to written language owes much to Carroll's original discussion of this issue.

Language learning occurs in a natural, informal, high-stimulus environment. The learning of reading, writing, and spelling, on the other hand, often takes place in a formal, unnatural, low-stimulus environment. Oral language learning requires no curriculum, books, or teachers. Learning happens naturally, partly because children are neurologically wired to learn oral language and partly because children are environmentally exposed to what is destined to be learned. Adults, siblings, and peers provide this exposure through conversations, experiences, and encouragement, all occurring in informal settings. The surrounding oral language is not "scoped and sequenced" into bite-sized pieces. The assumption is that children will extrapolate the rules of the language system, pace their own learning, and devise their own learning strategies. The possibility of failure is never entertained. Rather, it is assumed that success is inevitable. These are crucial and naturally occurring conditions for learning oral language.

By age 6, children can communicate with adults perfectly well. They learn the essential components of their native language in 5–7 years or less. Of course, refinements are made as children mature. Vocabulary, in particular, continues to expand. But the miracle is that children master all of the essential components of their native language in 6 years. All children learn to talk not through formal instruction but through listening, observing, and responding to the language of adults and peers. Smith (1983) puts it this way:

> There is an exquisite selectivity. Children first begin talking like their parents, then like their peers, and later, perhaps, like their favored entertainment or sporting personalities. They do not learn to talk like everyone they hear speaking, even those they may hear most. They learn the language of the groups to which they belong (or expect to belong) and resist the language of the groups that they reject or from which they are rejected. They learn, I want to say, from the clubs to which they belong. (p. 561)

Smith maintains that children learn because of their membership in particular groups he calls "clubs." This is an astute observation, and it helps account for some of the behavior of children as they join the literacy club—learning how to read and write. The adults and peers of the literacy club are the collaborators who help children learn to read and write.

On the other hand, in learning to read, write, and spell, everything is done quite differently, and rightly so, to a degree, for the processes are not altogether analogous. Still, it is possible to re-create in classrooms some of the conditions that lead to successful oral language learning. None of these ideas are complicated, and they can be implemented in classrooms. Teachers can construct settings that make the best use of the oral language heritage children often possess when they come to school.

Recording Oral Language

Record children's oral language in written form. Children can almost always read their own language more easily than they can read the language of others. Reading their own recorded language gives children an easy start in reading, and it provides many natural opportunities to examine the conventions of written language. Since recorded written language represents children's experiences as well as their language, there is a built-in guarantee that it will be understandable. How could it be otherwise? It expresses their own words, ideas, and experiences.

Respecting Language

Children bring the language of the home and the street to the classroom. Do not consider this language an impostor, but, rather, an ally. Good schooling enriches and supplements the language of home and street; the language of home and street enriches the more formal language of schooling. They are not enemies.

Using the Arts in Instruction

Make art, music, and drama part of the literacy experience. The arts are powerful motivators for learning. Children are more easily induced to learn when art, music, or drama are associated with the literacy experience. Few ideas can enrich instruction more readily than effective use of the arts in classroom instruction.

Banishing Failure

Regard failure as an impostor. Perhaps this notion has reached the dubious status of a cliché, yet I have found failure far less likely when teachers believe absolutely that children can learn. One need not subscribe to an uninformed emotionalism to understand the importance of hope and faith in the teaching–learning enterprise. Teachers must believe in children; children must believe in teachers. When this is the case, failure is all but banished.

Pacing Language Growth

Accept the individual pace at which children learn. We tend to define normal behavior far too narrowly: It is normal for some children to learn more slowly than others, to have more difficulty acquiring skills, and for some children to move rapidly and to have little difficulty acquiring skills. Some children talk early, others do not; some children read early, others late; some children write well from the beginning, others require more time. A late start or a slow start need not spell disaster, any more than an early, fast start always assures success. When we accept the idea that children learn at different rates, rather than fighting or denying it, we are in a better position to accommodate our instruction to the requirements of our children.

Making Language Learning Lively

Make literacy lively and enjoyable. A child who had just experienced 6 weeks of excellent reading, writing, and spelling instruction wrote, "We didn't do any reading or writing, but we've had a lot of fun in Mr. Rojo's class." Mr. Rojo was reluctant to show me this comment, because he thought I'd assume it was true. But I had visited Mr. Rojo's class every day for the past 6 weeks, and I knew that excellent literacy instruction occurred every day under his subtle direction. There was music, art, drama. There was reading, writing, spelling. There was language experience. There was oral language. There was reading to children; there was independent reading. What disguised this rich literacy curriculum was the sense of fun and enjoyment. Mr. Rojo was teaching children with reading difficulties in a summer reading program, kids who were used to boring lessons and failure, kids without hope. When they did not find what they had normally experienced, they concluded it must not be reading and writing—it must be something else. It must be fun! A teacher could hardly ask for a more glowing endorsement of his instructional technique.

Connecting Oral and Written Language

Inform children about the similarities and differences between oral and written language. When reading books aloud or discussing books children have read independently, help children understand how authors connect oral and written language. Such talk should be casual rather than didactic, brief rather than lengthy. A typical comment might go something like this: "The conversation between Jody and Sam sounds just like two friends talking on the playground. Why do you suppose the author made this conversation sound like a talk you might have with a friend?"

In order to read, write, and spell, children must learn the rules that govern written language, just as they learned the rules that govern oral language. Normally, written language conventions are formally taught. However, we might appropriately ask, "How much formal instruction is beneficial?" Certainly, there must be some formal teaching of the conventions of written language, but these structures are best learned in a context where meaningful reading and writing are a daily event. An inductive approach, in which children are encouraged to explore and experiment with written language, requires tolerance of trial and error and of wrong paths taken, perhaps more toleration than many of us are accustomed to allowing. Perhaps instruction should proceed on the assumption that sufficient exposure to written language will result in the inductive discovery of many of its conventions. This approach requires patience, but it may prove more fruitful than the overused, rule-oriented methods that are so often divorced from meaningful reading and writing experiences.

There are significant differences and similarities between learning oral language and learning to read and write. Some of the differences exist because of inherent differences between the two processes, but others exist because of arbitrary choices made by schools and society. It is the latter that should be modified to make reading, writing, and spelling more parallel and related to the manner in which oral language is acquired.

Written Language Experiences

Concept of Word

Written words consist of a series of letters serving to communicate meaning. They are bounded on both sides by space. They have three features: letters, sounds, meanings. Children do not automatically know that these features are needed to understand, concretely, what a word actually is. They may lack, in other words, a concept of *word.* They may, for example, think that a long word, such as *hippopotamus,* is two or three words; on the other hand, they may think *a lot of* is one word. As beginning reading, writing, and spelling instruction requires some knowledge of words, it is useful to determine where children stand regarding this concept.

Discovering whether children have a concept of what constitutes a word is quite simple, as Morris (1980) has shown. Have the child dictate a sentence. Record the sentence, and read it back to the child. Point to

---

TABLE 1.1. Acquiring Concept of Word

Has not acquired concept of word

1. Repeats the sentence and runs finger across the line of print out of sequence with the words.
2. Starts correctly with the first word or two, but loses track deeper into the sentence.
3. Reads longer words as two or three words. For example, *Mickey* might be understood as two words.
4. Reads two or more single words as one word. For instance, *shook hands* might be understood as one word.

Starts to acquire concept of word

1. Starts well and successfully tracks words halfway or more through the sentence.
2. Has difficulty on multisyllabic words, but then proceeds correctly through the rest of the sentence.

Has acquired concept of word

Can point and correctly stay with the text, word by word, throughout the entire sentence.

---

each word as you reread the sentence. Then ask the child to read the sentence aloud to you and to point to each word just as you did. Suppose the child has dictated this sentence: *"We visited Disney World, and I shook hands with Mickey Mouse."* As the sentence is reread, there are signs that will tell you where the child stands regarding the concept of word. Table 1.1 provides guidelines for judging children's acquisition of the concept of word.

It is ineffective simply to say to children, "This is a word." Children grasp the concept of word through functional exposure to print in a variety of settings. The following activities will help establish a concrete sense of what a word is.

1. While reading aloud, occasionally run your finger under the words so that spoken words are aligned with written words.
2. Take group- or individually dictated sentences or brief stories. As you reread, point to the words so that the spoken words and the written words are aligned. After reading and rereading the story several times, ask children to identify specific words within the story. If they cannot do so, reread the sentence from the beginning until the unidentified word is located and correctly identified.
3. Encourage writing using invented spelling. Writing is one of the best ways to advance children's concept of word.
4. Develop word banks using words learned from reading, writing, and spelling experiences. Have children practice classification activities with the words.

Scribbling

As early as age 1, young children begin to scribble on whatever surface is available, using whatever writing instruments are at hand. It is, therefore, a good idea to make paper and crayons available and to encourage this activity, although it may prove useful to urge your child not to scribble on recently painted walls. Years ago, I repainted a few walls for reason of random scribbling, but I now look back upon that childhood graffiti with exquisite pleasure. While it may have exasperated me a bit at the time, it was the beginning of writing for my three children, all of whom now write often and well.

Drawing

Children begin to draw pictures as soon as they achieve a measure of hand–eye coordination, which may occur at 18 months or even earlier. At first their drawings are unadorned, but children gradually add more detail and refine their representations of their world. Talking to children about their drawing will help you to understand something of how they make sense of their environment. It is also fascinating to see how children's drawings relate to the written language that often accompanies them.

Printing Letters

As children are exposed to environmental print, they begin to experiment with letters. They see letters and words everywhere in their world—*Sesame Street,* cartoons, toys, signs, books. Their attempts to make letters may occur as early as age 2, though more commonly it begins around age 3. Children's first efforts at printing letters usually involve attempts to represent their names. Their first efforts may include only a letter or two, but with encouragement more complete attempts will follow.

Mock Writing

Mock writing resembles traditional writing in certain respects, but it is not alphabetic: There is no connection between letters and sounds. For example, concomitant with beginning to print letters, children may draw wavy lines that resemble cursive writing, or they may write strings of letters. Children who produce mock writing think that their writing says something. They may ask you to tell them what their writing says; "What did I write?" is a question they sometimes ask. Take this question seriously, for it is an opportunity to establish a dialogue about writing—how it works and what it means. Mock writing is a sign that children have discovered that written language signals meaning. This is an event to be celebrated.

Children learn to scribble, draw, print letters, mock write, and learn what a word is through the literary experiences they receive at home or in preschool or kindergarten. They must hear and participate in conversations, stories, nursery rhymes, and language play. Further, the quality of these experiences is important. For instance, conversations initiated by children should focus on *their* meaning rather than yours. If Johnny comes into the kitchen grasping a ladybug in a dirty hand, don't bug Johnny about his dirty hands. Instead, answer his questions; talk about the things that are meaningful to him at that moment. Talk first, wash later. They must also be exposed to print: environmental print, print in books, print in their world of toys and television. Adults, older siblings, and playmates can enrich these experiences if the circumstances are right.

FIVE STAGES OF SPELLING DEVELOPMENT

Much of the research on the developmental aspects of spelling has been conducted by Edmund H. Henderson and his students, whose work is cited throughout this book. The most comprehensive description of spelling stages is contained in the second edition of Henderson's (1990) book *Teaching Spelling* completed just prior to his untimely death. The descriptions of the stages of spelling that follow owe much to Henderson's account, as well as those of his many students.

Learning to spell is a developmental process. The names of the stages of spelling development describe the major feature of each stage. Although the names of stages differ from one researcher to another, the substantive content of the stages remains essentially the same. Researchers have identified five stages. I have used the following names to describe each stage:

1. *Prephonetic*: The distinguishing characteristic of this stage is the absence of true alphabetic writing. There are no systematic connections between letters and sounds. Rather, children scribble, draw, make wavy, cursivelike lines, and write letters, usually in random order. Example: *AzESyuu.*

2. *Phonetic*: Children make systematic connections between letters and sounds that represent true alphabetic writing. This stage marks the beginning of writing that can be read by the writer and the writer's audience. Example: *sm* for *some.*

3. *Patterns within words*: Children learn the patterns to which letters and sounds correspond within single-syllable words. Children add sight words to their spelling repertoire, which provides the foundation for understanding more complex patterns within words. Example: *rane* for *rain.*

4. *Syllable juncture*: Children learn the structural principles that govern spelling at the point where syllables meet—their juncture. The most common juncture occurs when suffixes and inflected endings are added to words. Junctures also occur within words. Three patterns are significant: dropping, doubling, and changing. Examples: *takeing* for *taking, stoping* for *stopping, crys* for *cries.*

5. *Meaning derivation*: Children learn that words related in meaning are often related in spelling in spite of changes in sound within the related or derived form. This is a significant spelling principle, although it is often neglected in spelling instruction. Example: *nashunal* for *national*; teach relation to *nation.*

Understanding spelling development can help guide spelling assessment and instruction. Knowing what ought to happen at each stage can help you understand why children spell words in ways that may appear bizarre but that are reasonable linguistic approximations and developmentally appropriate. A detailed description of each spelling stage follows, as well as developmentally appropriate activities for each stage.

Prephonetic Stage

Description

I have used the term *prephonetic* to describe this stage, but it could just as reasonably be called *emergent,* as both of these terms describe essential characteristics of the prephonetic stage. All writing during the prephonetic stage is marked by an absence of letter–sound connections, hence the name *prephonetic.* It is characteristic of this stage that literacy is emerging in subtle ways that might easily be overlooked. For instance, given the opportunity, a 2-year-old will scribble. Initially these scribbles are random marks on paper, but they soon take on characteristics that resemble features of written English.

At first glance, this stage may seem to have little to do with spelling development, yet concepts crucial to literacy are formed during the prephonetic stage. What happens is reminiscent of the description of creation in the book of Genesis. In the beginning, concepts of oral and written language are "without form and void." These amorphous sounds and squiggles, however, soon take on a purposeful appearance. The infant gurgles and babbles, and soon these sounds take on form and shape. Oral language sprouts like a mushroom in a damp place, and somewhere between the ages of 1 and 3 the curious child picks up a crayon and scribbles on the wall. The child's first "writings" are random scribbles, but soon the shapes of written language begin to appear—curves, circles, straight lines, dots, joining strokes. Then, one day, as if by magic, the first written language occurs. A child, carrying a piece of paper and a crayon says, "I make a *J,* Mommy" (Figure 1.1). It is not magic, of course; it is the cultivated fruit of a literate environment. A literate home or an excellent preschool experience provides the air beneath a child's intellectual wings. The journey to literacy begins.

Developmentally Appropriate Activities

Teachers and parents can help children as they journey through the prephonetic stage. The help need not be formal instruction, but it should be constant and consistent. Some examples of activities follow.

Modeling While Reading Aloud. Read aloud from well-selected books, especially those with predictable patterns. Make reading aloud a pleasur-

FIGURE 1.1. "I make a *J,* Mommy"

able experience, with the child seated on your lap when possible. Place the book so that it is clearly visible for the child's perusal as you read from it. As you move through the book, talk about how print and illustrations work. Simple statements will suffice: This is the front of the book; this is the back; this is where the story begins; these words talk about this picture. As you read, occasionally move your finger along a line of print, but do not read in a slow, word-by-word fashion, as this will interfere with the natural rhythms of language.

Alphabet Books. Read alphabet books and books that contain rhyme. There are a surprisingly large number of ABC books with interesting illustrations and information to go with each letter.

Educational Toys. Provide toys that have a literacy component, such as alphabet blocks, crayons for drawing and writing, shapes that can be identified, pop-up books, and cloth, plastic, or board books that can be chewed upon, thrown about, and used for "pretend" reading.

Environmental Print. Draw attention to environmental print, such as signs, logos, cereal boxes, toys, cards with pictures of familiar objects, and other types of print-rich materials.

Making Grocery Lists. Make grocery lists and invite the child to write his or her own list. Never mind that the writing may not be readable. The child will "pretend" to read it for you, or you can be the translator.

Drawing and Labeling. After the child draws a picture, ask him or her to explain it to you. Write the child's name on the picture and add any words or a brief sentence that he or she might wish to dictate. Above all, show enjoyment and appreciation for the child's efforts.

Writing Names. Write your child's names on papers and drawings, calling attention to the letters in his or her name.

Thinking Games. Play games that encourage thinking. I often played a game with my children called "Thinking in the Room." I would think of an object in the room and encourage my children to guess what object I was thinking about. Their task was to narrow the range of possibilities by asking questions about the object's features and delimiting its possible location in the room. All questions were responded to with "yes" or "no" answers: Is it hanging on the wall? Is it bigger than the dog? Is it blue? Is it square? Is it made of wood? As the game progressed, my children then took their turn at "thinking" of an object while I asked the questions. Adult modeling helps children grasp the concept.

Telling Stories. Invent stories that children find interesting. In my home, one of my first stories was about the "Mouse Who Ate the House." Before long, my children were inventing their own "Mouse Who Ate the House" stories, an important development in the evolution from story listener to storyteller. I told stories about this greedy mouse for years, and a quarter of a century later the stories still resonate in my children's memories.

Categorizing by Contrasting Sounds. Develop categorizing activities that contrast short versus long vowel sounds, single consonant versus consonant blends. These activities can be accomplished with the whole class, groups, or individuals.

Phonetic Stage

Description

The phonetic stage, or letter name stage, as it is sometimes called, marks the beginning of spelling literacy. Letter–sound connections are made that result in true alphabetic writing. During this stage, children progress from barely decipherable invented spellings to a more advanced stage of phonetic spelling. It is reasonable, therefore, to think of the phonetic stage as progressing from a minimalist early stage to a more complete later stage. For this reason, some researchers discern two stages here—early and late phonetic. Progress within stages is described in great detail in *Words Their Way,* by Bear, Invernizzi, Templeton, and Johnston (1996). This book gives teacher-friendly information and activities for developing spelling and vocabulary knowledge, and represents the best information available on the topic of spelling stages and their instructional implications.

Henderson (1990) suggests that phonetic spellers are influenced by two factors: (1) the letter name spelling strategy, and (2) the influence of surrounding speech sounds on spelling.

Letter Name Strategy. A major influence on phonetic spelling is children's use of the letter name strategy. If the sound of a letter in a word resembles the name of that letter, children choose that letter to spell the sound. For example, they may spell *time* as *tm* or *tim* because the letter names *t, i,* and *m* closely resemble the sounds *t, i,* and *m* make in *time*. To understand how this works, say the letters *t, i,* and *m* aloud, then listen to

When you can only spell a few words, invented spelling is necessary for a beginning writer. This kindergarten student used the letter name strategy to write his story. Now he is illustrating his story.

their sounds in *time*. The letters say their names closely enough for children to discern their approximate spelling. Children perceive these letters and their sounds to be closely associated; hence, they match letter names to sounds. Most consonants have letter names that resemble their sounds in words, and long vowel sounds are, for all practical purposes, identical with the names of the letters *a, e, i, o,* and *u.*

Of course, the letter name strategy does not necessarily result in correct spelling of a sound in a given word. For instance, since long vowel sounds are often represented by two letters, as in *coat,* the letter name strategy, in this instance, would result in *oa* spelled *o.* At this stage, coat will likely be spelled *kt* or *kot*—the /k/ sound spelled *k,* the /o/ sound spelled *o,* and the /t/ sound spelled *t.* Short vowel sounds create a substantially different problem for young spellers, and accuracy in spelling short vowel sounds comes later.

Surrounding Speech Sounds. Read (1971, 1975), a linguist who studied children's invented spellings, has shown that the context in which certain letters and sounds appear within words determines whether they will be included or omitted when a word is spelled. For example, the letters *m* and *n* are often omitted before a final consonant. Thus, *band* may be spelled *bad* and *camp* may be spelled *cap,* the *n* omitted in *band* and the *m* omitted in *camp.*

Invented spelling seldom involves random guessing. On the contrary, Read's research has shown that young children's spelling behavior is driven by linguistically sophisticated reasoning. The words children spell during the phonetic stage often include the letters one would have predicted, but children sometimes include more or fewer than one might have guessed.

Children correctly represent most single consonants whose sound resembles their name. The following consonants have predictable and stable letter name matches: *b, p, f, v, m, n, t, d, s, k, j, z, l, r.* The consonants *c, g, h, w,* and *y* are slightly less predictable, yet they are soon learned and present only temporary problems (Temple, Nathan, Burris, & Temple, 1988). Consonant blends are more difficult than single consonants. Phonetic spellers tend to represent blends with one letter initially, but soon progress beyond this minimalist stage. Digraphs are a significant challenge for the phonetic speller since they have one sound but are spelled with two letters. Digraphs such as *th, sh, ch, ng* are often represented by a single letter except in those words or word parts already established in memory. Some typical consonant digraph spellings are illustrated in Table 1.2.

Phonetic spellers are much more likely to include consonant letters than vowel letters. Vowel letters are often missing or incorrect in the earliest part of the phonetic stage (Cramer & Cipielewski, 1995; Beers & Henderson 1977; Read, 1971, 1975). Toward the middle and end of the phonetic stage, however, noticeable progress in representing vowel spellings becomes evident. Table 1.3 presents examples of spellings produced by a first grader during the first week of school. These spellings are typical of the phonetic stage.

Developmentally Appropriate Activities

The following activities will help phonetic spellers make progress toward more conventional spellings. The activities in this stage consist of a mix of word study activities along with opportunities for daily writing. Writing does more to hasten spelling development than any other single activity.

Establishing and Maintaining Word Banks. A word bank consists of a stock of known words drawn from reading and writing experiences. Only known words are appropriate candidates for a word bank. There are many potential sources for establishing individual word banks: group or individually dictated accounts, known words from reading sources, poems, word-walls, rhyming words, and words from written accounts.

Have children work as partners to select known words from familiar texts or other sources, and write them on 3" × 5" cards. The words are

TABLE 1.2. Early Consonant Digraph Spellings		
Digraph	Spelling	Example
ch	*h*	*wht* for *watched*
sh	*c, s, h*	*ce* for *she, sep* for *ship, weh* for *wish*
th	*t, v*	*ta* for *they, mvr* for *mother*

kept in a file or shoe box. As words accumulate, it is a good idea to show children how to alphabetize their words within their containers.

Children usually forget some of their words; this is quite natural and should be expected. One way to minimize forgetting is to have children write, when possible, the page number and source from which they have drawn words. They can then return to the original source to review the context from which the word was originally drawn.

Categorizing Words. Once word banks have been started, begin word categorizing activities. These activities may be practiced at specified times as well as during children's spare time. Words can be categorized by meaning, sound, and structural patterns. Word sort categories can be suggested by the teacher; these are called closed sorts. Words can also be sorted by categories thought up by children; these are called open sorts.

Journal Writing. Introduce children to journal writing. There are many options for using journals as part of a reading–writing program. After examining options, determine what type of journal writing might work best for your children. One type is a dialogue journal, a composition book used to carry on private written conversations between teacher and student. Topics in dialogue journals are self-generated. While dialogue journals have been used from first grade to college-level courses, they are particularly effective in the early stages of learning to read and write. Teachers who have used dialogue journals often report improved communication between themselves and their students as well as improved discipline. Dialogue journals work well when teachers are able to read and respond regularly. Trouble occurs, however, when a response does not match student expectations, as this second grader's disappointed journal entry shows: "I won't write no mor til yuo write me back" (Goodman & Goodman, 1983, p. 596).

Scheduling time to respond to student journals is crucial. On the other hand, when teachers respond, enthusiasm for writing runs high. Palmer

TABLE 1.3. Examples of Early Phonetic Spellings		
nth for *north*	rne for *raining*	s for *saw*
y for *why*	etn for *eating*	ap for *up*
uv for *of*	wt for *went*	wth for *with*
trn for *turn*	wan for *when*	wt for *what*
ovteh for *over to*	tgr for *tiger*	rop for *rope*
bne for *bunny*	wz for *was*	u for *you*

and Coon (1985, p. 61) describe the excitement of writing when journal writing is well managed on both sides of the written dialogue:

> TEACHER: My students can't wait to get into the classroom every morning to begin writing.
>
> CHILD: Dear Mis Part [Parent] I like your ruden [writing].

In the beginning, journal writing is simple. For example, Eric, a first grader, started by filling whole pages with neat rows of capital letters. His teacher wrote: "Dear Eric, This is very neatly done. Could we talk about it?" Eric's third entry went like this:

> DXSLSLXDLS
> It.park.was.no.a.hill [The park was on a hill]
> XDSKL

Eric's teacher responded: "Dear Eric, This is great! I'm so excited that you are writing words that I can read" (Palmer & Coon, 1985, p. 61).

Start an Author's Chair-Sharing Experience. The ambiance of a special place is important to children. What child has not built a fort to nourish a need for a place with a little magic of its own? Respond to this childhood need by creating a special place from which writing is shared with the class, such as an author's chair, podium, or platform. Establish rules for sharing and receiving writing. Model sharing techniques by volunteering to share your writing with the children. Take the first risk, and children will eagerly follow in your footsteps. Set the example for critical listening by giving thoughtful attention to the writing children share. What you say and how you say it will be remembered and modeled by the children. Give praise, recognition, and respect. Above all, make sharing pleasant and safe.

Publish Books. There are simple and efficient ways to have children publish books. Avoid complicated, fancy bookmaking except for special purposes. If bookmaking becomes so complex that only teachers or parents can "make" books, some of the pleasure and spontaneity of bookmaking will disappear. Parents and volunteers can be helpful in making fancier books for special occasions, but for everyday purposes keep it simple.

Dramatize Writing. Produce some of the plays, skits, and stories children write. Elaborate productions are not necessary, although they are occasionally appropriate. Effective drama can be produced spontaneously by children working together in small groups with some teacher supervision.

Develop In-School Audiences. Find interested audiences for children's writing within your school building. Natural audiences include principals, administrators, children in other classrooms, and visitors. Planning is necessary to make best use of these natural audiences.

Develop Out-of-School Audiences. Out-of-school audiences for writing are limited only by your imagination. Parents are an excellent audience, particularly if they are apprised of the purposes of the writing program. Other outside audiences include senior citizens, newspapers, children's magazines, and the Internet.

Patterns within Words Stage

Description

During this stage, children come to understand that English spelling is not based on a simple one-to-one letter–sound correspondence. They learn that something more complex is involved in spelling English words. The distinction between the phonetic stage and the patterns within words stage is summarized by Bear et al. (1996):

> In the Letter Name stage, students learned about short vowel patterns, starting with word families. Throughout this beginning stage students became competent reading single syllable short vowel words, and many long vowel words. In spelling, these beginners examined the orthography using their letter name knowledge and a linear strategy in which each letter represented one sound. In contrast, students in the Within Word Pattern stage move beyond a letter name strategy; they learn long vowel patterns and other abstract vowel patterns, and their knowledge in spelling r-influenced single-syllable words and consonant blends and digraphs is substantial. (p. 248)

The patterns within words stage comprises several key events and instructional activities, including (1) the appearance of the silent vowel marker in misspelled words, (2) growth in correctly spelled short vowel patterns, (3) growth in correctly spelled consonant blends and digraphs, and (4) emphasis on teaching–learning of long vowel patterns.

Silent Vowel Marker. A sign that children are moving beyond the phonetic stage is the appearance of the silent vowel marker, which signals a long vowel spelling. Long vowels are "marked" or "signaled" by the presence of a silent vowel letter. The silent vowel in each of the following words signals a long vowel spelling: *cake, meet, boat, time, shoe.*

Children tend to spell long vowel sounds with a single vowel letter during the phonetic stage: *cak* for *cake; met* for *meet; bot* for *boat; tim* for *time; shu* for *shoe.* At the beginning of the patterns within words stage, children show they now understand that something more complex is involved in spelling. In other words, they now understand that spelling is not simply a one-to-one match of letter to sound, as they thought during the phonetic stage. Thus, look for long vowel words to be spelled correctly or for a "marking" vowel to appear in a misspelling. For example, *boat* may be spelled *boet, cake* may be spelled *caik.* Bear et al. (1996) have called this behavior "using but confusing."

The appearance of a marking vowel is a reassuring sign since it indicates a step forward in understanding the English spelling system. The marking behavior is a good example of how spelling errors can sometimes be understood as signs of growth rather than as negative events signaling ignorance.

Short Vowel Patterns. Another sign that children have moved beyond the phonetic stage of one-to-one letter–sound matching is the consistent appearance of correctly spelled short vowel patterns in single-syllable words. Short vowel spellings are more consistent than long vowel spelling patterns. The short vowel mismatch errors, common during the phonetic stage, are gradually abandoned. Mismatches such as *rad* for *red, hem,* for *him,* and *hit hot* are replaced with correct short vowel spellings.

Consonant Blends and Digraphs. Yet another indicator that children are progressing satisfactorily through the patterns within words stage is the appearance of correctly spelled consonant blends and digraphs. Words such as *then, sing, ship, chin, stop,* and *trip* are likely to be spelled correctly. High-frequency words that fall into this category are the ones most likely to be spelled correctly. More complex patterns, as in *taught* and *enough,* come along more slowly.

Long Vowel Instruction. An important goal during the patterns within words stage is to provide consistent instruction in spelling long vowel patterns. The instructional emphasis during this stage is on single-syllable long vowel patterns. Long vowel patterns must be learned, but how? Perhaps the least useful way is to teach vowel rules. The infamous rule "when two vowels go walking the first one does the talking" has too many exceptions to be useful, and this is true of many vowel rules. If teaching vowel rules seldom works, what will help children discover vowel patterns? We can take a lesson from oral language learning. Many of the rules that grammarians use to describe oral language are too complex to be taught, but they are learned, nevertheless, primarily through consistent exposure to rich oral language. Few of us could articulate, for example, the rules that describe the grammar of our spoken language. Yet we apply these rules every day without conscious thought. So it is with spelling rules. Spelling rules are learned by meaningful and practical exposure to the written language. While reading and writing are crucial components of an effective spelling approach, they are unlikely to accomplish the job alone. Add systematic spelling instruction and engaging word study to this mix, and spelling knowledge will grow.

Developmentally Appropriate Activities

Studying Vowel Patterns. A small number of vowel patterns yields a large number of words. Many words can be formed by adding an initial consonant to the phonograms listed in Table 1.4. Words representing many vowel patterns can be formed using vowel patterns. Stahl (1992) indicates that about 500 words can be derived from the vowel patterns shown in Table 1.4.

Teacher-Directed Words Sorts. In teacher-directed word sorts, the teacher selects the categories that will be explored and provides appropriate words that fit them. A teacher might write two words on the board with contrasting vowel sounds, such as *boat* (long vowel sound) and *hot* (short vowel sound). Students then sort the given words into vowel categories. Potential sources for word sorts are (1) word cards made by the teacher, suitable for a variety of sorts, (2) word cards drawn from children's word banks, and (3) words drawn from reading or spelling lists. After children have become accustomed to sorting words into only two categories, noncategory words may be added to the

---

TABLE 1.4. Vowel Patterns

-ack	-ain	-ake	-ale	-all	-ame
-an	-ank	-ap	-ash	-at	-ate
-aw	-ay	-eat	-ell	-est	-ice
-ick	-ide	-ight	-ill	-in	-ine
-ing	-ink	-ip	-ir	-ock	-oke
-op	-or	-ore	-uck	-ug	-ump
-unk					

sort. This is an additional challenge that should be used only after students have acquired some skill in sorting words. Students can sort words individually or in small groups.

Student-Directed Word Sorts. In student-directed word sorts, the categories for sorting are selected by students instead of the teacher. Procedures for student-directed word sorts are similar to those outlined for teacher-directed sorts.

Word Study Journals. Word journals have a variety of purposes. For example, after students have participated in teacher- or student-directed sorts, they can record the words used in their word journals. These journals can be used for vocabulary development as well as for studying spelling patterns. Words may be organized in journals under various headings. There can be sections devoted to meaning sorts, word structure sorts, vowel pattern sorts and so on. For example, a journal might have a meaning section in which students have separate pages for words related to sports, food, school, or any other meaning category. Categories can be divided into subcategories within sports, such as basketball, skating, and soccer. Activities for word journals can be enriched by encouraging children to brainstorm for additional ways in which they can use their word journals. It is amazing how many ideas children can produce that an adult might never have considered.

Games. There are many games that can be adapted and used to broaden children's knowledge of word meaning, word structure, and spelling patterns. For example, the classic television game *Jeopardy* can be adapted for word study purposes. In addition, spin games, racetrack games, and card games of many varieties can be used. Detailed descriptions and directions for using such games appear in *Words Their Way* by Bear et al. (1996). Morris (1982) and Gentry and Gillet (1993) have also suggested ways in which word sorts can aid reading and spelling.

Syllable Juncture Stage

Description

A syllable juncture is the place within a word where syllables meet. Letters are often dropped, doubled, or changed at the juncture of syllables. By the time children reach the syllable juncture stage, they have a basic spelling vocabulary and they have control of many long and short vowel spelling patterns. Spelling errors frequently occur at syllable junctures, especially where inflected endings or suffixes are joined to base words. Spelling problems also arise within the internal structure of a word where syllables meet, and this often results in spelling errors. Deciding whether a word requires one consonant or two is difficult; for poor spellers this decision is often their Waterloo. Henderson (1990) suggests that the core principle of the syllable juncture stage is the doubling of consonants to mark the short vowel. Two concepts must be grasped to understand this principle, according to Bear et al. (1996).

1. The final consonant is doubled when adding *-ed* or *-ing* to a word that has a consonant–vowel–consonant pattern (CVC) as in *hop— hopping.*
2. The final *e* is dropped when adding *-ed* or *-ing* to a word that has a consonant–vowel–consonant-silent *e* pattern (CVCe) as in *hope— hoping.*

According to Templeton (1991), children acquire a firm grasp of syllable juncture principles during this stage. He states that "The basic clue to doubling, dropping, or changing letters depends on the structure within the joined syllables. For example, *sit* has a short vowel pattern, and when you add a suffix that begins with a vowel, you must double the final consonant in *sit.* Otherwise, you have a different word—*siting (site + ing)*" (p. 422).

Table 1.5 gives examples of the types of errors that typically occur at syllable juncture points.

The words in Table 1.5 illustrate three errors common during the syllable juncture stage. Column 1 illustrates the failure to drop the final *e*

TABLE 1.5. Syllable Juncture Errors

Dropped	Doubled	Changed
caring, careing	bagged, baged	cried, crys
firing, fireing	boring, borring	galleries, gallerys
loving, loveing	ceiling, ceilling	easiest, easyest
lying, lyeing	necessary, neccesary	mysteries, mysterys
taking, takeing	chimney, chimmney	parties, partys
tapes, taps	always, allways	juries, jurys
minutes, minuits	almost, allmost	injuries, injerers
named, namd	beginning, begining	bunnies, bunnyes
claimed, claimd	planned, planed	earlier, earlyer

when adding inflected endings such as *-s, -es, -ed,* and *-ing.* Column 2 illustrates the pervasive problem of doubled consonants. Doubling errors occur when affixing a word as well as within words, when single consonants are doubled or double consonants are spelled with only one letter. Column 3 illustrates the failure to change *y* to *i* when inflected endings such as *-s, -es, -ed, -ing, -er,* or *-est* are added.

During the syllable juncture stage, children show significant progress in understanding and applying the rules governing dropping, doubling, and changing letters. For some children, however, spelling problems associated with dropping, doubling, and changing letters may persist into the early meaning derivation stage. Nevertheless, most of the conventions associated with these spelling issues are learned during the syllable juncture stage.

Developmentally Appropriate Activities

Word Study Journals. Word study is essential for developing vocabulary and spelling knowledge, and students should keep journals in which they record activities associated with word study. For instance, after students have participated in an individual or group sorting experience, the results of their work can be recorded in their journals under appropriate categories. If students have recently worked on compounds, inflected endings, and plurals, for instance, they should have pages in their journals for recording the results of their sorting experiences. These journals not only provide a handbook for vocabulary and spelling study, but also provide an opportunity for writing the words, a useful activity for retention of spelling words.

Compound Words. Working with compound words helps students understand how words are combined to form new meaning units. The individual words within a compound typically retain their spelling when combined, a stabilizing factor in leaning to spell compounds. Choose several compound words to illustrate how each word in a compound word contributes to the new meaning. For example, *basket* and *ball* combine in *basketball* to name a game that uses a *basket* and a *ball*. Each word contributes a component of meaning; each word retains its original spelling. Stability in spelling compounds is typical, although there are some exceptions.

Here is an activity that can be used when working with compounds. Arrange single words in columns and have students work in small groups to make compound words.

fly	any
thing	time
yard	back
work	shop
one	grand
room	him
self	mate
body	every
father	any
mother	side

First, have students make as many true compounds as they can and define their meanings. Then challenge them to create a list of pseudocompounds: compounds that do not currently exist in the English language but might exist if a need for such a word arose. For example, one can imagine a flyshop—a place where flies shop, or a place where airplanes are repaired. Word study exercises dealing with compounds should focus on the influence of combining on meaning, and on spelling.

Plurals. The most common plural endings are -*s* and -*es*. Words that end in *x, s, ss, ch, sh,* and *tch* usually take the -*es* plural ending, whereas all other words generally take the -*s* ending. Irregular plurals are exceptions to this generalization. The following activity can be done individually or in small groups. In the former case, students sort the words into two columns: words that take the -*s* ending and words that take the -*es* ending. If students are working in groups, they can make word cards and sort the words into appropriate categories. Individual and group work can be followed by having students record their work in their word study journals.

Meaning Derivation Stage

Description

The final stage of spelling maturity occurs when children have reached the Piagetian stage of formal operations, that of logical operations and abstract thinking. Children who have progressed through the earlier stages are now prepared to examine polysyllabic words. Many of the words that must now be learned are derived from Greek and Latin roots. The spelling of these words is based largely on meaning and derivational principles.

Words have an important spelling–meaning relationship. Words related in meaning are often related in spelling in spite of changes in sound within the related form. The spelling–meaning relationship is illustrated in these three meaning-related words: *reside, resident, residential.* Say these words aloud and you will notice that the long /*i*/ in *reside* is reduced to an unstressed, indistinguishable vowel sound (*schwa*) in the derived forms— *resident* and *residential.* Yet despite the change in the vowel sound in the derived forms, there is no change in the spelling of the vowels. That is, the spelling remains stable in the derived forms despite changes in sound. The English spelling system is consistent, though not perfect, in this respect. Imagine how much more difficult it would be to spell polysyllabic words if the spelling of derived forms changed with every shift in stress and sound. This is one reason, among others, why a one-to-one correspondence between letters and sounds would not be the perfect system that spelling reformers have imagined it would be. This spelling–meaning principle is illustrated in the words shown in Table 1.6.

The spelling–meaning relationship illustrates the importance of vocabulary study as an essential part of the reading and spelling curriculum, particularly in Grades 4–8. As children progress through the grades, they encounter more and more polysyllabic words. If each new word had to be learned individually, without understanding the meaning relationships that exist among words, reading and spelling would be much more difficult. The student who has studied some of the history and etymology of English will discern meaning patterns that enhance both reading and spelling power. For example, knowing the meaning of *please* will enable students to make an educated guess that *pleasant* is a related form, thus improving the chances of correctly deducing the meaning and the spelling of this related form. Simply relying on sound to spell *pleasant* would result in incorrectly spelling the word *pleasant.*

These observations suggest that spelling instruction is premised on a broad-based knowledge of the English language, whose extraordinary

TABLE 1.6. Spelling–Meaning Connection

Base word	Derived form
marine	mariner
confide	confident
reserve	reservation
collide	collision
assign	assignation
compose	composition
parish	parishioner
suppose	supposition
solemn	solemnity

diversity is largely derived from other cultures, with Greek, Latin, and French foremost among them. Effective spelling instruction cannot stand alone; no spelling book will suffice to inform students of the history of the English language, though surely such study ought to be incorporated into spelling books. No spelling curriculum can fully succeed without acknowledging the contribution that wide reading and systematic study of the English language can provide. Word study therefore ought to be a significant component of the reading, spelling, and language arts curriculum.

Developmentally Appropriate Activities

Illustrate How Meaning Aids Spelling. Tell students that words related in meaning are often related in spelling, and illustrate the concept using examples such as those shown in Table 1.7. While it is true that root words remain essentially constant in spelling, children need to know that spelling changes often occur at the point where word endings are joined with the root word. For example, when adding *-ion* to words ending with *t* (*educate*, *education*) you drop the *e* and retain the *t*. But there are other variations of the *-ion* ending (*-sion*, *-tion*, *-ation*) that cause spelling changes that depend on how the root word ends. This stipulation applies to many other suffixes. The most common spelling change involves dropping the silent *e* marker (*convulse*, *convulsion*) and changing *y* to *i* (*apply*, *application*). Other, less predictable changes also occur. How a base word is modified usually depends on how the base word ends.

TABLE 1.7. Greek-Derived Prefixes

Prefix	Meaning	Word
a-, an-	without, lacking, not	amoral, anemia
amphi-	around, about	amphibian
ana-, an-	up, back, again	analysis
anti-, ant-	against, opposite	antithesis, antonym
apo-, ap-	away, from, off	apogee
cata-, cat-	down, backward, against	cataract
dia-, di-	through, across	diagnose, diabetes
dys-	bad, difficult	dyslexia
en-, em-	in, into, within	endemic
hyper-	over, above, beyond	hyperactive
meta-, met-	along with, besides	metaphor
para-, par-	besides, alongside	parapsychology
peri-	around, surrounding	perigee
pro-	before, in front of	prologue, prognosis
syn-, sy-, sym-	with, together	synthesis, symbol

Greek-Derived Prefixes. Table 1.7 lists English prefixes derived from the Greek language, along with English-derived words to which the prefix is attached. Have children add to this list as a small group or individual activity.

Writing Activities. The following activities revolve around writing. Writing and spelling must be connected so that spelling words can be practiced in meaningful writing environments.

Activity 1: Choose a familiar character from history, books, or TV. Decide on a title and write a story about your character. Here are some ideas for "revising" history a little:

   a. The Day Tom Sawyer Painted My Fence
   b. Christopher Columbus Tells How He Goofed
   c. My Gunfight with Pecos Bill

Activity 2: Beginnings are hard in almost any endeavor, and this is especially true in writing stories. Here are some story starters you might want to try:

   a. Its head was huge; its arms and legs short and stubby.
   b. I slipped out of my room and made my way past the first danger point.
   c. I kept wondering, "How will I explain this to Dad?"
   d. Tinga, the old crippled tiger, crept through the tall grass.
   e. "He's the meanest person in the world," I decided.
   f. "Get going, legs," I commanded. But they refused to budge.

Activity 3: Here are a few questions that may help you get started writing a story of your own:

   a. Would you rather live in a tree or a cave?
   b. How would you survive alone in the forest?
   c. What would it be like to be boss of your home for a day?
   d. Would two heads really be better than one?
   e. Do Martians eat pizza, mizza, or what?

Activity 4: You are on a spaceship traveling to another galaxy. You were born on the ship and now you are 10 years old. Describe a day in your life. Consider these questions: What is life like on your spaceship? What do you wear and eat? Do you go to school? What subjects do you study?

Activity 5: You discover a tiny lady with her arm caught on a branch of an apple tree in your backyard. You set her free and you are given two wishes as a reward. There is just one problem; you must live with the consequences of your wishes, which may be different than you had thought. Write a story about this adventure.

Activity 6: Think of some of the "bad guys" in fairy tales you have read. For instance, there is:

a. The Wolf in "Little Red Riding Hood."
b. The Giant in "Jack and the Beanstalk."
c. The Troll in "The Three Billy Goats Gruff."

Could it be that these three vile creatures are not villains at all but merely victims of unfair, one-sided publicity? Tell their story from their point of view.

Activity 7: When people write books or stories about themselves it is called *autobiography*. Write a book about yourself. Make a page for each of these topics:

a. A brief sketch about me in 100 words
b. Friends and enemies
c. Favorite music and TV programs
d. What I do when I'm not in school
e. What I like and dislike
f. What's really important about me
g. Dreams about my future life

PERSPECTIVE AND SUMMARY

Chaim Potok starts off his novel *In the Beginning* with these words: "All beginnings are hard." I am challenged and intrigued by these words. On the one hand, I believe they are fundamentally true. On the other hand, I see no need to make beginnings hard on purpose. As parents and teachers we should do everything in our power to make the beginnings of literacy pleasurable and interesting, yet challenging.

The cradle of spelling is rocked by parents and teachers who under-stand that the lullaby of literacy makes the loveliest music a child will ever hear. It is incumbent on us, therefore, to rock the cradle with gentleness, yet not fear to challenge children to participate in the language game. Learning to read, write, and spell are monumental tasks. There is no biological inheritance to support the acquisition of literacy, as may well be the case with oral language. But most children manage the journey into literacy quite well, especially if the beginning of this journey is supported at home and in school.

This chapter has presented the following main ideas:

• The beginnings of spelling are nourished through experiences centering around aural, oral, and written language: listening, speaking, and writing.
• Aural language experiences are nourished by being read to, by listening to stories, and by exploring the world of letters and sounds.
Children learn oral language through meaningful practice and use. Oral language lays the foundation for the journey into literacy.
• Written language is acquired through exposure to literate environments, exploration, and direct instruction. Children need experiences with scribbling, drawing, nursery rhymes, language play, and exposure to print in a variety of settings.
• Learning to spell is developmental. Children go through five stages of spelling growth: (1) *prephonetic*: literacy emerges through scribbling, drawing, forming letters and mock writing, all without letter–sound connections; (2) *phonetic*: alphabetic writing begins when children first begin to make systematic letter–sound connections, using invented spelling; (3) *patterns within words*: children discover rule-governed spelling patterns within words; (4) *syllable juncture*: children examine the changes that occur at the juncture of syllable—the dropping, doubling, and changing that occurs at juncture points in words; and (5) *meaning derivation*: children learn that words related in meaning are often related in spelling in spite of changes in sound within the related form.

REFERENCES

Bear, D. R., Invernizzi, M., Templeton, S., & Johnston, F. (1996). *Words their way: Word study for phonics, vocabulary, and spelling instruction.* Englewood Cliffs, NJ: Prentice-Hall.

Beers, J. W., & Henderson, E. H. (1977). A study of developing orthographic concepts among first grade children. *Research in the Teaching of English, 11*(2), 133–148.

Carroll, J. (1966). Some neglected relationships in reading and language learning. *Elementary English, 43,* 577–582.

Cramer, B. B. (1985). *The effects of writing with invented spelling on general linguistic awareness and phonemic segmentation ability in kindergartners*. Unpublished doctoral dissertation, Oakland University, Rochester, MI.

Cramer, R. L. (1968). *An investigation of the spelling achievement of two groups of first-grade classes on phonologically regular and irregular words and in written composition*. Unpublished doctoral dissertation, University of Delaware, Newark.

Cramer, R. L., & Cipielewski, J. F. (1995). Research in action: A study of spelling errors in 18,599 written compositions of children in grades 1–8. In *Spelling: An overview of research and current research information and practices* (pp. 11–52). Glenview, IL: Scott, Foresman.

Gentry, J. R., & Gillet, J. W. (1993). *Teaching kids to spell*. Portsmouth, NH: Heinemann.

Goodman, K. S., & Goodman, Y. (1983). Reading and writing relationships: Pragmatic functions. *Language Arts, 60,* 590–599.

Gould, S. J. (1981). *The mismeasure of man*. New York: Norton.

Henderson, E. H. (1990). *Teaching spelling* (2nd ed.). Boston: Houghton Mifflin.

Morris, D. (1980). Beginning readers concept of word. In E. Henderson & J. Beers (Eds.), *Developmental and cognitive aspects of learning to spell* (pp. 97–111). Newark, DE: International Reading Association.

Morris, D. (1982). Word sort: A categorization strategy for improving word recognition ability. *Reading Psychology, 3,* 247–259.

Palmer, G., & Coon, G. (1985). Kids write right away. *Early Years, 14*(9), 61–63.

Read, C. (1971). Pre-school children's knowledge of English phonology. *Harvard Educational Review, 41*(1), 1–34.

Read, C. (1975). *Children's categorization of speech sounds in English* (NCTE Research Reports No. 17). Urbana, IL: National Council of Teachers of English.

Stahl, S. A. (1992). Saying the "p" word: Nine guidelines for exemplary phonics instruction. *Reading Teacher, 45*(8), 618–625.

Stanovich, K. E., Cunningham, A. E., & Cramer, B. B. (1984). Assessing phonological awareness in kindergarten children: Issues of task comparability. *Journal of Experimental Child Psychology, 38,* 175–190.

Temple, C., Nathan, R., Burris, N., & Temple, F. (1988). *The beginnings of writing* (2nd ed.). Boston: Allyn & Bacon.

Templeton, S. (1991). *Teaching the integrated language arts*. Boston: Houghton Mifflin.

Chapter 2

•◆•

The Beginnings of Writing

All my life I've been frightened at the moment I sit down
to write.

—GABRIEL GARCÍA MÁRQUEZ

INTRODUCTION

Perhaps you are asking yourself why a book about spelling devotes an
entire chapter to the beginning of writing. I'm glad you asked. Writing
and spelling are like Abbott and Costello, Tarzan and Jane. You can't think
of one without evoking the other. This book has two recurring themes:
Spelling becomes meaningful only in the context of writing; reading
provides the background information needed to become a competent
speller. Thus, reading, writing, and spelling are inextricably linked, although this crucial link is not always obvious in the manner in which we
move children toward literacy.

Writing is especially relevant to spelling because it is the playing field
on which spelling must be practiced. The stages of beginning writing
overlap with the stages of spelling growth described in Chapter 1. Further,
the principles of beginning writing, as described by Clay (1975) and
reviewed in this chapter, illustrate the way in which emergent writing
converges with the beginnings of spelling.

A LITERACY STORY

I watch Amy as she grasps a pencil in her small, delicate hand and begins
to draw and write with great confidence. I am fascinated. Can this tiny

3-year-old unravel the mysteries of written language? Is she too young for this adventure? Will she enjoy doing what many older children and some adults dislike and find difficult? A piece of cake! She delights in writing. And just as Amy can write, so can the millions of children like her who populate our preschools, kindergartens, and primary grades. Young children tackle writing with the confidence of an Olympic athlete. Instead of fearing the challenge, they anticipate victory. Why not? They have mastered their oral language with the ease of a gifted shortstop fielding a ground ball. They can also master the written language, and teachers are in the best position to help them do it. Teachers are the cornerstone of the writing edifice. Teachers create the environments in which writing and writers can flourish.

The story of emergent writing is an adventure and a mystery. How do young children learn so much so quickly? What stimulates their imaginative powers? Young writers venture to the moon and back and face dark dangers in strange lands. They travel with the Cowardly Lion and the Tin Man to the Land of Oz. Their topics range from gravity to grandma, from gnus to zoos. And just as there is adventure in their stories and poems, there is mystery and majesty in their writing prowess. As I watch young children write, I am often reminded of the time I first stood in a grove of ancient redwoods. Quiet dignity. The mystery and the majesty were overwhelming. So too is the writing of young children. Writing with young children is exciting. Classrooms where young writers are at work are among the most enchanting places on earth. Cultivating classrooms into gardens where writing flourishes is a challenging and rewarding task.

It was just such a classroom where Lori wrote a lovely poetic piece about the sun, flowers, and love (Figure 2.1).

PREPARING CHILDREN FOR INDEPENDENT WRITING

Athletes train for the events in which they compete, the better they prepare, the greater the likelihood they will succeed. Likewise, children must prepare for the task of writing. In order to write on their own, children must be able to use their own words and experiences, write the letters of the alphabet, and associate letters with sounds. None of these prerequisites need be fully mastered. It is sufficient to have a moderate level of capability in each.

Words and Experiences

Some children see the world from the back of a migrant worker's truck, others from the comfort of an air-conditioned Cadillac. Some children know

FIGURE 2.1. Poetic expression: Lori's story; between kindergarten and first grade; 1989, late summer.

only the mean streets of urban poverty, others know the tranquility of rural roads. Regardless of circumstances, children's words and experiences deserve to be received with dignity and respect. Thoughtful teachers know that all children have words and experiences worth sharing. It is the teacher's job to see that they are shared in an atmosphere of approval and trust.

Words are the tools children use to possess their experiences, to know themselves, and to know the world around them. Good teaching enriches and extends children's words and experiences, enticing them out of the crevices of students' minds and onto paper. Hughes (1967), an English poet interested in children's writing, describes the importance of words and experiences to writers:

Because it is occasionally possible, just for brief moments to find the words that will unlock the doors of all those many mansions inside the head and

express something—perhaps not much, just something—of the crush of information that presses in on us from the way a crow flies over and the way a
man walks and the look of a street and from what we did one day a dozen
years ago. Words that will express something of the deep complexity that
makes us precisely the way we are, from the momentary effect of the
barometer to the force that created men distinct from trees. Something of
the inaudible music that moves us along in our bodies from moment to
moment like water in a river. Something of the spirit of the snowflake in the
water of the river. Something of the duplicity and the relatively and the
merely fleeting quality of all this. Something of the almighty importance of
it and something of the utter meaninglessness. And when words can manage
something of this, and manage it in a moment of time, and in that same
moment make out of it all the vital signature of a human being—not of an
atom, or of a geometrical diagram, or of a heap of lenses—but a human being,
we call it poetry. (p. 124)

Language is the key to learning, and the reception children's language
receives is closely linked to success in writing. It is important to remember
that language differences among children are not synonymous with language deprivation. Language differences are common, whereas true language deprivation is rare. Distinguishing the appearance of language
deprivation from its reality is crucial. Language differences may make
some children hesitant to express themselves freely in classrooms, even
though they may have much worth saying. Mearns (1929) speaks of the
unexpressed feelings and thoughts of children in these words:

> Power of language they undoubtedly had, I mused, terrific power; but no one
> had apprised them of that gift, I suspected, for it is not the sort that would
> pass as creditable among teachers generally. It was the clipped, colloquial
> idiom of youth, hot, prejudiced, rebellious; ungrammatical, and impolite;
> highly absurd from an adult standard; but beautifully fitting as an instrument
> to convey genuine feelings. (p. 18)

The language power heard on the streets can be harnessed for
classroom purposes. Brilliant thoughts can be conveyed in ungrammatical
sentences. Beautiful feelings can be expressed in colloquial idiom. Elegant
ideas can be couched in impolite language. Language changes as a
consequence of learning, not as a precondition to it. Apprise children of
their language gifts and encourage them to use their native gift of
language no matter how unconventional it may be. Language as it exists
is the key to learning; language as you wish it to be is what comes later.
Billy Joe and Mary Sue may not shine today, but they can sparkle like
diamonds tomorrow.

Writing enriches and extends the words and experiences children possess. When they have finished writing, these children share their writing with their classmates.

Lack of confidence is sometimes a deterrent to participation in language activities. Build children's self-confidence by removing social, cultural, or personal barriers that inhibit the flow of language. The delightful surprise of discovering a diamond in the rough and polishing its many facets is one of the great joys of teaching.

The Alphabet, Handwriting, and Punctuation

Writing the letters of the alphabet is prerequisite to independent writing. With patient instruction, most children can learn to write the letters well enough to begin independent writing within a few weeks of entering first grade. Some children can begin as early as preschool or kindergarten. Knowing the letter names and being able to write them makes it possible for children to invent the spellings of many words, and that is where handwriting instruction comes into the picture.

Handwriting practice should accompany learning to write, and should incorporate meaningful language experiences, for best results. Independent writing provides many opportunities for meaningful handwriting instruction. Individual handwriting tips can be given during brief, informal conferences as children write. For example, as children are writing, stop at a particular child's desk and say, "Your story is coming nicely. I love the way you started your story. Here, let me show you how to make the letter *k*. You're having a little trouble with it, aren't you?" Encourage other children similarly.

Teachers sometimes worry that instruction in handwriting and the mechanics of writing will interfere with the content of writing, but such worry is justified only when content is ignored or seldom considered. Without question, content is the first concern of writing instruction. Nevertheless, handwriting and the mechanics of writing must be taught. Ms. Smart, a marvelous first-grade teacher from whom I learned much, expected legible handwriting, so she taught handwriting. She expected proper punctuation, so she taught punctuation. And her children wrote the most fluent, creative compositions I have ever seen produced by first-grade children. Much of the writing could easily be taken for advanced fourth-grade writing. She praised; she shared; she created real audiences for writing. Content was her first concern, yet she never hesitated to teach the mechanics of writing. She was always gentle and frequently informal in her approach. She preferred on the spot one-to-one instruction, yet when her class needed more extensive help on a particular skill she taught it, usually to the whole class. Ms. Smart convinced me that there is no fundamental conflict between legible handwriting and composing well, nor between the mechanics of writing and content.

Associating Letters with Sounds

I have discussed in detail how children come to associate letters with sounds in Chapter 1, but a brief reminder is relevant here. Before children enter school, they learn to distinguish whispers from shouts, laughter from tears, angry voices from friendly ones. They have also learned the speech sounds, the phonetics, of their native language—the proof is that they can talk. That phonetic knowledge is put to use when children write. To be ready for independent writing, children must learn auditory discrimination (in the current jargon, *phonemic awareness*), the ability to distinguish one speech sound from another, as well as learning to associate speech sounds with the letters that represent them.

WRITING FOR THE FIRST TIME

Beginnings are hard, and the hardest beginning of all is the one you make alone. But lessons learned alone strengthen confidence. Beginning writing will test any teacher's mettle. You will experience victory and defeat. You will sometimes be dismayed by the frail and feeble writing your children produce. On losing days you may ask yourself, "Why did I ever start this writing program?" However, you will win more often than you will be defeated, and you will be delighted by the vigorous and vibrant writing your children produce.

Writing has many beginnings, but perhaps the most difficult beginning of all is writing for the first time. The stories in Figure 2.2 were written by first-grade children in November. The teacher, Ms. Cosma, had recorded a few group and individually dictated experience stories for 10 weeks prior to the writing of these stories. One day, while visiting in her

Story as written	Translation
My Dad And me wr bltting a Hos it was A Big Hos. David	My dad and me were building a house. It was a big house. David
I play in the grass And I play with my frads And I play with Debbie. Mary	I play in the grass. And I play with my friends. And I play with Debbie. Mary
Wane the poho Wan evng wane wt iut to get some hane he kalimd and kalimd for hane he fnd hane. John	Winnie the Pooh One evening Winnie went out to get some honey. He climbed and climbed for honey. He found honey. John
My Dad is nice My Mom is nice My sistrss is nice Danielle (first story)	My dad is nice. My mom is nice. My sisters is nice. Danielle
I like to play on the siweing with my bruthrs and Sistr. Danielle (second story)	I like to play on the swing with my brothers and sister. Danielle
I kak my had I fel off the bed My Mom tok me to the hsptl. Nathalie	I cracked my head. I fell off the bed. My mom took me to the hospital. Nathalie

FIGURE 2.2. Stories by David, Mary, John, Danielle, and Nathalie: First independent writing.

classroom, I asked Ms. Cosma if her children had started independent writing. "No," she replied, "none of my children are ready to write." I suspected that some could write, if given an opportunity, so I asked if any of her children could read. I knew that children who can read can nearly always write. She named five children who were readers: Mary, John, Danielle, Nathalie, and David.

I gathered the children around a table in the back of the room, and asked, "Have any of you written a story by yourself?" Their answer confirmed my suspicions: "We can't write," one of them said. Nevertheless, I believed they could. We talked a bit about writing. Finally, David asked, "What could we write about?" His question gave me an opening, so we talked about writing topics, and I recorded their ideas on the board.

When I knew that everyone had something to write about I said, "There will be some words you will want to use but don't know how to spell. When that happens, I'll help you." I expected that there would be many such words, and I wanted them to ask for help so that I could show them how to work through a word they didn't know how to spell. To give them a head start, I showed them how to invent the spelling of my name. We worked our way through my name in three steps: How do you think it starts? What do you hear next? What comes last? Together, they came up with *K-r-m-r*—a good effort.

They began writing. Soon, John asked, "How do you spell *evening?*" Perhaps he thought I would tell him how to spell *evening*; instead, I took him through an instructional routine that helps children focus on the beginning, middle, and ending of the word they want to spell. I wanted John and the other children to learn this routine. It went like this:

MR. CRAMER: Listen as I say the word *evening*. What's the first sound you hear in *evening*? (*I pronounced* evening *with a slight emphasis on the first sound.*)

JOHN: I hear an *e*.

MR. CRAMER: Good, John. Write the *e*. Now listen again. What's the next sound you hear in *evening*? (*This time I emphasized the second sound.*)

JOHN: I hear a *v*? (*Uncertainty registered in his voice.*)

MR. CRAMER: That's fine, John. Write the *v*. What is the last sound you hear in *evening*? (*This time I emphasized, ever so slightly, the last sound.*)

JOHN: Is it *ng*? (*Uncertainty again.*)

MR. CRAMER: That's excellent John. *E-v-n-g* is close to the way *evening* is spelled. Every time you have a word you want to write but you don't know how to spell it, spell it just like we did together.

Invented spelling procedures should focus attention on the beginning, middle, and ending of a word: How does the word start? What comes next? How does the word end? I repeated this three-step routine each time one of the children asked for help. David, John, and Nathalie were soon inventing their own spellings, while Danielle and Mary needed much encouragement. Independent writing is greatly hampered when children are reluctant to risk making spelling errors. Most children catch on to invented spelling quite easily, and delight in running their own show. Other children, like Danielle and Mary, may be uncomfortable with invented spelling. There are children who would rather not use a word at all than spell it incorrectly. Patience and supportive teaching helps such children overcome their initial reluctance. Gradually, as children experience the rewards of fluent writing, they accept and even enjoy inventing their own spellings.

When the children had completed their stories, they read their stories to the principal, a supportive administrator, who asked the children if he could display their stories on his bulletin board. The children were reluctant to part with their stories, and asked that copies be made. When we returned to the classroom, the children read their stories to the class. It was a proud moment for them. As I was leaving, the other children asked me to return to write stories with them, which I did.

There is a relationship between content and spelling in these stories. For example, I think one could reasonably argue that John's story is the most lively and interesting, even though it has the highest percentage of spelling errors. About 62% of the words in John's story are misspelled. The relationship of spelling errors to story content is not accidental. Generally speaking, the children who took the greatest risks produced the best writing (David, Nathalie, John) They were not intimidated by the spelling demands inherent in the writing task. Consequently, they subordinated spelling to content, and the result was better writing.

I will push the point a little further. Mary's and Danielle's first story are less interesting, and they have the highest percentage of correctly spelled words. Danielle and Mary played it safe and used only those words they thought they could spell. Inevitably, this "play-it-safe" attitude adversely influences content because it inhibits the full use of available language. Danielle's second story is more interesting than her first, if only slightly. As she began to feel more comfortable with invented spelling, she took greater risks.

To write effectively, children must be able to use all the words and experiences at their command. If teaching methods restrict the flow of words and experiences, writing will be impoverished. Children who are just beginning to write have an abundance of words and experiences. Most first-grade children have an oral vocabulary ranging from 5 to 20,000 words, yet can spell less than 1% of these words. When spelling and other concerns are removed, children can concentrate on content. Later, after fluency is well established, they can learn to revise, edit, and proofread their writing for a public audience.

··•··

FOUR WRITING STAGES

Writing begins as play. Children begin writing the moment they put crayon to wall. Understanding its origins requires an act of imagination. Imagine Amy: At 18 months she walks, talks, and tumbles. She is a delightful nuisance! Alone in her room one day, she picks up a crayon and moves it vigorously across her bedroom wall. Behold, marks appear! She wonders, "What is this magic?" Of course, Amy's earliest marks are experimental and random. She loves making marks, and so she scribbles on every object in sight. It's great fun!

Amy's mom and dad encourage her scribbling while substituting paper for wall. They read to her and hang her "writings" on the refrigerator door, making much fuss over their beauty and importance. Sometimes Mom writes *A-m-y* on Amy's papers, points to the letters, and says, "Amy, these letters spell your name." By age 4, Amy is an emerging writer who has developed a magnificent obsession. Her writing is no longer random, although it is still exploratory and experimental. Now she writes with an *intent to convey meaning*. Yesterday Amy "wrote" a grocery list "just like Mom's," she said. When Amy and Mom went shopping, each had a grocery list. Today Amy scribbled a note to her daddy. Amy read it to Dad: "It says, 'I love you, Dad.' " Dad gave Amy a hug. Literacy had emerged as an important part of Amy's landscape. Her writing conveys messages, and she knows that her messages say important things. What began as play, scribbling on the bedroom wall, has evolved into complex learning.

Four stages of writing development may be observed among emerging writers such as Amy: scribbling, drawing, letter strings, and invented spelling. The first three stages are prephonetic and the fourth is phonetic. Prephonetic writers have not yet grasped the connection between letters and sounds, whereas phonetic writers have. Phonetic writers use invented spelling to approximate the correct spelling of words.

Scribble Stage

Elsie is 5 and in kindergarten. One morning she approached her teacher, Ms. Mead, with a story she had "written."

ELSIE: This story is about my dog.

MS. MEAD: Tell me about your story.

ELSIE: This is Scat (*she points to a figure*). Scat and I like to play. He chases me and I chase him.

Elsie pointed to specific marks on her paper indicating the events of the
story. Later, from the author's chair, Elsie "read" the same story, described
the same events, and pointed to the same figures as when she had shared
her writing with Ms. Mead. Elsie is in the scribble stage of writing, but she
knows that her drawings and lines have meaning, because she intentionally
invests her "writing" with meaning.

Between ages 3 and 5, most children know that marks on paper have
meaning. These marks are often called *scribbling*, but perhaps the term
scribble is misleading because it conveys the inaccurate impression that
scribble writing lacks purpose. This is not so; the scribble stage of writing
is purposeful. For the 1- or 2-year-old child, scribbling may be primarily a
pleasurable physical activity, but for children 3–5, scribbling and drawing
take on meaning.

During the scribble stage, children imitate adult writing, producing
cursive and printlike forms. Scribble writing shows connections with
conventional writing. For example, there is evidence of left-to-right and
top-to-bottom orientation and a kind of mock writing that resembles print
and cursive writing. Letters are sometimes interspersed among drawings
and lines. Most importantly, there is an intent to communicate ideas,
although a specific message is not always intended (Clay, 1975). Erin's
writing (see Figure 2.3) exemplifies the scribble stage of writing, showing
cursivelike scribbles moving left to right. Erin tells her teacher that her
writing says: "Here comes a big Indian. Let's make a run for it."

Drawing Stage

Dyson (1983) describes this conversation with a young writer:

> "Barry," I asked, "What do grown-ups write?"
> "Oh, letters . . . like J, G, H, K," replied the five year old.
> "What do you write?" I continued.
> "I just write houses and stuff." (p. 886)

Barry "writes" with pictures. Why not? Picture writing is the original form
of writing, many thousands of years older than writing with letters.
Further, there are practical reasons why Barry began writing with drawings
rather than print. First, he had not yet learned the alphabetic system—
writing with letters and sounds. Second, he has learned to represent
meaning through pictures. Third, he viewed drawing itself as a form of
writing, a reasonable alternative to writing with letters.

Drawing is a form of early writing. For young writers, like Barry and
Erin, drawing and writing are one. Children's first letters and words often

FIGURE 2.3. Erin's story: Scribble stage.

appear among pictures they have drawn. Young children have greater control over their drawings than they do over written language. Sometimes children "write" in pictures alone; other times their drawings include letters and copied words. Children give meaning to their drawing and writing by talking about them. For the young child, drawing and writing are closely related ways of communicating meaning (Dyson, 1988).

Drawing is an important adjunct to writing growth. Even after children have learned conventional forms of writing, drawing continues to play a supporting role in writing. Drawing supplements the written messages of young writers; stimulates recall, making it easier for children to read and reread their writing; benefits children independent of its contribution to writing, since art is an expressive medium unto itself. The drawing stage of writing is illustrated in Tanita's work (Figure 2.4.) Notice that three sight words (*witch, broom, ghost*) are included in this drawing. These words were copied from a source, as the writer was still in the prephonetic stage of spelling development.

Letter-String Stage

Once children have learned to make letters and numbers, they write strings of letters to communicate their messages (Figure 2.5). Letter-string writing indicates that children have grasped the generative principle of writing. Once children discover that words can be generated using only a few letters in varying combinations, they begin writing strings of letters that they suspect say something. A child might think of it like this: "Hey, I can write lots of words and ideas with just a few letters." The letter-string stage is still prephonetic writing, since there is no intentional connection between letters and sounds. As in the scribble and drawing stages, certain features of conventional writing are present in the letter-string stage. These features include letters, names, copied words, punctuation marks, directional orientation, and perhaps a few known sight words. Figure 2.5 illustrates a

FIGURE 2.4. Tanita's story: Drawing stage

number of Clay's (1975) principles. Some of the letter arrangements suggest letter-string work; others suggest the flexibility principle, that is, experimenting with a variety of letter forms; some of the letters suggest the recurring principle—repeating certain forms. There is no end to the inventiveness of children as they explore the world of letters and words, trying to discover how it works, how they can master it, and what purpose it may be made to serve.

Clay (1975) describes the prephonetic child's sense of writing like this: "The child seems to say, 'I hope I've said something important. You must be able to understand what I've said. What did I write?'" (p. 24). The scribbling, drawing, and letter-string stages are examples of prephonetic writing that are intended to communicate meaning. Absent, however, is any connection between letters and sounds. When children begin making such connections, they move into phonetic writing.

Invented Spelling Stage

Once children understand that letters can represent sounds, they can make educated guesses about how to spell words. In learning to talk, children

FIGURE 2.5. Lynette's story: Letter-string stage.

have acquired a thorough knowledge of phonetics, the speech sounds of language. This knowledge enables children to invent or approximate the spelling of unknown words remarkably well at an early age (Cramer, 1968, 1970; Chomsky, 1971; Read, 1971). Young children are excellent at listening to the sounds they hear in words and matching letters to sounds. As spelling growth continues, children develop additional spelling strategies, as discussed earlier.

When children invent spellings, every letter is intended to stand for a sound they hear. Watch a first-grade child invent spellings and you will see an amateur linguist at work, as in Temple, Nathan, Burris, and Temple's (1988) description: "If you watch a youngster invent spellings, you will see and hear him exaggerating the production of speech sounds: whistling her S's, stabbing repeatedly at her D's, choo-chooing her H's. On a working level she is exploring place, manner, and voicing. But if you ask her what she's doing—'Writing you a letter,' she says!" (p. 64). Writing with invented spelling is a boon to emerging literacy. The exploratory nature of invented spelling teaches children much of what they need to know about written language. Just as taking away exploration from oral language learning removes a crucial mechanism for learning to talk, taking away exploration from written language learning removes a crucial mechanism for learning to read, write, and compose. An example will illustrate this assertion.

Lynn, a prolific first-grade writer, tells of an adventure she experienced with her toys and her cat (Figure 2.6.) There is no word for which Lynn cannot invent an appropriate spelling. Follow the original text and compare it with the "translation." You will find that her spelling is quite extraordinary.

PRINCIPLES OF BEGINNING WRITING

In the early 1960s, a distinguished scholar published research on the writing of intermediate grade children. He explained his lack of data for children in Grades K–3 by suggesting that children at these levels either do not write or write only under duress. Old myths die hard. However, a new day has dawned. There is no excuse today for believing that young children cannot write. Evidence to the contrary is overwhelming.

Clay (1975) has identified a number of concepts and principles that describe young children's early efforts to write, help define the nature of their writing, and provide clues for nurturing it, as well. Some of these concepts and principles are obvious to the casual observer, while others are more subtle. Teachers can benefit from some of the ideas embedded in the principles identified by Clay and elaborated by others. I review

Clay's ideas—the meaning, exploration, sign, generative, directional, inventory, and spacing principles—while adding my own understanding of what these concepts might imply for the teaching of writing to young children.

Meaning Principle

At age 3, my daughter Amy learned her first written word, *Pepsi*. She liked to drink it , and so did I. When traveling, she knew where to stop to get a bottle of Pepsi. At the grocery store, she unerringly distinguished her favorite from the also-rans. How did she "read" this word? Initially, the context of a red, white, and blue logo containing a five-letter word enabled her to "read" *Pepsi*. Gradually, *Pepsi* became a sight word known outside of its logo context. Why did Amy learn *Pepsi* so readily? Because it had powerful meaning for her.

The preeminence of meaning is the most pervasive characteristic of

Original story	Translation
"The Big ivs"	"The Big adventure"
Page 1: I like to pl with my	I like to play with my
ts wn day my ts	toys one day my toys
wt ta I as my mom	weren't there I asked my mom
af sy nw wa ty wa tn	if she knew where they were then
lfa o.c. my cat wi my	I found o.c. my cat with my
ts. I td my mom	toys. I told my mom
tat I fd my ts.	that I found my toys.
Page 2: my mom sd gd I am	my mom said good I am
ga tat you fd your ts	glad that you found your toys
and sa gv me a big hg	and she gave me a big hug
Page 3: the nx day I td	the next day I told
my dad abt the	my dad about the
big ivs and ha	big adventure and he
liked ti	liked it
Page 4: I ct on ti pb	I kept on telling people
ab the big ivs	about the big adventure
Page 5: sa I nva ft	so I never forgot
the big ivs	the big adventure
Page 6: and I rmb it	and I remember it
all my lfe.	all my life.

(continued)

FIGURE 2.6. Lynn's story: Invented spelling stage.

FIGURE 2.6 *(continued)*

(continued)

Sd I nva ft at
the big ivs

and I rmb it
all my lfe.

FIGURE 2.6 *(continued)*

emerging literacy. Children expect written language to be meaningful (Dyson, 1983; Harste , Woodward, & Burke, 1984; Newman, 1984; Sultzby & Teale, 1985; Sultzby, 1986); this expectation is deeply embedded in our culture. Everything children know about written language tells them that writing conveys meaning. Clay (1975) describes just how acutely aware a 5-year-old can be about the meaningfulness of writing: "Peter produced a string of letter signs, intermingled with drawing artistically presented in green and orange crayon. He thought it probably contained an important message after the care he had taken with it, and he delivered it into my hand with the instruction 'Give this to your children, and learn them it cause it says a lot of fings!' " (p. 50).

Children are prepared by our popular culture to recognize oral and written language as meaningful. They are bombarded with print in books and buses, supermarkets and subways. Today, most children know that two golden arches and a particular configuration of letters means *McDonald's*. Take a preschooler to the supermarket and he or she may read the specific or generic names of well-known products: cookies, Oreos, cereal, Froot Loops. Popular culture transmits this knowledge through commercials, signs, toys, and even the clothing we wear.

It is not surprising, therefore, that meaning pervades children's earliest writing attempts. What adults call scribbling is meaningful writing to children. Only at the earliest ages are written marks on paper random. Between age 3 and 5, writing becomes purposeful. Children begin to produce lines that looks like cursive writing and block letters that resemble print. They discover that their names can be written, an important early experience demonstrating the meaningfulness of print. Such experiences with oral and written language prepare children to write at an early age.

Exploration Principle

Ben, age 4, waited in the yard while his dad crossed the street to the neighbor's house. Dad's quick return took Ben by surprise: "What took you so *short*?" he asked. Ben could not have heard this expression in adult speech. It simply does not occur in adult language. So where did he learn it? All language learning is exploratory, whether spoken or written. Ben's expression is a language experiment. He explored the possibility of reversing a familiar adult expression, "What took you so long?" Later, he will discover that his sensible analogy is not used in mature speech. In the meanwhile, it communicates perfectly well. Gradually, Ben will sort out the conventions that govern his native language, but first he must explore the possibilities. The more he explores, the more likely he is to learn the conventions rapidly and with ease.

Just as children explore oral language, they also explore written language when given the opportunity. Exploration is a necessary condition for writing growth. Therefore, acceptance of the beginning writer's errors is essential. Where taking a risk brings censure, writing will be timid. Where mistakes earn only scorn, writing will lack imaginative force.

When Alisha finished her first written story (Figure 2.7), she said to her teacher, Ms. Motrik, "I've told lots of stories, but this is the first one I wrote. I like writing stories." Alisha wrote "One Lonely Bear" in February

Original story	Translation
Page 1: One night thar was a sad bear he was so sad that he cad cri. one day he wat away to fid hany	One night there was a sad bear he was so sad that he could cry. one day he went away to find honey
Page 2: Bet he sdred to cri so he datat no wat to do so he sayd "yi am I so an happy?" sa din Lee he hrd a vos he lot a rad he dete see ahne thg	But he started to cry so he didn't know what to do so he said "why am I so unhappy?" suddenly he heard a voice he looked around he didn't see anything
Page 3: Bet than he sa samthen in has shado he lact and he sa a snail tacen to haim the snail "sayd you r so sad b cas no bdey lics you no't" sayd the Bear	But then he saw something in his shadow he looked and he saw a snail talking to him the snail "said you are so sad because nobody likes you why not "said the Bear
Page 4: Bet the snail cate halp the Bear so the snail wat away Bet sapthen als was in has shado at was a racoon the racoon sayd "nan av the ahnm can halp you"	But the snail couldn't help the Bear so the snail went away But something else was in his shadow it was a racoon the racoon said "none of the animals can help you"
Page 5: (*Dictated to the teacher*) So you know that sooner or later you'll have to go to a new forest. And when you leave all of the animals will say good by to you.	

(continued)

FIGURE 2.7. Alisha's story, "One Lonely Bear": Exploration principle.

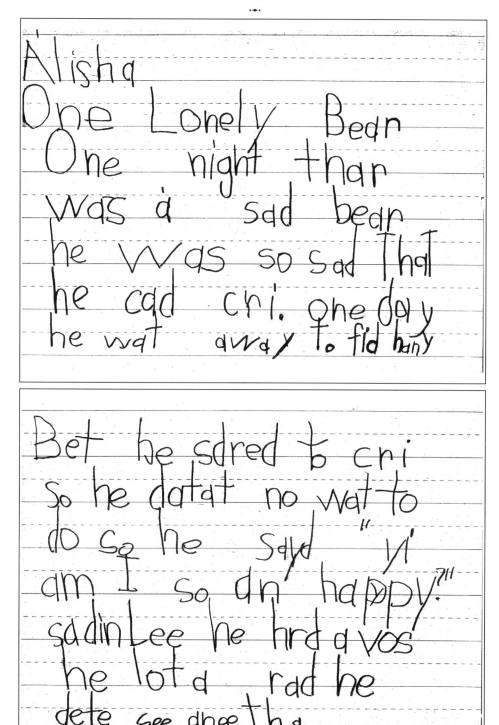

Alisha
One Lonely Bear
One night thar
was a sad bear
he was so sad that
he cad cri. one day
he wat away To fid huny

Bet he sdred to cri
So he datat no wat to
do so he sayd "yi
am I so an happy?"
sadinlee he hrd a vos
he lot a rad he
dete see dhee tho

(continued)

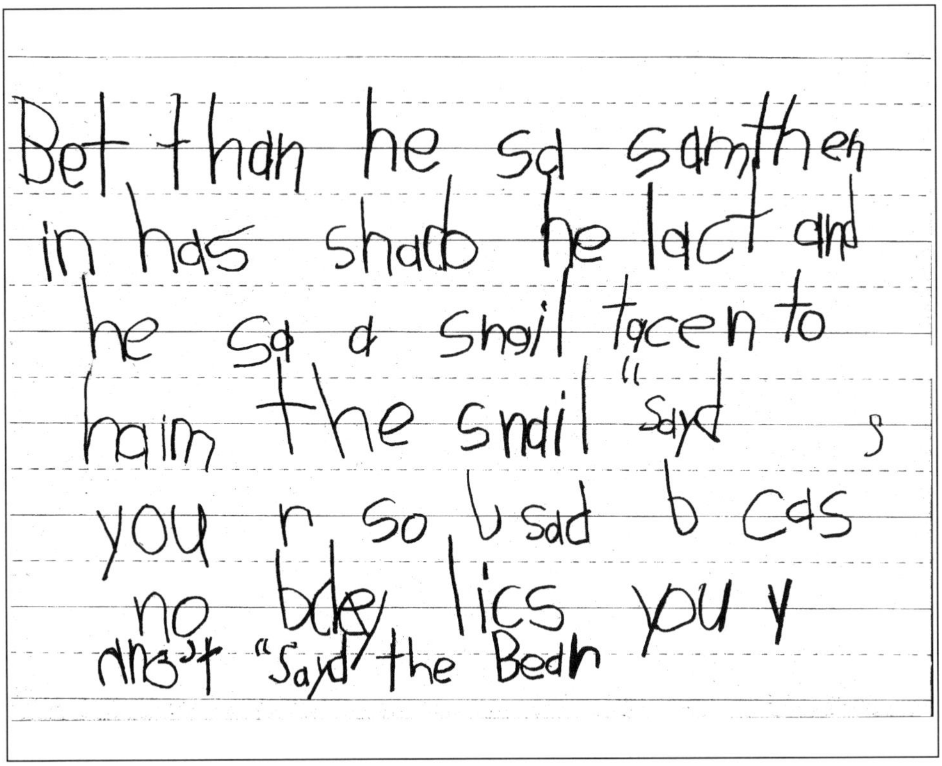

Bet than he sd samthen
in has shacb he lact and
he sd a snail tacen to
haim the snail "sayd   ,
you r so v sad b cds
no bdey lics you y
nns-t "sayd the Bean

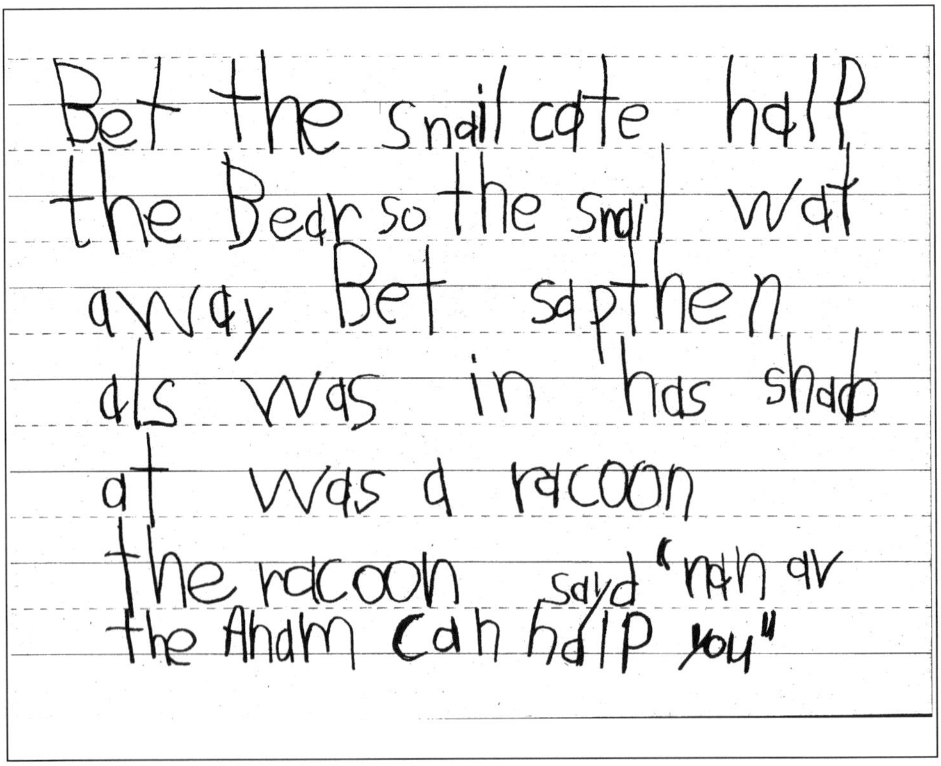

Bet the snail cate half
the Bear so the snail wat
away Bet sapthen
als was in has shacb
at was a racoon
the racoon sayd "nah av
the Anam cah halp you"

FIGURE 2.7 (continued)

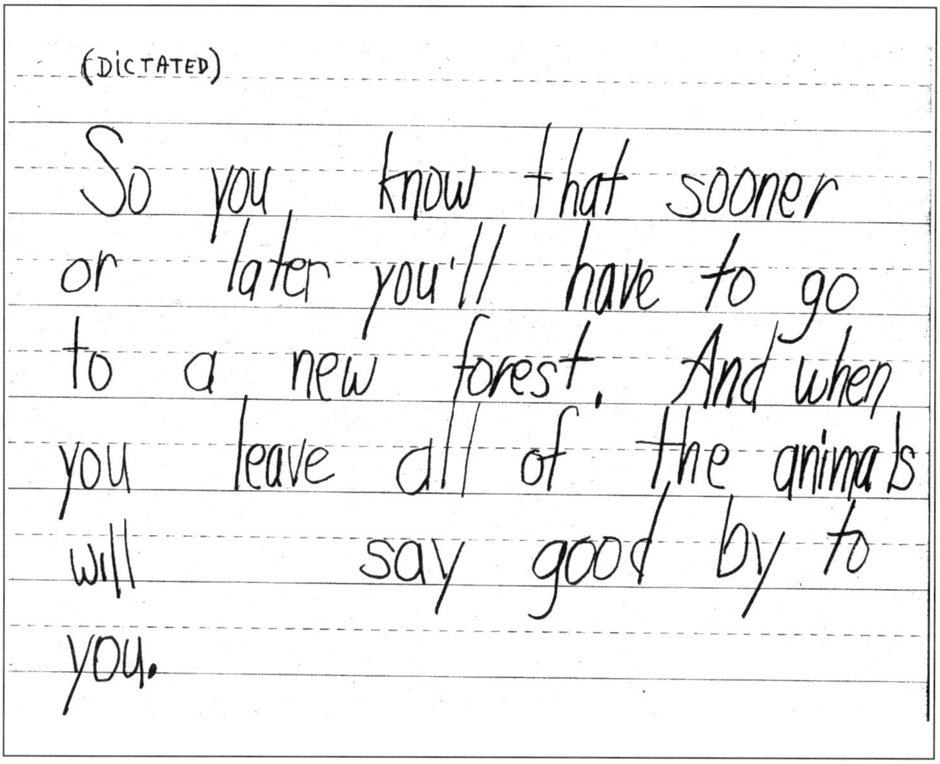

(DICTATED)

So you know that sooner
or later you'll have to go
to a new forest. And when
you leave all of the animals
will say good by to
you.

FIGURE 2.7 *(continued)*

of her first-grade year. At the time, she read at a first-grade level. It took Alisha nearly an hour to write her first story—five pages of text, thoughtfully worded, using invented spelling as she went.

This was the first time Ms. Motrik had asked any of her first graders to write independently, although they had often taken group and individually dictated stories. After Alisha had written four pages on her own, she tired. So Ms. Motrik took the last page (p. 5) of her story in dictation.

Two lessons may be drawn from the circumstances surrounding the writing of "One Lonely Bear." First, it pays to take risks, like Alisha and Ms. Motrik did. Ms. Motrik wasn't sure Alisha was ready to write, but she risked trying an unfamiliar idea. Alisha risked writing a story without knowing how to spell many of the words she would need and uncertain of most written language conventions. Without Ms. Motrik's support, Alisha would not have written "One Lonely Bear" and surely would not have discovered her gift for writing so early. Ms. Motrik's support made the risks acceptable.

Teachers support students, but who supports teachers? Who makes the risks acceptable for the Ms. Motriks of the teaching profession? Teaching is a lonely job. Ms. Motrik had my moral support, but that is cold comfort when faced with daily classroom decisions. Unfortunately, she had little support from colleagues and school administrators. Nevertheless, Ms. Motrik profited from this experience. She learned the value of writing and discovered that she had underestimated the writing potential of her students. Such teachers are the heroes of their profession, possessing the courage to take risks. Fortunately, risk taking pays dividends for children as well as teachers.

The second lesson is that dictation prepares children for independent writing. Alisha's writing shows that she had some understanding of certain conventions of written language. She occasionally used a period or a question mark. One one occasion she used a contraction, incorrectly, but in an appropriate context (*no't*). When Alisha used quotation marks, she did so within the context of a conversation. For instance, *said* is not incorporated into a quotation in one instance, but is on another. Even when she made a mistake, she came close to correct usage.

Alisha's writing also shows a remarkable knowledge of spelling. Where did she learn so much about writing without having written? She learned it from reading and from her dictated accounts, most likely. Alisha's reading instruction had included frequent opportunities to dictate stories. Dictation played an important role in her knowledge of punctuation and spelling, giving her many opportunities to see her oral language converted into written language, along with the appropriate written language conventions.

Give beginning writers many opportunities to write without undue concern for correctness, particularly during first draft writing. For the beginning writer, the mechanical aspects of writing are formidable. Beginning writers are still mastering pencil and paper, hand–eye coordination, and letter–sound associations. These are complex tasks that slow down writing. Beginning writers need patience, purpose, and an appreciative audience. Give them a well-balanced mix of reading and writing along with targeted instruction as needed. Above all, focus on meaning.

Sign Principle

Children must learn the many signs of the English language in order to read and write: letters, numbers, and punctuation marks. There are 26 letters, (52 if you consider upper- and lowercase) a dozen or so punctuation marks and 10 numbers, which can be used in an almost infinite number of combinations. Children discover early that writing stands for something besides itself, although they may not know just what. Learning these signs requires that children experiment—and they do. Early writing is full of invented shapes: blocks, circles, squiggles, reversals. Children invent new signs and elaborate on traditional ones as they learn the writing system.

Their explorations lead to mastery of letters, punctuation, and word meaning. Clay (1975) describes the importance of young writers' explorations this way: "Left to experiment with letter forms children will create a variety of new symbols by re-positioning or decorating the standard forms. In this way they explore the limits within which each letter may vary and still retain its identity" (p. 43).

Children grasp the sign principle readily when their environment is filled with meaningful, pleasurable exposure to print, as in the following examples. Jenny, age 4, bursts into the living room waving a piece of paper containing a string of letters. "Dad, what does this say?" She thinks it must say something wonderful, perhaps because Mom and Dad have read many wonderful stories to her. Reading to children and encouraging their "writing" soon gives them the idea that print, not the pictures, is the source of the stories they've been listening to. Once children make this crucial discovery, they have understood the sign principle that writing stands for something besides itself, and that it can be used to convey meaningful ideas. From Jenny's perspective, her piece of writing is much like the books read to her and the books she pretends to read. Dad accepts Jenny's offering as a legitimate piece of writing and solemnly reads it to her. Soon, Jenny is back with another piece of writing. This time *she* knows what it says: "Dad, this says, 'I love you very much' " (Figure 2.8).

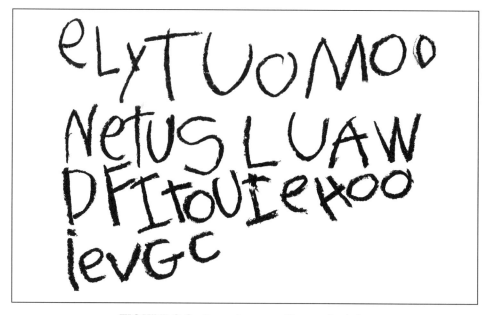

FIGURE 2.8. Jenny's story: Sign principle.

Generative Principle

Carla, a kindergarten youngster, wrote a string of letters in her journal and drew a picture (Figure 2.9). Her string of letters tells about the beautiful building she had drawn. Once children discover that a few letters, used in varying combinations, can generate many words, they have understood the generative principle of writing. Children often show they have understood this idea well before they can write authentic words. Carla's letter string, an example of prephonetic writing, suggests that she understands this idea. Prephonetic writers make no connections between letters and sounds and cannot, therefore, spell words. Sometimes, however, they copy words or write their names. These letter strings represent real writing to writers such as Carla. They think they have discovered how to write real messages, and they are partly right. They have discovered a basic principle by which writing is generated, and this is an important beginning. As reading and writing skill grows, children add letter-sound associations to their knowl-

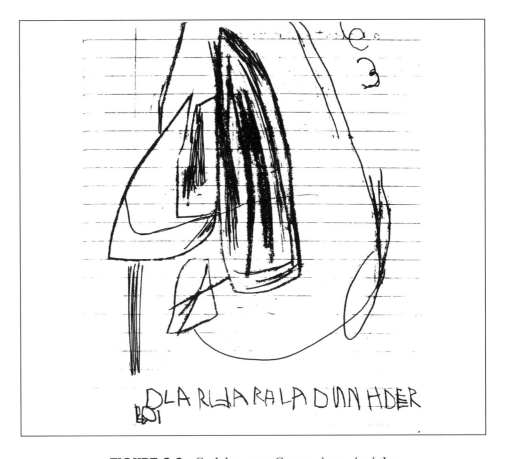

FIGURE 2.9. Carla's story: Generative principle.

edge base, enabling them to generate real words using invented spelling. When this happens, conventional writing begins.

Directional Principle

Melissa, a precocious 5-year-old, wrote everything backwards. Melissa's mother suspected dyslexia and asked a neighbor, a former teacher, for advice. She sat down with Melissa and said, "Sweetheart, when you write you start on this side (she pointed to the left-hand margin of the paper) and write in this direction. Like this." Then she demonstrated where to start, how to move from one line to the next, and which direction to orient the letters. "Oh, so that's how you do it!" said Melissa, taking the pencil and writing in the normal way. Melissa subsequently exhibited only the occasional lapses into directional confusion that normally accompany learning to read and write.

Directional confusion, such as Melissa's, causes great anxiety among teachers and parents. The popular press and much of the learning disabilities literature have given the impression that directional confusion is symptomatic of perceptual disability, learning disability, and that hydra-headed monster, dyslexia. The following discussion addresses issues related to directional confusion, including its normality, causes, misidentification with learning disabilities, and correction.

The Normality of Directional Confusion

Directional confusion is common, and it doesn't end in the primary grades. Ask any drill sergeant. As a raw recruit in basic training, I kept my left thumb pressed tightly into my index finger. I did this to orient myself to left–right movements during rapid order drill. I learned this trick from a drill sergeant who "suggested" it after I had marched off in the opposite direction from the rest of the platoon on several memorable and embarrassing occasions. And if you have ever driven in England, you will certainly appreciate the normality of directional confusion. You soon learn the new system, but the slightest inattention can cause you to revert to the old system. With practice, errors diminish and then seemingly disappear. Months or even years later, however, you find yourself driving on the wrong side of the road again. You have reverted to an old habit.

Children have similar problems with the directional structure of English, which is written from left to right and top to bottom. This directional pattern is arbitrary. Hebrew, for instance, is written from right to left, and traditional Chinese is written from right to left and vertically. While learning to orient their writing according to the directional principles of English, children have periods of confusion in which they find it helpful to experiment. For example, they try a variety of arrangements of print on the page, reversing letters and words and orienting print in the wrong direction. In short, they experiment and learn, and, like a raw army recruit, they occasionally march off in the wrong direction. These minor lapses may last for years for some children.

Causes of Directional Confusion

Most directional problems are caused by factors present in the writing situation. Knowing what these factors are can help you understand why they occur and how to correct them. There are at least six prominent causes of directional confusion.

Focusing. Writing presents several major tasks that must be confronted simultaneously: meaning and message, spelling and mechanics, letter formation, and page arrangement. Writing requires a balance between conflicting obligations. On the one hand, writers must attend to all aspects of the writing task. On the other hand, they must give special attention to meaning. Experienced writers have an enormous advantage over inexperienced writers. They can put the mechanics of writing on automatic pilot while attending to meaning.

Young writers do not have this option. They face a double bind. If they focus on meaning, as they should, mechanical errors will certainly occur. If they focus on meaning and mechanics, mechanical errors will likewise occur. Either circumstance results in a variety of writing difficulties more severe for young writers than for mature writers. Young writers are especially prone to directional confusion, a matter that rarely troubles the mature writer.

There are solutions to the double bind that young writers face. Above all, wait patiently for young writers to mature. As they mature, directional confusion will diminish, as will other mechanical errors. Then, as you teach revision, etch on children's consciousness that no mistake need be permanent; mistakes take on an entirely different character when this is understood and practiced.

Different Learning Rates. George was in the third grade, reading at a sixth-grade level. While other third graders read books of 20 or 30 pages, George read books of 200 or 300 pages. Even so, when writing he sometimes reversed letters and words. Should Ms. Kaufman, George's teacher, worry? No. Why not? George's pace as a reader is far faster than most third graders. On the other hand, his pace in mastering directional concepts is slower than other third graders. His reversals are the residual traces of past confusion. They will continue to surface for an indeterminate period of time. Eventually, they will disappear entirely. Since George reads and writes perfectly well, no specific remediation is necessary.

Misinterpretation of Instructions. Even when instructions are seemingly clear, children often misinterpret them. Misinterpretation of directions can result in directional confusion, as happened with Gerry. Ms. Ellis, a first-grade teacher, wanted her children to conserve paper, so she said, "Write *to* the bottom of the page." Gerry thought Ms. Ellis meant start *at* the bottom of the page. Gerry started on the bottom line, right margin, and reversed the letters and words as she wrote. Later she explained why: "Ms. Ellis said, 'Start at the bottom of the page.' " Gerry's misinterpretation of perfectly reasonable directions is not unusual. Children can invent more ways to misinterpret directions than teachers can forecast. When directional confusion occurs, look for natural explanations first; never assume that a perceptual problem has caused the confusion. While perceptual problems have become a favorite explanation, they are seldom the culprit.

Immature Visual–Motor Coordination. Coordinating pencil, paper, and the complexities of writing is a formidable task. The younger the child, the more immature the visual–motor skills. Kindergarten, first-, and second-grade children are especially vulnerable to mistakes resulting from visual–motor immaturity. Children gain control of visual–motor tasks at different rates. Consequently, instruction geared to children's individual learning rates is necessary.

Conserving Space. What does an inexperienced writer do when the page ends before his or her thoughts are complete? He or she writes uphill, downhill, or anyplace there is room to finish the thought. Primary-grade children think this makes sense, and it accounts for some strange arrangements of print. Patient explanation of alternative solutions eventually solves this minor problem.

Momentary Forgetfulness or Confusion. In a moment of inattention or confusion, a child may reverse a letter or word. Forgetting what is correct is perfectly normal, especially during the early stages of learning. Distinguishing *m* from *w* or *p* from *q* is easily forgotten or confused when these concepts are still new. Maturity resolves the problem in the long run, but occasional gentle reminders are useful in the meanwhile. For example, when Billy reverses the letter *d* say, "Billy, watch while I make the letter *d*. Notice, the circle points in this direction."

These six causes of directional confusion discussed cover most cases. Occasionally, directional problems are of a more serious nature, but rare problems must not be confused with the garden-variety directional confusion many children experience during the early stages of learning to read and write.

Directional Confusion and Learning Disabilities

Learning disability theorists, including dyslexia enthusiasts, have assumed that reversals and directional confusion are important indicators of perceptual deficit. Actually, they are seldom more than temporary manifestations of immature reading and writing skill. Learning disability theorists have taken normal developmental behaviors to be indicators of damaged or deviant mental processing, whereas, on the contrary, reversals and directional confusion are far more likely to reveal perceptual flexibility than disability. Letter and word reversals, for example, signal children's effort to discover the proper way to perceive these signs. In effect, children ask themselves: How should letters be oriented in space? In what direction should letters and words be sequenced? What will happen if I turn this letter around? Should letters and words be perceived like other familiar objects?

In the perceptual world the child is familiar with, a shoe remains a shoe no matter how it is positioned in space. Turn a shoe upside down or sideways and it is still a shoe. But do letters, numbers, and words work in the same way? No. Writing is one of the few areas of experience where spatial orientation or sequence signals a change in identity. Move the letter *b* around in space and it becomes *p*, *d*, or *q*; write *on* right to left and its identity changes to *no*; rotate *9* on its axis and it becomes *6*. Young writers and readers have to learn these new identity concepts, a confusing task.

Correcting Directional Confusion

The right way and the best way to learn these new and difficult identity concepts is to explore how letters and words work by manipulating them. Writing provides this opportunity. It takes time and experience to orient oneself to the arbitrary direction of print. Some children catch on quickly and exhibit few reversal or directional problems, while other children are slower in gaining a stable sense of directional orientation. Most children exhibit some reversals or directional uncertainties throughout kindergarten, first grade, and into second grade. A few children exhibit directional problems as late as third or fourth grade. Indeed, directional problems can persist into adulthood, but in such cases they may signal insufficient achievement in reading and writing rather than perceptual problems. When growth is exceedingly slow or nonexistent, directional problems may continue indefinitely. Even in these cases, they are a symptom of the problem, not the problem itself.

Experimenting with letter shapes, directionality, and letter sequence is normal developmental behavior that involves reversals and other directional errors. Such errors may be common for a period of time, as was the case with Juanita who is in first grade (Figure 2.10). She reverses two words: *is—si* and *of—fo,* as well as the *g* and *d* in *gold.* The reversals Juanita

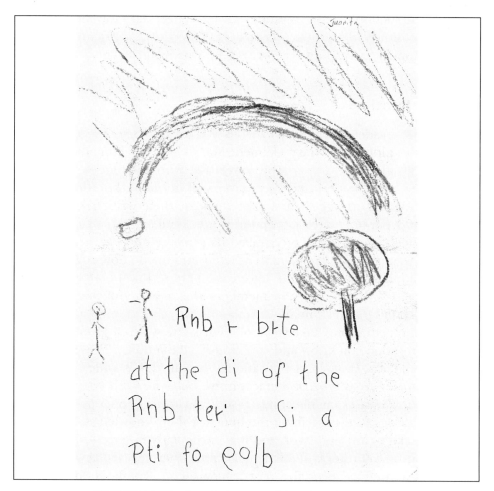

FIGURE 2.10. Juanita's story: Directional principle.

exhibits are normal and developmental. Children need reminders about how to orient their letters and words, but it should never be assumed that such reversals are a sign of a perceptual problem.

When helping children with orientation problems, this four-step procedure may be useful.

Step 1: Start at the top left position of your paper.
Step 2: Move left to right across the page.
Step 3: Return sweep down and to the left.
Step 4: Locate the next starting point.

In addition to these basic steps, show children how to use lined paper, how margins work, how to move to a new page, how to arrange print on a page, and other directional conventions related to specific situations. Informal instruction should continue as long as necessary for children who learn more slowly than their classmates. Directional difficulties nearly always disappear as reading and writing knowledge grows.

Inventory Principle

Mary, a first grader, handed Ms. Ames a booklet: "See, I know all the letters of the alphabet," Mary claimed. Mary's booklet contained all the letters of the alphabet, upper- and lowercase, with each letter illustrated by a picture. Mary had created an inventory of her letter knowledge. Even children as young as age 3 or 4 take stock of their writing knowledge. Teachers and parents of young children are familiar with this behavior, although they may not have recognized its purpose and characteristics.

Young writers enjoy assessing their letter and word knowledge. Typical inventories include upper- and lowercase letters, known words, words beginning with a certain letter, or members of a meaningful category, such as friends, family, and animals. Inventory lists vary, but their common characteristic is that they take stock of what is known in a given category.

Knowing what you know and consciously taking note of it is important learning behavior. In current educational jargon, this is called *metacognition*. Inventories are a type of metacognitive behavior with two important uses. First, inventories enable children to evaluate their own progress and gain satisfaction from describing the limits of their knowledge. Self-evaluation is crucial to any endeavor, and it is particularly important in writing. When children take stock of what they know, they can set new goals for themselves as well as recognize past achievements. Young children enjoy testing their knowledge, and if encouragement and support are abundant, they are likely to surprise you. Recently, for instance, I gave a book to a 3-year-old who was visiting my office with her grandmother, a graduate student. A few days later I received this thank-you note: "Dr Dictr cramer tank you for the book. I wal red at. you are nis. love Victoria."

Second, inventories give teachers information about children's progress that can be used to plan future instruction. Even more important, inventories inform teachers of progress already made. Encourage inventories. Now and again ask children to write all the letters or words they know. Encourage them to include a drawing along with their word or letter inventory. When children inventory some aspect of their writing knowledge, praise their effort, and share it with the class. Figure 2.11 is Rebecca's inventory of her alphabet knowledge.

Spacing Principle

We are accustomed to spacing between words; it seems so natural and sensible that it is difficult to imagine any other arrangement. Withoutspaceswordsruntogether. Thismakesreadingmoredifficult. However, many ancient languages, such as some ancient Greek manuscripts of the Bible, did not have spacing between words. Spacing between words is a relatively

FIGURE 2.11. Rebecca's story: Inventory principle.

new idea, a convenience for readers. Surprisingly, one can learn to read without spaces rather easily.

Some beginning writers leave little or no space between words. Others invent special devices, like stars and drawings of various kinds, to mark the boundaries between words. Darren (Figure 2.12) uses periods to indicate word boundaries in a little testimonial about his school—"And . this . the . best . school . I . ever . had." Difficulty with spacing does not necessarily mean children are unable to distinguish word boundaries. For children who can write, distinguishing word boundaries is a problem easily overcome.

Some teachers have children leave a space between words the width of their finger, pencil, or strip of thin cardboard. These devices provide a handy physical solution to the problem of word spacing. This temporary aid is usually spontaneously abandoned once children get the hang of word spacing. Now and again a child will need encouragement to abandon the spacing device, but this is easily accomplished through the use of praise and rewards. Some educators say that using a finger or pencil is a crutch. True! But remember that crutches are useful, even necessary, on certain occasions.

STRATEGIES FOR BEGINNING WRITING

Successful teachers of writing use many instructional strategies. The following ones have proven effective for many teachers. Persistence is a virtue when trying out a new instructional idea. If a new strategy seems not to work, consider the possible causes of the failure. Perhaps you need to adjust the strategy to suit your circumstances, personality, or teaching style. Other times you might have to give a new idea time to work or just fine-tune it. After a fair trial, of course, a strategy that does not work should be abandoned.

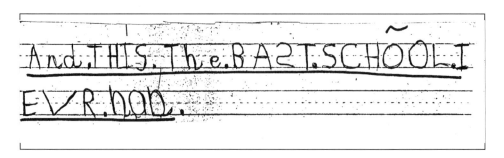

FIGURE 2.12. Darren's story: Spacing principle.

Recording Oral Language

Recording children's language through dictated accounts is good preparation for writing. It has several significant advantages. First, it is an excellent way to model the writing process. Many of the elements that go into graphically representing speech are modeled through dictation. Children can observe the transformation of oral into written language, such as left-to-right direction of print, the return sweep, punctuation, spelling, organization and sequencing of ideas, and revisions resulting from student-initiated changes. Best of all, they experience the wonder of their own talk transformed into print.

Second, dictation makes the connection between reading and writing easy to observe. After dictation, the account is reread. Rereading closes the circle between talking, writing, and reading, and illustrates this simple premise: "What I say can be written. What I write can be read."

Third, dictation provides an opportunity to model the four stages of the writing process. Prior to dictation, the children choose a topic and brainstorm ideas for their account. When ready, children dictate a first draft. Sometimes the first draft is the only draft, but often children add, delete, or rearrange information in the account. Dictated accounts are usually illustrated and shared with classmates. Thus, dictation paves the way for independent writing by giving experience in the writing process: planning, drafting, revising, and presenting writing.

Fourth, dictation increases composing fluency, a basic objective in writing. Having practiced composing through dictation, children come to writing confident in their ability to compose and well practiced in topic selection and development. Experience in oral composition prior to independent writing provides children a margin of comfort that facilitates independent writing.

Reading Aloud

I have never forgotten that my second-grade teacher, Ms. Ives, read to us every day. The books she read transformed a modest country classroom into a magic kingdom of "Let's Pretend." The benefits I derived from being read to are inestimable: a sense of story, an ear for language, a love of books, an appreciation for fine writing. All this from merely being read to? Yes. Small beginnings start avalanches. Ms. Ives started just such an avalanche of lifetime reading habits for me, which was augmented by other learning experiences.

Reading aloud demonstrates to children how marvelous a pleasure reading can be, as well as enriching language, building background knowledge, increasing print awareness, and sparking imagination. It lays the foundation on which the superstructure of writing is erected. Reading aloud prepares children for writing in ways no other activity can match. Listening to stories and poems read aloud is a vital component of literacy instruction. Read to children every day.

Consider your own likes and dislikes as well as those of your children when selecting read-aloud literature. Your tastes in literature are your legacy to your students. Young children appreciate interesting characters, simple plots, and an easily understood writing style. Show enthusiasm for what you are reading. Make certain the classroom is conducive to listening. Quiet the children, ensure their comfort and freedom from distractions, and see that the temperature and ventilation are properly adjusted.

Use vocal devices to suggest mood and tone. Inflection, volume, dramatic pause, and reading rate add to children's pleasure and understanding. Physical gestures also heighten interest. For instance, if you are reading the words of a wicked witch, facial expression and bodily posture help establish the witch's character. Younger readers especially enjoy the physical aspects of reading aloud. Finally, maintain eye contact and position yourself so that the children can easily see you.

Modeling

"Hey, Mr. Cramer, welcome to Maine-Endwell." Ed Ferencik, a sixth-grade teacher, welcomed me to my first teaching position in rural, upstate New York. Ed was my first graduate course in education. He was a model of what a teacher ought to be: caring, thoughtful, informed. We shared common teaching experiences: success and failure, frustration and satisfaction, joy and disappointment—the ups and downs that good teachers face every day. Ed was my mentor and role model in teaching. Through observation and conversation, I learned all that this good man had to share with a new teacher who wanted to be, like Ed, a good teacher.

As Ed was a model for me, so I became a model for my fifth graders. Like adults, children learn much by closely observing behavior exhibited by adults and peers. Model reading and writing behavior for your children. As you read, explain what you do, show how you do it, and tell why you enjoy it. As you write, show how ideas fit together, how writing decisions are made, how punctuation works, and why you enjoy writing. Don't be afraid to make mistakes in your writing when modeling for children. Making mistakes is normal, and kids need to know this. It also gives you an opportunity to show how you correct mistakes. Comment casually on the components of writing you want children to appreciate and practice. Help children see that they, too, can be readers and writers.

"Do as I do," is the motto of the role-modeling teacher. Above all, write something now and then that is just for your students. When I teach writing to my graduate students, I write stories and poems and share them before I ask them to share their writing with me. This makes my students much more willing to share their own writing. I wrote the following poem for one of my graduate classes and shared it with them.

Kenny: A Teacher Remembers

"Adios, Mr. Cramer," you whispered
As you hurried
From my fifth-grade classroom.
Long past, your whispered words,
And still they echo in my mind.
Kenny, you are a wound
That will not heal,
A memory that will not fade.

Thirty-seven years have glided past
Since last I saw you in the flesh.
I saw your face again today,
Dark and brooding,
Fire in the eyes,
Smoldering resentment,
Anger not yet fanned to flame.

You hated school and teachers,
And had good reason.
In class, you tested limits,
Grew interested in science,
Won a small prize in the science fair.
I worked to earn your trust,
You responded with the gift of trust.

You were a man–child
Poised on the cusp of life,
Ready to follow whatever model prevailed,
Good or bad, right or wrong.
Unaware of having chosen,
You chose death.

Death claimed you early,
A victim of angry men
Penned up with savage guards,
Even more savage inmates.
Death came in the cellblocks
Of Attica Prison.

You railed against a society
Which first wronged you,
And you returned that wrong
In fullest measure.
You robbed and murdered
Not ten years gone
From that fifth grade classroom
Wherein I sought to save your soul,
To rescue your fertile mind.

Perhaps my methods were not
Well suited to the task,
My understanding not yet mature.
But my heart went out to you,
As I sought to heal the hurt
Inflicted by a brutal father.

I let you down, Kenny,
It hurts to confess this truth.
So many deeds I did not do,
Words I did not say that might
Have turned your feet from
That dread path that led to
Early death for you and others.
If only I'd had the wisdom,
The goodness, the foresight.
"Adios, Kenny."

Connecting Drawing and Writing

Art helps children explore the connections between written and spoken language and the graphic world of art. Children can compose with words as well as pictures, language as well as lines. Crayons and paper, paint and brush are simple tools, but children can use these tools to create and re-create their own world of thought and imagination. Even children in the earliest stages of writing can combine drawings with letters and words. More advanced writers should also illustrate their writing.

Help children connect their drawings to spoken and written language. The connection is easily made. Talk with children about their drawings. Explain and illustrate the importance of drawing as a way of organizing and expressing ideas. Take dictation from those who cannot write independently. Label their drawings with words, phrases, or sentences. This helps children associate the ideas expressed in their drawings with those expressed through oral and written language. Encourage children to make their drawings as complete as possible so that their ideas are fully expressed. The more vivid and complete the drawing, the easier it is for children to recall their written and dictated language. Dyson (1988) points out that many children who elaborate their drawings also elaborate their written texts. She also discovered, however, that this did not hold true for all children.

Figure 2.13 is an excellent illustration of the connection between drawing and composing. Lynette, a kindergarten child, dictated "The Little Girl and Her Turtle." This three-part saga accompanied her lovely picture of a girl and her turtle. The string of letters is Lynette's independent contribution to the writing act, exemplifying the letter-string stage of prephonetic writing.

Conferencing

Linda, a second grader, had just completed a four-page story called "My Babe Bruthr." It took her 2 days to complete a first draft, during which time she had conferred with her teacher, Ms. Jordan, and had read parts of her draft to classmates. The questions and comments that arose during these on-the-spot conferences motivated Linda to continue drafting. Now, however, Linda had completed a draft and needed a more formal conference with her teacher.

Ms. Jordan started the conference by having Linda read her draft aloud. Then she retold the story to Linda. Retelling showed Linda that Ms. Jordan listened carefully, and it gave Linda an opportunity to consider whether the retelling was correct. It also helped Linda to consider how an outside audience understood her story, an important skill for writers. The retelling experience moved Linda in that direction.

Ms. Jordan also asked questions to help Linda reflect on her draft and to consider revisions. These are the kinds of questions that Ms. Jordan asked.

> What's it like having a new brother in the house?
> What part of your story do you like best?
> Tell me more about your baby brother.
> What do you think of your story so far?
> Do you think you'll add anything to your story? If so, what might you add?
> What are you going to do next with your story?

Writing conferences often stimulate revision. While Ms. Jordan did not put undue pressure on Linda to revise, her goal was to help Linda improve her writing. The conference accomplished this goal. Linda reflected on what she had written and revised her story. A day later she announced with finality, "This story is done!" Linda's remark made it clear that she had taken this piece as far as it should go. Ms. Jordan, a wise and experienced teacher, complimented Linda on her story and arranged for her to read it from the author's chair. Later, with the assistance of parent volunteers, Linda made her story into a book.

Dictation of story: "The Little Girl and Her Turtle"

Page 1: Once upon a time a girl was walking her turtle. One day she walked too far, and she got lost. Stayed tuned for Part 2 of the "Little Girl and Her Turtle."

Page 2: The little girl was so worried she had to lay down to rest. Stayed tuned for Part 3.

Page 3: While the little girl was sleeping, she didn't notice that her turtle was running away. He was leaving because she held his leash too tight. Stayed tuned for Part 4. (Author's note: Lynette decided not to compose Part 4.)

FIGURE 2.13. Lynette's story: Connecting drawing and writing.

Predictable Books

Modeling benefits writers. For hundreds of years, artists from every discipline have learned their craft from the works of others. For instance, Winston Churchill attributed his command of the English sentence to his imitation of Thomas Babington Macaulay and Edward Gibbons. Their command of the English sentence enticed him to imitate their style. Some find the word *imitating* too strong for their taste, but I consider it an honest assessment of the ancestry of most of our ideas, knowledge, and skills. Hundreds of other writers and artists have testified to similar experiences.

Children's books often feature a recurring pattern of language and a set of predictable story events. Such predictability makes the books easier to read, and children enjoy them immensely. Repetition is a familiar and much-loved device in children's literature. There are many books with predictable components that serve as excellent models for writing. Bill Martin's (1969) *Brown Bear, Brown Bear* is a classic among this genre. Predictable books also provide excellent oral language experiences for young children and are especially useful for choral readings, chants, and listening enjoyment. They also provide opportunities to predict story outcomes, an excellent way to develop inference skills in listening and reading.

Predictable books add a valuable dimension to a writing program when used thoughtfully and in moderation. Modeling helps writers use literary patterns to shape and guide their writing. Modeling is useful even if young writers make only minor variations in the pattern when they produce their own writing. Predictable books provide models for writing that are easy to follow. For instance, the repeated adventures of "The Gingerbread Boy" show young writers how a continuing narrative unfolds. It gives them a model of how repeated events can create interest and tension in a story. "The Three Billy Goats Gruff" exemplifies the building of suspense and drama through the use of recurring language patterns

Writing conferences stimulate revision. These students share their writing with one another. Later, they will make changes in their writing as a result of their discussion.

and story events. The chief value of modeling lies in exposing children to good writing that stimulates interest and makes writing enjoyable.

While predictable books make useful writing models, they can be overdone. Writing based on literary models should never replace self-selected writing topics. The heart of an excellent writing program resides in children selecting writing topics that mirror their personal interests and experiences. Even the youngest children are capable of selecting their own topics and writing about them in thoughtful and interesting ways. Give young writers great leeway in selecting their own writing topics and discourse modes, but do not hesitate to assign writing topics or discourse modes that you believe will strengthen your writing program. Instructional experiences that broaden children's writing repertoire are always worth considering. Predictable books are one of many instructional strategies that can broaden and strengthen children's writing knowledge.

The following steps described are suggested for a writing experience using a carefully chosen predictable book or poem as a model. This activity will require three to five writing sessions if all seven steps are followed.

1. Read the book or poem aloud once or twice. Use tone and gesture to add to the liveliness and enjoyment of the reading.
2. Choral read or chant the story or poem. If possible, give everyone a mimeographed copy.
3. Discuss the story or poem. Invite comments and ask questions.
   a. What part did you like best?
   b. What part is easiest to remember?
   c. What surprised you?
   d. What did you notice about the way it begins? ends?
   e. What part is repeated more than once?
4. Invite the class to write a group story or poem similar to the one they have read. Start the piece by writing the first lines yourself.
5. Invite class members to offer their lines. Take as many lines as time permits.
6. The next day, revise and edit the piece together. Then make the group story or poem into a book. Have the children illustrate it.
7. Finally, have the children write their own story or poem using the original source as a model.

The poems that follow were written by third-grade children. The teacher, Ms. Harmon, first modeled the poem *What Is Red.* The poems were published in simple handmade books constructed by the children.

What Is Black

Black are the clouds, black as can be.
Black is coal in a coal mine.
Black might be a blackboard, shiny and clean.
Black is gooey and sticky tar.
Black is skin

Amy, Grade 3

What Is Yellow

Yellow is the middle of an egg, which is very tasty indeed.
It feels mushy when you touch it with your finger and it
doesn't sound like anything. It is so quiet.
Yellow is a grapefruit, tangy and sweet.
Yellow is the sun on a sunny summer day.
Yellow is a pineapple, tasty as can be.

Elrod, Grade 3

What Is Red

Red is a fire truck rushing by
Red is the sun in the evening sky.
Red is my nose on a chilly day,
Red are the mittens I wear for play.

Ruth, Grade 3

Writing Folders

Keep writing folders for your children. There are two types of folders to
consider: the cumulative writing folder and the working-draft folder. The
cumulative writing folder is for maintaining a record of progress over the
school year. It can be the beginnings of a writing portfolio. The working-draft
folder contains writing in progress and other resources used in daily writing.

Cumulative Writing Folder

Larry spent 20 minutes rereading some early pieces in his cumulative
writing folder. When finished, he said to his second-grade teacher, "This
is how I used to write. I'm a better writer now, don't you think, Mr. Rubin?"
Mr. Rubin agreed. Both of them could see his progress.

Once every week or two, have children choose pieces of their writing
for inclusion in their cumulative folder so that a representative sample of
writing is maintained for each child. The cumulative folder has two impor-

tant uses. First, it gives teachers a means of evaluating writing progress. Over time, a profile of individual and class progress can be charted. This information can be used to apprise children of how they are doing. Second, a cumulative folder provides diagnostic information that can guide future instruction. For example, evaluation of representative pieces from cumulative folders will reveal strengths and weaknesses in composition and mechanical skills. Instructional decisions can then be made accordingly.

The cumulative folder should be kept in school. The information it contains is too valuable to risk losing. Furthermore, its value depends on its ready availability. Naturally, children need access to their own folders. Encourage them to look through their writing at regular intervals. This helps them gain perspective on the progress they have made. Children enjoy comparing the way they currently write with past performance. From time to time, have children choose a piece of writing from their folder to rewrite. Often enough, this results in an entirely new piece, but, even so, it gives writers a sense of mastery to discover how they can handle a writing topic now compared to an earlier performance.

Working-Draft Folder

Children need folders in which to keep drafts of work in progress. As they proceed through the steps of the writing process, their current work is likely to go through several stages, ranging from prewriting notes to revised drafts. Keeping work in a folder avoids the problems of lost drafts and other mishaps that befall children's written work. In addition to housing current writing, the working-draft folder may also contain other writing aids. Inexpensive folders are available commercially. A folder with two inside pockets works well. Works in progress are kept on one side, while the opposite side contains writing aids such as a topic list and a writer-at-work handbook (described in the next sections).

Topic List. Make a topic list and run off copies for children to keep in their writing folder. Conduct a brainstorming session early in the year. Write the resulting list of topics on the board. Have children choose topics from the list to add to their own lists. From time to time, discuss topic selection with the class and urge children to add topics to their lists as ideas occur to them. Good writing topics often arise during class discussions and writing conferences. When this happens, remind children to add these topics to their lists. A bit of early attention to topic lists will soon result in more topics than there is time for writing about them.

Writer-at-Work Handbook. A collection of other writing aids, is what I call a writer-at-work handbook. How many aids you include in your handbook depends on the grade level you teach and the priorities you wish to stress in your writing program. You might include any or all of the following:

1. Teacher conference guidelines.
2. Peer conference guidelines
3. Revision guidelines
4. Editing and proofreading symbols
5. Editing and proofreading questions
6. Clustering map
7. Waiting-time activities
8. Bookmaking instructions
9. Word lists of various kinds
10. Writing skills mastery list

Student Editors

Interruptions during conferences should be discouraged except in special circumstances. Nevertheless, students sometimes need help when the teacher is busy conferencing. One way to reduce or eliminate interruptions is to train student editors. Student editors take their responsibilities seriously when properly trained and motivated. Teachers who have tried this idea find that students learn writing skills more thoroughly as a result of working as student editors.

Determine which categories of editorial help—for example, punctuation, word selection, sentence sense, story leads, and spelling—are most often needed. Assign one or more students to each editorial role; select students who are most capable of performing a given editorial task. Train the student editors in the technical and social aspects of their work. When other students need help and you are busy, they can consult with the appropriate student editor. You can gradually bring other students into this activity by appointing assistant editors. The chief editor for punctuation, for example, will then have two responsibilities: to help students having difficulties and to train the assistant editor. Every 6 weeks or so the chief editor will "retire" and the assistant editor will take over as chief editor. Then it will be the new editor's job to train an assistant. Thus, training student editors is an extension of peer editing.

PERSPECTIVE AND SUMMARY

Early literacy experiences can be harsh or sweet. Winston Churchill found the beginnings harsh, although he wrote humorously about the mysteries and miseries of learning to write and cipher.

•◆•

We continued to toil every day, not only at letters but at words, and also at
what was much worse, figures. Letters after all had only got to be known,
and when they stood together in a certain way one recognized their formation
and that it meant a certain sound or word which one uttered when pressed
sufficiently. But the figures were tied into all sorts of tangles and did things
to one another which it was extremely difficult to forecast with complete
accuracy. You had to say what they did each time they were tied up together,
and the Governess apparently attached enormous importance to the answer
being exact. If it was not right, it was wrong. It was not any use being "nearly
right." In some cases these figures got into debt with one another: you had
to borrow one or carry one, and afterwards you had to pay back the one you
borrowed. These complications cast a steadily gathering shadow over my daily
life. (Gilbar, 1989, p. 39)

Though beginnings are often hard, beginnings can sometimes be
joyful. Mary Frances Kennedy Fisher's baptism into literacy was not of fire
but of bliss. Her grandmother read the Bible to her; her Mother read aloud
whatever she was reading if Mary was anywhere within earshot; her father
read the headlines at the breakfast table. Books were household companions and reading a shared and joyful experience. Reading and writing were
never a mystery or misery to her, quite different from young Winston's
experience. Teachers have the high privilege of helping make the beginnings of literacy sweet for children, just as M. F. K. Fisher's family and
friends did for her.

This chapter has presented the following main ideas:

• Independent writing can begin once children are able to write the
letters of the alphabet and make connections between letters and sounds.
   • Emergent writers move through four stages: (1) the scribble stage,
wherein children produce cursive and printlike forms; (2) the drawing
stage, wherein children produce pictures and may include letters and sight
words; (3) the letter-string stage, wherein children write strings of letters;
and (4) the invented spelling stage, wherein children produce true alphabetic writing.
   • Seven early writing principles were described: (1) the meaning
principle: expecting written language to be meaningful; (2) the exploration
principle: learning the conventions of writing through risk-taking and
discovery; (3) the sign principle: discovering that writing stands for
something besides itself; (4) the generative principle: understanding that
an unlimited number of words and sentences can be produced with only
a few letters used in varying combinations; (5) the directional principle:

learning how letters, words, and lines of print are oriented and ordered in written English; (6) the inventory principle: taking stock of what is known by cataloging, itemizing, or listing known letters and words; and (7) the spacing principle: discovering traditional conventions of spacing between words and lines of print. These principles help define what children discover about writing as literacy emerges.

• Eight beginning writing strategies and their rationales were suggested: (1) recording oral language through dictated accounts introduces children to the conventions of print, provides models of written language, and improves writing fluency; (2) reading aloud motivates writing and enhances language and ideas for writing; (3) modeling reading and writing behavior shows children how these processes are carried out; (4) connecting drawing and writing encourages children to compose with words and pictures; (5) conferencing with writers provides encouragement and instruction; (6) using predictable books as models stimulates writing; (7) keeping two types of writing folders maintains a record of growth and achievement (cumulative writing folders) and houses writing in progress (working-draft folders); and (8) training students to serve as peer editors.

REFERENCES

Chomsky, C. (1971). Reading, writing, and phonology. *Harvard Educational Review, 40,* 287–309.

Clay, M. M. (1975). *What did I write?* Portsmouth, NH: Heinemann.

Cramer, R. L. (1968). *An investigation of the spelling achievement of two groups of first-grade classes on phonologically regular and irregular words and in written composition.* Unpublished doctoral dissertation, University of Delaware, Newark.

Cramer, R. L. (1970, February). An investigation of first grade spelling achievement. *Elementary English, 47,* 230–237.

Dyson, A. H. (1983). Research currents: Young children as composers. *Language Arts, 60,* 884–891.

Dyson, A. H. (1988). Appreciate the drawing and dictating of young children. *Young Children, 43,* 25–32.

Gilbar, S. (1989). *The open door.* Boston: Godine.

Harste, J. C., Woodward, V. A., & Burke, C. L. (1984). *Language stories and literacy lessons.* Portsmouth, NH: Heinemann.

Hughes, T. (1967). *Poetry in the making: An anthology of poems and programmes from listening and writing.* London: Faber & Faber.

Mearns, H. (1929). *Creative power: The education of youth in the creative arts.* New York: Dover.

Newman, J. (1984). *The craft of children's writing.* Portsmouth, NH: Heinemann.

Read, C. (1971). Pre-school children's knowledge of English phonology. *Harvard Educational Review, 41*(1), 1–34.

Sultzby, E., & Teale, W. H. (1985). Writing development in early childhood. *Educational Horizons, 64,* 8–12.

Temple, C., Nathan, R., Burris, N., & Temple, F. (1988). *The beginnings of writing* (2nd ed.). Boston: Allyn & Bacon.

Chapter 3

Invented Spelling

It's a damn poor mind that can only think of one way to spell a word.

—ANDREW JACKSON

INTRODUCTION

Alisha, a first grader, wrote *shado* for *shadow* in one of her earliest stories. Her teacher, Ms. Motrik, encouraged Alisha to spell any unknown words, "as best you can." Not knowing how to spell *shadow,* but encouraged to invent its spelling, Alisha made an educated guess. When children like Alisha use their knowledge of the language to approximate the spelling of a word they cannot spell, they are temporarily *inventing* its spelling.

Invented spelling is controversial. Major television networks have run interviews with advocates and critics; major newspapers and magazines have written articles describing its pros and cons. It is used as a club to berate teachers and belittle schools. It has become a symbol of what critics call "dumbing down our schools." Unfortunately, its advocates often defend it on its weakest premises, while its critics are uninformed, and often uninterested in being informed, about its purpose and place in learning to read, write, and spell.

Invented spellings are best guesses about letter–sound relationships, on the same order as a 2-year-old's guesses about how to pronounce words. Invented spelling has gone by different names: temporary spelling, place holders, approximations, spelling-as-best-you-can, and so on. All these terms express the idea that partially spelled words are a temporary solution to this question: How can we enable children to write while they are still acquiring knowledge of spelling principles and as yet have only a small spelling vocabulary? This chapter answers that question and discusses related issues.

This chapter covers seven invented spelling topics: (1) defining and defending invented spelling; (2) Patty's excellent adventure; (3) prerequisite knowledge for invented spellings; (4) how invented spelling works; (5) how invented spelling influences growth in writing, reading, and spelling; (6) the relationship of invented spelling to standard spelling; and (7) explaining invented spelling to parents.

DEFINING AND DEFENDING INVENTED SPELLING

Defining Invented Spelling

Invented spelling describes children's first efforts to spell words they have not yet mastered. Children who cannot read, or who are in the beginning stages of reading, have a large oral vocabulary. A kindergarten or first-grade child, for instance, may have an oral vocabulary of 5–20,000 words, an enormous store of language knowledge, but it takes years before a child's spelling vocabulary grows to a size useful for writing. Further, spelling vocabularies are never as large as oral vocabularies. In decades past, it was assumed by many in the educational community that children therefore should wait until third grade or so before they started to write.

The acquisition of literacy, it was thought, followed this sequence: First you learn to read; then you learn to spell; then you learn to write. Although it seems logical, this view is based on an underestimation of children's capabilities. In addition, this sequence cannot realize the full benefit that arises out of learning to read, write, and spell in an integrated approach to teaching–learning the language arts.

Delaying writing and spelling until a foothold has been acquired in reading is wasteful of children's time and talent. Why not write on the first day of school? Why not write even before school begins? Children possess a wealth of oral language a resource that can hasten and enhance the long journey to literacy. But one big obstacle stands in the way—spelling. "You can't write if you can't spell," the skeptics insist. But this is not quite the case. The real question is "How well must you spell before you can begin to write?" The answer is relative to the circumstances. Patty's "WNSUPATM" story, presented later in this chapter, demonstrates that young children can write well, even when misspellings outnumber correct spellings 5 to 1.

Consider the issue of spelling from the writer's perspective. Many writers draft in a white-hot heat, concentrating only on meaning. Journalists, for instance, work on deadline. Their drafts are often sent electronically from the field to the office. It wouldn't shock me to learn that many reporters, under deadline, send drafts to the office containing spelling errors, even given the convenience of a spell checker computer program. If you doubt this, ask the person who works the rewrite desk, as I have. Would it make sense to say to journalists, "You can't write unless you can spell every word correctly"? In this context, it is patently absurd to even consider the issue as pertinent to writing. If spelling must always be correct, only pedants would be permitted to write. What we can expect from writers is increasing maturity in spelling as one grows in age and experience. What we should expect is something close to perfection in spelling when writing reaches a public audience, and even this is subject to age, experience, and circumstances.

Writing should begin as soon as children can approximate the spelling of words they wish to use in their writing. It doesn't matter how many of those words, if any, are spelled correctly. For example, consider this piece of invented spelling: EFUKANOPNKAZIWILGEVUAKANOPENR (If you can open cans I will give you a can opener; Chomsky, 1979). Visit classrooms where writing is well taught, where invented spelling is encouraged, and you will find that children who write early make rapid progress in spelling because they are learning to read simultaneously, not in spite of invented spelling but because of it.

Defending Invented Spelling

What I have said will irritate, if not infuriate, the critics of invented spelling. But critics, please read on. Some of your criticism is justified. Spelling instruction has been neglected in many schools over the past decade or so. Invented spelling is not a permanent substitute for correct spelling, nor is it a conspiracy to delay or deny the importance of learning to spell. On the contrary, invented spelling can, if properly directed, hasten and enhance the development of reading, writing, and spelling. Invented spelling is not a sufficient substitute for consistent and vigorous instruction in standard spelling. When such instruction is provided, invented spelling will not confuse children, nor will it conflict with standard spelling instruction. Rather, it will enhance spelling knowledge.

The critics' major complaint is that invented spelling will leave children handicapped in spelling, leading to habitual misspelling. They fear that children who misspell words in their formative years will not overcome these "bad habits" later. If this were true, I'd move over to the side of the critics in a New York minute—but it is not true. Nevertheless, the concerns that parents, politicians, business leaders, and teachers have raised about invented spelling must be addressed.

Research on Invented Spelling

Is invented spelling just another name for tolerating misspelling? Is there evidence to suggest that invented spelling leads to poor spelling habits in the mature learner? No and no. Does invented spelling make a significant and valuable contribution to the acquisition of literacy? Yes.

I conducted perhaps the first extensive classroom research involving invented spelling. The study examined the effects of invented spelling on standard spelling achievement (Cramer, 1968, 1970). In the 1960s, invented spelling was called *spelling-as-best-you-can*. The term *invented spelling* was popularized by Carol Chomsky and Charles Read, both of whom conducted extensive studies on the issues of spelling and early writing.

I found that first-grade children who had extensive experience in early reading and writing using invented spelling quickly became superior spellers. At the midpoint and end of their first-grade year they performed significantly better in every measure of spelling achievement than their counterparts who did not use invented spelling. Children in invented spelling classrooms spelled better on lists of phonetically regular words; they spelled better on lists of phonetically irregular words; most importantly, they spelled better in written compositions.

The same children also performed better in reading and writing (Stauffer & Hammond, 1969). More importantly, they not only became superior first-grade spellers, readers, and writers, but they maintained their superior achievement across the 6 years in which their performance was tracked (Stauffer, Hammond, Oehlkers, & Houseman, 1972). It should be noted that these studies were conducted within the context of a larger study on the effects of a Language Experience Approach to literacy instruction. Language Experience puts a premium on early writing and wide reading in self-selected literature, two conditions that facilitate spelling growth.

Read (1970, 1971, 1975) provided the first linguistic explanation of invented spelling. While invented spelling had been used in classrooms prior to Read's seminal studies, no one knew what linguistic mechanisms made it possible. Read's elegant studies provided a linguistic explanation for this phenomenon and helped bring invented spelling into the mainstream of educational practice. In studying the invented spellings of preschool children, he discovered that different children invented the same system of spelling, and that particular spellings were systematic and uniform from child to child. Read's studies demonstrated that children classify sounds into categories on the basis of perceived similarities, and that children used their knowledge of letter–sound relationships to produce approximations of words that were remarkably consistent with the underlying phonemic system of English. He also found that invented spelling flourished where parents enjoyed and appreciated their children's writing.

Clarke (1988) studied the effects of invented spelling versus traditional spelling among first-grade children, measuring reading, writing, and spelling achievement. While achievement in reading was similar for the two groups, children using invented spelling showed superior spelling and phonetic analysis achievement over children using traditional spelling. Interestingly, low-achieving children showed the greatest benefit from invented spelling. Clarke suggested that invented spelling may help children shift from visual to phonetic processing of words much earlier than they might otherwise have done. She also noted that the invented spelling group showed progressive development toward correct spelling.

Healy (1991) compared the effects of invented spelling and traditional spelling on growth in reading and writing among first-grade children. Children in the invented spelling group produced better writing and more writing than children in the traditional spelling group. Healy did not find significant differences between the two groups in reading growth.

Garcia (1997) investigated the effects of invented spelling and a high word-frequency spelling program on first graders' reading, writing, and spelling growth. Results showed that invented spelling had a statistically significant beneficial effect on growth in word attack skills and vocabulary knowledge, though not on comprehension. Invented spelling also had a significant beneficial influence on writing. Children in the invented spelling group wrote longer compositions, used more T-units, and wrote more words classified as above the first-grade level.

Writing behaviors were also markedly different between the two groups. The invented spelling group did more rereading of their writing, helped or asked friends for help with spelling more often, and illustrated their writing more frequently. Children in the high word-frequency spelling program, as one might expect, consulted their dictionaries more often looking for correct spelling.

No significant differences were found between groups on the number of words spelled correctly on lists of regular and irregular words or in written compositions. Garcia's findings tend to corroborate most of Clarke's (1988) findings and some, though not all, of Healy's (1991) findings regarding the influence of invented spelling on reading, writing, and spelling.

These studies suggest several generalizations about invented spelling that have implications for teaching young children to read, write, and spell.

1. Children in an invented spelling regimen spell better than their counterparts in traditional spelling programs, or at least as well. No reliable or replicable research has shown that invented spelling has a negative influence on spelling achievement.

2. Children in an invented spelling regimen read better than their counterparts in traditional spelling programs, or at least as well. No reliable or replicable research has shown that invented spelling has a negative influence on reading achievement.
3. Children in an invented spelling regimen produce more and better writing than their counterparts in traditional spelling programs. Period. No reliable or replicable research has shown that invented spelling has a negative influence on writing.
4. The most significant benefit invented spelling conveys is improving the quality and quantity of the writing children produce. This is not surprising, since the purpose of invented spelling is precisely to enable children to write early and often. It accomplishes this goal and in the process conveys benefits of varying degrees to reading, writing, and spelling growth.

There is a substantial body of spelling research closely linked to invented spelling, including developmental stages of spelling, the relationship of spelling to the acquisition of literacy, word study, spelling orthography, and structural and meaning principles in spelling. Over the past quarter-century, the late Edmund Henderson and his colleagues, mostly graduates of the University of Virginia, have stimulated a renaissance of research on spelling and its influence on learning to read and write. I have cited most of the principal contributors to this resurgence of spelling research throughout this book, but it seems appropriate to mention some of them here, since their findings support the major themes described in this book and specifically support the idea advanced in this section that research substantiates the valuable contribution of invented spelling to learning to read, write, and spell. The roll call of University of Virginia spelling researchers includes, but is not limited to, the following individuals: James Beers, Carolyn Beers, Donald Bear, Richard Gentry, Tom Gill,

These students use invented spelling in first draft writing. Later, they will correct misspellings when editing their writing for public presentation.

Jean Gillet, Marcia Invernizzi, Francine Johnston, Darryl Morris, Robert Schlagal, Charles Temple, and Shane Templeton.

Oral Language Learning as Analogous to Written Language Learning

Invented spelling is to writing what toddler talk is to speaking. Understanding how oral language learning occurs offers clues to how written language might be learned, although it is important to note that learning to talk and learning to read have many differences as well as many similarities. When children first begin to pronounce words, they mispronounce every word they use. Nine-month old Amy doesn't start out saying, "Dad, I'd like a glass of milk." Rather, she says something that sounds like "Dah. Mook," with a few other unintelligible consonant and vowel sounds thrown in. Her parents had no trouble understanding this noise as, "Dad, I want milk." They did not say, "Amy, your enunciation is incorrect. You can't have any milk until you say, 'Dad, I'd like a bottle of milk.'" More likely, Dad not only gave Amy milk, but a kiss and a pat on the head. Like most dads, this dad said, "Barbara, did you hear what Amy just said? *She said she wants milk.* Isn't that terrific! What a bright child we have. She must take after my side of the family."

Amy's parents did not worry that mispronouncing words in the early stages of oral language growth would condemn her to habitual mispronunciation for the rest of her life. What prevented this? The quality of the surrounding oral language influenced the outcome. Children who are surrounded by rich oral language learn to speak the language well. On the other hand, if the oral language environment is impoverished, the result may also be impoverished. Children learn their oral language best in a context of social acceptance of the idea that beginners make "mistakes." It is not damaging for children to go through an extended period during which an incalculable number of "mistakes" are made. Indeed, one can imagine no other way for language growth to occur. Gradually, language is shaped to the surrounding language environment.

As with oral language, so, too, with written language. Surround children with a rich written language environment and you are likely to get excellent growth in literacy. On the other hand, if the written language environment is impoverished, you are likely to get impoverished literacy development. Making "mistakes" at the beginning of any learning process is normal and universal, but this does not mean that the beginner's mistakes will be the mistakes of the mature learner. Indeed, it is doubtful if learning can take place at all in the absence of mistakes.

The word *mistake*, incidentally, often has a negative connotation, although I do not regard it as negative when used in the context of learning. Rather, a mistake in a learning context should be regarded as a misunderstanding arising out of unfamiliarity with the new territory the learner is exploring. Mistakes for the beginning learner are of little consequence if the learning environment is supportive. We learn from our mistakes, perhaps more than we learn from our correct responses. What matters in beginning learning is the quality of instruction, the frequency of practice, and an instructional environment where learners can take risks, indeed, are encouraged to take risks.

Creative Spelling or Creative Written Expression

Some advocates of invented spelling have argued that requiring children to spell correctly stifles their creativity. The inference drawn from the "stifled creativity" argument is that the invented spelling itself is creative. Not so. When a 4-year-old boy writes *R U DF* (Are you deaf?), he is making remarkable use of his limited knowledge of letter–sound relationships (Bissex, 1980), but it is stretching the point to call this creative activity. As he grows in his knowledge of the spelling system, it will not stifle his creativity if he is taught to spell words correctly. Indeed, it will make his writing more fluent. As he gains mastery of the mechanics of written language, he will express his ideas more fluently, thus opening the door wider to written creative expression.

Automaticity in spelling is as desirable as it is in reading. But automaticity comes later and gradually. Invented spelling gives children early access to the written language. With access, it becomes possible, but not inevitable, for children to produce creative works. It is the product, the story or poem, not the spelling, that expresses a child's creativity. Thus, I would argue that Patty's "Once Upon a Time" story (Figure 3.1), which follows, contains elements of creativity that are resident in the text itself, not in the spelling.

PATTY'S EXCELLENT ADVENTURE

Children are often our best teachers. Watch them closely. Listen to their voices, whether written or oral. You can learn important lessons from children that are not available elsewhere. I learned a lesson from Patty. At age 5 she wrote a "WNSUPATM" ("Once Upon a Time") story. At age 6 she wrote "The Pet," which she described as "not a story." Read Patty's stories in Figures 3.1 and 3.2.

Patty loved to write. She wrote "WNSUPATM" in kindergarten. Look closely at her invented spellings, and consider the quality of her ideas. She

Original text	Translation
wnsupatn	Once upon a time
thr ws a ltl grl	there was a little girl
hos nm ws Jan	whose name was Jan
n Jan ws absulte	and Jan was absolutely
a btfl prns	a beautiful person
wn da Jan sad	one day Jan said
I am so brd that	I am so bored that
I am gng ot	I am going out
n the wrd to fin	in the world to find
sum avtr	some adventure
I tnk Im gon	I think I'm going
in spaz to catg	in space to catch
mi duter	meteor
sooo Jan fld	so Jan found
a str bem	a star beam
nd when hi n	and went high in
awtspaz.	outer space
ef u wt to	if you want to
no mor abt Jans	know more about Jan's
avnturs red	adventures read
the nect cpt	the next chapter
in my bk.	in my book.

FIGURE 3.1. "WNSUPATM": Patty, kindergarten.

The cat
The cat is a pet.

FIGURE 3.2. "The pet": Patty, first grade.

has the prerequisites needed to write, and the evidence is present in "WNSUPATM." Her ideas are interesting; the story reveals imagination. Invented spelling enabled Patty to express her creative capabilities. But the real creativity here is her focus on meaning, her story, not her spelling. The spelling is merely the vehicle through which her creativity is expressed.

Patty stopped liking to write when she got to first grade. After writing "The Pet," she drew a big X across her story and said, "This is not a story." It was clear to Patty, if not to others, that this piece had no message, no meaning, no interest. Written creative expression is impossible when one is limited to a very small number of known spelling words. Patty is right. *This is not a story.* This might do as an exercise in handwriting practice. But it is not writing. It is supposed to be a story, and it is not. Patty knew this; I wonder if her teacher did?

Contrast the ideas and words used in "The Pet" with those used in "WNSUPATM." Patty the kindergartner wrote words such as *absolutely, beautiful, person, adventure, outer space, meteor, chapter.* She used whatever words she needed to express her ideas; no word was too long, too difficult, or too complex for Patty to attempt, and of course she misspelled them all. Her kindergarten story contains 77 words in all, or 57 different words.

Ten words were spelled correctly; all other spellings were invented. For every word she can spell there are four or five she cannot spell. But notice that her modest spelling vocabulary did not slow her down and did not interfere with her focus on meaning.

Patty the first grader writes a quite different piece in "The Pet." There is nothing imaginative or creative about it. She uses just five words: *the, is, a, cat, pet*—all spelled correctly. But it was clear to Patty, and should be clear to teachers and parents everywhere: This is not a story.

As a first grader, Patty is not encouraged to use invented spelling. Denied the use of this tool, Patty finds meaningful writing impossible because she doesn't have a sufficient vocabulary of known spelling words to create imaginative stories such as "WNSUPATM." She can write a few simple words, but she cannot access her wealth of ideas or her cornucopia of oral language. What happens to children like Patty who are deprived of the opportunity to use invented spelling? An early start on writing is withheld; an early start on understanding the spelling system is denied; an opportunity to extend reading knowledge is prevented. This is certainly unfortunate, but perhaps not disastrous.

Maybe the random wheel of fortune will stop at their number, and a good teacher or parent will intervene somewhere farther down the line. Ignore their ability, deny it, and it may not resurface. There are, as Mearns (1929) once suggested, those predestinate artists for whom the urge to express is superior to all rebuff. But many children are easily rebuffed; they suffer when they are denied access to their talent. Native talent may be repressed, or it may disappear altogether. Patty is "absolutely a beautiful person," capable of growing into literacy rapidly, as are so many children. But teachers and parents must show they believe in children's potential by putting the tools for creative expression at their disposal as early as possible. The earlier and more often a young eagle flaps its wings, the greater are its chances of soaring off into the blue sky that beckons beyond the safety of its aerie. Potential must never be wasted, denied, or delayed.

PREREQUISITE KNOWLEDGE FOR INVENTED SPELLINGS

Children need at least four interconnected capabilities in order to invent spellings. They must be able to write the letters of the alphabet; they need phonemic awareness, particularly the ability to segment sounds; they need to know some letter–sound relationships; and they need to understand that letter–sound relationships are written sequentially, left to right, in English spelling. They need only a beginners' knowledge of all of these prerequisites to start writing using invented spelling.

Knowledge of the Alphabet

The best predictor of reading success in first grade is knowing the letters of the alphabet. It does not follow, however, that the magic wand for learning to read and write is to teach letter names. Nevertheless, the alphabet should be learned early to get children off to a good start. Obviously, they cannot invent spellings until they can form at least some of the letters of the alphabet. Acquaint children with the alphabet in as many ways as possible. They should recognize upper- and lowercase and begin to write the letters early. In the beginning, children prefer to make uppercase letters, and there is no reason to urge them to abandon this strategy in the early stages. Gradually they should be taught basic handwriting techniques through functional and simple instruction. Some commercial handwriting programs are useful, but are not essential; teachers can devise their own handwriting practice routines. Whatever materials and procedures are used, legibility is the most important handwriting characteristic, and handwriting itself, although important, is subordinate to the larger goal of meaningful communication of ideas.

Learning to write the letters of the alphabet should begin as early as preschool or kindergarten, although this need not be formal instruction. By early first grade, consistent, formal instruction in writing, recognizing, and naming the letters of the alphabet is crucial. Letter formation practice should be limited to short periods of time suitably spaced throughout the week. Group handwriting instruction can be given in small doses, and individual practice can be provided as needed, while circulating among the children as they are writing. The best first-grade teacher I have ever known, Ms. Smart, did it this way while consistently producing children who could read, write, and spell with extraordinary excellence. Even the slowest children in her classroom always managed to read, write, and spell beyond what anyone might have anticipated.

Phonemic Awareness

Phonemic awareness is prerequisite to learning to read and write. It is typically defined as awareness of the sounds that make up spoken words. Beginning readers and writers need to recognize and distinguish one speech sound from another in order to decode and encode the written language. Recognizing and distinguishing speech sounds is necessary to making letter–sound connections in writing. There is an abundance of research supporting the importance of phonemic awareness for reading and writing, some of it focusing on phonemic awareness as a prerequisite and predictor of reading success (Bradley & Bryant, 1983; Ehri & Wilce, 1987; Ball & Blachman, 1991; Ayres, 1993), and some on the role of invented spelling in developing phonemic awareness (Cramer, 1985; Stanovich, 1988; Mann, Tobin, & Wilson, 1988; Housel, 1989; Moriarty, 1990).

Invented spelling makes it possible to combine practice in letter formation with the development of greater phonemic awareness. When Patty wrote *I am so brd,* she segmented *bored* into three parts and made three letter–sound connections—b–r–d. Although *bored* has more than three phonemes, Patty demonstrated that she can manipulate sounds within words. Without this capability, she could not write. It is quite clear now, and has been for decades, that children who have received phonemic awareness training or already possess it can write early in their school career.

Chomsky (1971, 1979) has argued that writing ought to precede reading. Her point is that children gain greater knowledge of the written language through writing than they do through reading. Chomsky is probably right; at the very least reading and writing ought to commence at the same time, with equal instructional time and attention given to both. Someone once called writing the royal road to reading, an apt description.

Letter–Sound Relationships

Knowledge of letter names and sounds is related to success in learning to read, write, and spell. Familiarity with letters and sounds eases the way to beginning reading and writing. Adams (1990) says, "A child who can recognize most letters with thorough confidence will have an easier time learning about letter sounds and word spellings than a child who still has to work at remembering what is what" (p. 12).

Children who can talk have learned the phonology of their language, but it does not follow that children automatically apply their knowledge of phonology to reading, writing, and spelling. Most children must be taught, or at least encouraged, to apply what they know about phonology to what they know about letters. Once children have acquired basic phonemic awareness, either directly or indirectly, and know some of the letters of the alphabet, they are ready to write. The letters that say their names are the easiest to represent (Beers & Henderson, 1977; Beers, 1980; Templeton, 1980). Thus, a child trying to spell *I went fishing* may produce *I WT FEHNG.* While the letter string is not complete, the letter names are produced quite accurately and in sequence.

Sequential Order of Letters and Sounds

English words are spelled in sequential order, left to right. Children must understand the sequential nature of representing sounds with letters

·•·

before they can approximate the spelling of words. Many children learn to spell their names and can often copy words correctly, placing the letters in their appropriate sequence, without understanding the sequential nature of representing letter–sound relationships, which is more than just the idea of one thing following the other. It is a meaningfully connected series, one thing following another in logical progression as one spells or approximates the spelling of English words. During the prephonetic stage, children do not exhibit this understanding. However, as they move into the phonetic stage of spelling growth, it becomes clear that they have grasped the sequential principle of representing letter–sound relationships.

HOW INVENTED SPELLING WORKS: ITS LINGUISTIC FEATURES

The features of early invented spellings are described and summarized here as extrapolated from research reported by Read, Henderson, Beers, Gentry, Temple, and Bear and colleagues, all of whom are referenced throughout this book.

- Long vowels are spelled by the name of the letter that matches the sound, sometimes called the letter-name strategy: *rak* for rake; *got* for *goat*; *tru* for *true*.
- Short vowels are spelled by the letter-name that has the sound closest to the one being replaced: *fes* for *fish*, *git* for *got*.
- Two nasal sounds, *m* and *n*, are omitted when they occur just before another consonant: *bopy* for *bumpy*, *plat* for *plant*.
- Syllable sonorants *l*, *m*, and *n* carry the vowel sound in a syllable: *batl* for *battle*; *btm* for *bottom*; *opn* for *open*.
- R-controlled vowels are omitted: *grl* for *girl*; *hrd* for *heard*.
- Past tense marker *-ed* is spelled with a *t* or *d*: *lokt* for *looked*, *stpt* for *stopped*; *klid* for *climbed*; *brd* for *bored*.
- Sounds made by double letters *t* and *d* are spelled with one letter: *ltl* for *little*; *mdl* for *middle*; *padl* for *paddle*.
- Affricative sounds such as *dr*, *tr*, and *ch* are spelled *jr*, *gr*, *chr*, and *h*: *jran* for *train*; *griv* for *drive*; *chran* for *train*; *wht* for *watched*.
- One or more letters may stand for an entire word. This is called letter-name spelling: *u* for *you*; *r* for *are*; *yl* for *while*; *nhr* for *nature*.

It is important to understand that the features identified in children's invented spelling are generalizations that apply in many instances, but not all. You will undoubtedly notice variations among children. Thus, while one child will spell *train* as *jran,* another may spell it *trn* or *tran.* How children spell a given word depends on the stage they are in, the progress they have made within a given stage—early, middle, late—and the variation attributable to individual differences. An excellent book to consult on issues related to spelling stages and word study is that written by Bear, Invernizzi, Templeton, and Johnston (1996).

As children move through the stages of spelling growth, they become less dependent on sounds and more dependent on broader spelling concepts: within-word patterns, syllable juncture rules, and meaning derivation principles. It is not necessary to know all of the technical details in order to understand how spelling growth occurs. It is useful, however, to understand some of the basic concepts outlined in this section. For instance, if you see *bumpy* spelled *bopy* and *troubles* spelled *chribls,* you might think the child is way off in understanding how to connect letters with sounds. But an understanding of how children invent spellings will show you that there is a linguistic reason for these seemingly strange choices. Children in the earliest stages of spelling growth are closer to the actual sounds of language than adults, and sound clues are their major spelling strategy. Children can hear sounds in words that a linguistic could identify but most of us would miss or ignore. Mature spellers, on the other hand, no longer depend on sound as the major spelling strategy and may, therefore, be less attuned to the actual sounds in words.

HOW INVENTED SPELLING INFLUENCES GROWTH IN WRITING, READING, AND SPELLING

Invented spelling conveys significant instructional benefits. If this were not so, there would be little, if any, value in using it as an early introduction to literacy instruction. But its value is clear, and this is no mere assertion: It is backed by research and successful experience in classrooms. Invented spelling supports reading, writing, and spelling. This section describes how and why this is so.

Invented Spelling Supports Writing

Most children believe they can write. Graves (1983) estimates that about 90% of entering first-grade children believe they can write. Children who are encouraged to draw and scribble at an early age later read and write more readily and effectively than children who are denied these important formative experiences. Most children have experience writing their names and drawing pictures. They move through stages of scribbling, mock writing, and experimentation with alphabet letters and words (Clay, 1975; Temple, Nathan, Burris, & Temple, 1988). Young children can write, even when they can form only a small number of letters. With or without direct encouragement, they may begin to invent spellings, as was the case with the preschool children studied by Read.

Invented spelling supports writing, for several reasons. First, invented spelling gives children the idea that writing is connected to thought. Writing makes thought visible and permanent in a way that oral language cannot. One can examine a written thought, revise it, extend it, or reject it. The spoken word, on the other hand, is soon forgotten.

Second, the earlier children write, the more practice they will have in putting their ideas on paper and the better writers they will become. Children who do not write until age 9 or 10 miss years of writing practice. Children who write from the first day of school have an advantage in time on task.

Third, writing and reading are so closely connected as to be insepara-ble. Children who write do a great deal of rereading of their own works (Garcia, 1997) and are also likely to spend significant time reading the writing of their peers. Children who write know where writing comes from. It is not magic, as one 7-year-old thought. He assumed a machine was turned on and continued working until it had produced a book. After writing his own book he realized that authors write books, and that it is interesting and challenging work done by people just like him (Calkins, 1986).

Healy (1991) compared traditional spelling development versus in-vented spelling. While her study had many interesting findings, one of the most telling was productivity. On average, journal writing entries for invented spellers were 3 times as long as entries for traditional spellers: 30 versus 10 words per entry, respectively. More importantly, the invented spelling writers included more detail, elaboration, and imaginative lan-guage; the quantity and quality of their writing were superior. If you are not encouraged to invent spellings, the inevitable consequence is reduced fluency, which constrains other potential.

Invented Spelling Supports Reading

Chomsky (1979), one of the earliest and most thoughtful writers on invented spelling, gives an excellent account of the contribution it makes to reading. Her analysis is more detailed than the following quote can represent, but many of the ways in which spelling contributes to reading are foreshadowed in this brief comment.

The inventive spellers, during the months that they engage in their writing activities, are providing themselves with excellent and valuable practice in phonetics, word analysis and synthesis, and letter–sound correspondences. In addition, they are experiencing a sense of control over the printed word. There is an independence that is gained with print and a sense that print–sound relationships are something that one works out for oneself. This practice and this attitude serve them well when it comes time to read. The initiative and self-reliance developed through writing carry over into learning to read. The children expect to take an active role in learning to read, as they did with writing. In my opinion, this attitude is a crucial element in reading. Since the children are prepared to go ahead on their own, what they need is adequate input from the environment. They need to be exposed to large quantities of print. (p. 48)

Stauffer (1970) was among the earliest researchers to understand and demonstrate that reading instruction gets a powerful boost when it is combined with early writing using invented spelling. Stauffer was an advocate of the Language Experience Approach to reading, which had all of the elements later described as Whole Language Philosophy. His approach combined early writing using invented spelling, language experience stories, oral language development, self-selected literature for reading, comprehension instruction, and word recognition training that emphasized auditory and visual discrimination training. These elements provided an integrated language arts approach to teaching reading.

The connection between reading and spelling goes back several centuries in American history. Early instruction in reading can hardly be distinguished from spelling instruction. Noah Webster's *Blue Back Speller* served as both speller and reader. This connection, forgotten by many, had an element of wisdom that needs to be remembered. Spelling involves writing, which boosts emergent reading capabilities. That is precisely what invented spelling provides. Analysis of the relationship between invented spelling and reading suggests nine factors that play a contributing role in learning to read.

Phonetics

In beginning reading development, children use rudimentary phonological cues from printed words to make educated guesses about how to pronounce words. Since children who have used invented spellings have had the experience of going in the other direction, from speech to print, going from print to speech gives them a leg up in making the transition from writer to reader.

Phonemic Awareness

Phonemic awareness is the awareness of the sounds that make up spoken words. Studies have established that phonemic awareness is a better predictor of reading success in first and second grade than IQ, age, or socioeconomic status, and it can be trained. Some degree of phonemic awareness must be present before a child can read or write, but it need not be fully developed. Engaging in writing through invented spelling further develops whatever phonemic awareness is present when children first begin to write. Invented spelling also focuses children's attention on isolating sounds and coming up with letters to represent the sounds they hear in words. Further, since writing is a highly meaningful activity, general literacy development is also well served.

Letter–Sound Relationships

Early writers must make connections between letters and sounds. Invented spelling provides the place and the opportunity for children to practice and improve their understanding of just how the relationship between letters and sounds works.

Word Analysis and Synthesis

Analyzing words into their constituent parts is what readers must do when they encounter an unknown word. They must then blend the elements together to pronounce the word—analysis and synthesis. Children who write at an early age have much practice analyzing and synthesizing words. This practice adds to children's word knowledge and leads to increased reading fluency.

Control

When we are in control of a situation we have power or authority over it. There is a sense in which young readers must be in control of the printed word or the printed word will control them—that is, frustrate them. A look at Patty's writing (Figure 3.1) gives one the sense that nothing about words overwhelmed her. She was in control. Thus, she wrote whatever her thoughts directed her to write.

Confidence

Confidence and control go hand in hand. To be certain of one's capabilities is the hallmark of confidence. Children who invent their own spellings gain confidence in their writing and subsequently in themselves as writers.

Hypothesis Construction

Children construct hypotheses and try them out to see what works, as Piaget (1955) has shown. This is what children are doing when they invent spellings. They begin to do as Haley (Figure 3.3, discussed in detail later) did when she wrote several words two ways. Is *of* spelled *uv* or *ov*? She tried out both. Is *slipped* spelled *slipt* or *slpt*? One is more complete than the other. This may have seemed significant in her thinking. All sorts of questions arise as children try to figure out the written language system: Does this sound require one letter or two? Does this word have three letters or four? Does the vowel sound in *shoe* have one letter or two? It is the asking and answering of these questions, even when wrong, that enables children to arrive at a better understanding of how words work. Hypothesis construction about how reading and writing work is one of the most useful activities invented spellers engage in.

Curiosity

When children are read to and given the opportunity to write, they soon become curious about the marks they have put on paper; even when these are scribbles or randomly arranged letters, children want to know what they have produced. They know from their experience as a listener that writing is supposed to make sense. So they ask, "What did I write?" This is an expression of children's natural curiosity, encouraged and enhanced by invented spelling. This curiosity will serve them well as they grow and develop in their understanding of the written word.

Heightened Activity

Children love to keep busy, especially when they are busy with what is meaningful to them. Writing involves the physical activity of depicting the written word and illustrating it with drawings. Writing is also a mental activity, engaging children in thought. Similarly, reading is an active process whose most difficult aspect is mental activity, the interpretation and elaboration of meaning.

Invented Spelling Supports Standard Spelling

Let's look at the invented spelling of Haley, a first grader. Haley calls her story "Klmz Bny." On a cold February morning her teacher, Ms. Church, gave Haley a copy of "Clumsy Bunny," a 14-page book with a picture on each page. Haley wrote her own text to go with each page, as shown in Figure 3.3.

Haley is a confident writer. By midyear, Haley had acquired a small set of function words that she could correctly spell, and she had a substantial oral language vocabulary, little of which she could spell. Ms. Church's encouragement of invented spelling enabled Haley to overcome the spelling barrier, with the results shown in Figures 3.3, 3.4, and 3.5.

Haley's invented spelling success derives, at least partly, from the knowledge she had gained from the reading instruction she had received. In addition, Haley possessed the prerequisites needed to write: She could write the letters of the alphabet, had a strong sense of phonemic awareness, understood the alphabetic principle of sequencing letter–sound relationships left to right, and had a solid knowledge of letter–sound relationships. Seven significant observations can be made about Haley's work and her progress in spelling.

1. At early stages of spelling growth, incorrect spellings may out number correct spellings, although this may depend on whether you count

Page	*1.*	Klmz woke up and strcht out his rms.
Page	*2.*	And thn he fl out ov bed. Bonk!
Page	*3.*	He lkt ndr his bed and sl his shu.
Page	*4.*	He wz ptn his shu on and he had to ti it.
Page	*5.*	Klmz lkt for his uthr shu. He fnd it undr his drsr.
Page	*6.*	Por Klmz. He hit his head on the drsr wen he recht for his shu.
Page	*7.*	Wil Klmz wz ptn on his ovrals, one uv his strps snapt.
Page	*8.*	Then he wz gna put tothpst on his tothbrsh. It klgd up and it skwrted in his fas.
Page	*9.*	Wil Klmz wz wshn hz hnds and fas, the soap slpt out uv hz hnds.
Page	*10.*	It hit hz mrer. Klmz wz skrd.
Page	*11.*	Then he wz gna get a glas uv wtr and it spld.
Page	*12.*	Klmz Bne tht he wz rde for brkfst and he wkt out ov the bthrm.
Page	*13.*	Klmz slipt on the soap and he fl down the strs.
Page	*14.*	He wnt roln down the stars. Por Klmz.
Page	*15.*	Shesh!O bruthr!

FIGURE 3.3. Haley, age 6, Grade 1: "KLMZ BNY."

a	he	out
and	head	shesh
bed	his	soap
bonk	hit	the
down	in	then
for	it	to
get	on	up
had	one	woke

FIGURE 3.4. Haley's 24 correctly spelled words from "KLMZ BNY."

the number of different words used or the number of running words, that is, every word used in the piece. Out of 74 different words used, Haley correctly spelled 24 and misspelled 50, a 2 to 1 ratio of invented to correct spellings. On the other hand, out of 165 running words, Haley correctly spelled 80 and misspelled 85, an almost even ratio.

arms, rms	ready, rde
bathroom, bthrm	rolling, roln
breakfast, brkfst	saw, sl
brother, bruthr	scared, skrd
bunny, bne, bny	shoe, shu
clogged, klgd	slipped, slpt, slipt
clumsy, klmz	snapped, snapt
dresser, drsr	spilled, spld
face, fas	squirted, skwrted
fell, fl	stairs, strs, stars
found, fnd	straps, strps
glass, glas	stretched, strcht
going to, gna	then, thn
hands, hnds	thought, tht
his, hz	tie, ti
looked, lkt	toothbrush, tothbrsh
mirror, mrer	toothpaste, tothpst
of, ov, uv	under, ndr, undr
oh, o	walked, wkt
other, uthr	was, wz
overhauls, ovrals	washing, wshn
poor, por	water, wtr
put, pt	went, wnt
putting, ptn	when, wen
reached, recht	while, wil

FIGURE 3.5. Haley's 50 words with invented spelling from "KLMZ BNY."

2. Haley exhibits significant spelling strength, even in the words she misspells. She spells consonant sounds with exceptional accuracy, as these examples illustrate: *strcht, skwrted, strps, spld, strs, snapt, tothbrsh, tothpst, klgd.* She has outstanding command of letter–sound relationships.

3. During early stages of invented spelling, many children can spell one-, two-, and three-letter words correctly. Haley shows great strength in correctly spelling such words. If the word is five letters in length or more, she always resorts to inventing it.

4. Haley is moving toward more correct spelling and greater aware-ness of spelling principles. Notice that she spells certain words two ways: *bny* and *bne, hz* and *his, ndr* and *undr, strs* and *stars, slpt* and *slipt.* This indicates that she is aware of the variability in letter–sound relationships, crucial knowledge for understanding the English spelling system.

5. Invented spelling allows Haley to experiment with how the spelling system works. This is hypothesizing—trying out ideas, rejecting or accept-ing hypotheses as she goes along. Haley is well on her way to becoming a competent speller.

6. Invented spellings do not remain static over long periods of time. Transitions are gradually made from less complete to more complete, from incorrect to correct. There is evidence that Haley is well aware of spelling options. Inconsistencies in invented spellings signal growth more often than confusion. Words spelled two ways suggest that a transition may be about to take place. Inconsistencies in invented spellings tend to appear in the following three circumstances, and are more often signs of progress than regression:

   a. When words are in transition from incorrect to correct—*hz, his; thn, then;*

   b. When words are in transition from less complete to more com-plete—*ndr, undr; slpt, slipt;* and

   c. When children experiment with irregular or variable letter–sound relationships within words—*bne, bny; ov, uv.*

7. Words available in the immediate print environment may, never-theless, be invented, probably because children find this more efficient than copying words from a source. We know that children use environ-mental print to aid them in their writing, but we do not know the particulars about how such models are used. Haley invented spellings for words that were available in the book she used. Eight words appeared in her book: *bump, shoe, snap, squirt, splash, what, a, day.* She did not use four of the available words: *bump, splash, what, day.* She used *shoe* but spelled it *shu;* she spelled *squirted* as *skwrted;* she used *snap* in its inflected form *snapt;* and she spelled the base word, *snap,* correctly.

Now that you have read Haley's story and perused the data in Figures 3.3, 3.4, and 3.5, think about the following questions, and make your own judgments about what can be learned from Haley's work.

1. What is the most important idea you have gained from Haley's work?
2. What predictions can you make about Haley's future as a reader and writer?
3. Will Haley become a good or poor speller? What evidence would you cite for your prediction?

THE RELATIONSHIP OF INVENTED SPELLING TO STANDARD SPELLING

Three issues are pertinent to discussing the relationship of invented spelling to standard spelling. (1) Does invented spelling lead to poor spelling habits? (2) Does invented spelling lead to confusion regarding standard spelling? (3) How do children make the transition to standard spelling? These issues were touched upon earlier in this chapter, so here I will review the major points.

Does Invented Spelling Lead to Poor Spelling?

There is no reliable evidence that invented spelling leads to poor spelling. On the contrary, invented spelling leads to better spelling, as discussed earlier. This seems counterintuitive until one considers how children learn their native language. In most cultures, children need 5–7 years to master all of the features of oral language except vocabulary, which continues to grow throughout one's lifetime. This seems to be a universal norm. Understanding how native oral language is learned gives us some insight into how children may learn their written language. Children can only approximate the language that surrounds them and consequently, make thousands upon thousands of "mistakes" in learning their language. It doesn't harm children to go through this long period of approximating the oral language that surrounds them, and it is unavoidable. It is the only way to learn language.

Invented spelling enables children to learn the written language in a manner similar to the way they learned their oral language. Invented spelling is based on the premise that spelling words "as best you can" will produce literacy faster and better than following the traditional model in which writing was delayed until spelling had been acquired.

Does Invented Spelling Lead to Confusion Regarding Standard Spelling?

Most children know that their invented spellings are not correct or final spellings and are perfectly willing to accept that the conventional spelling system is different from their approximations. They are capable of figuring out differences and similarities between standard spelling and their best guesses. As Chomsky (1979) maintains, "The printed word 'belongs' to the spontaneous speller far more directly than to children who have experienced it only ready made. For once you have invented your own spelling system, dealing with the standard system comes easy. A considerable amount of the intellectual work has already been done" (p. 49). Wide reading provides the correct models. Formal spelling instruction does likewise, but more gradually.

I want to emphasize that we must not give children the impression that correct spelling doesn't ultimately matter. It matters, but it must be acquired at an appropriate pace. Good models are just as important in learning written language as they are in oral language. As time goes on, young children figure out that the oral language in their environment is different from their own rendition of it. As a consequence, they gradually shape their language to the language of their parents, peers, and teachers. Gradually, their immature language disappears, replaced by mature language. It works the same way with written language when the instructional atmosphere facilitates it.

Children understand language concepts best when they construct their own understandings of how things work. In effect, they reinvent the language, oral and written, as they learn. Read's (1970, 1971, 1975) studies show us that children's invented spelling are, in effect, a reinvention of the English spelling system. Children's invented spellings are consistent and linguistically sophisticated. Read's findings buttress my faith in children's capacity to learn and demonstrate that English spelling, far from being the chaotic beast of popular mythology, is a rule-governed system.

How Do Children Manage the Transition to Correct Spelling?

Although I haven't yet found *the* answer to an important question teachers often ask me—"When do you stop allowing invented spelling and require children to spell words correctly?"—I have two responses to it.

First, we stop *allowing* invented spelling as it is replaced with correct spelling. In other words, we don't disallow invented spelling—instead, we systematically teach correct spelling. Thus, as time goes on and spelling achievement matures, there is less and less need for children to invent spellings. We want children to spell correctly the words they know. We want them to invent spellings for the words they do not yet know how to spell. We teach them to search for correct spellings when they revise their writing, particularly when writing reaches a public forum or is to be presented to an audience where the expectation is for correct writing.

The second answer to the question may shock you. We never stop *allowing* invented spelling. (Keep reading.) Invented spelling never goes away because it is always necessary to invent the spellings of unknown words during the drafting stage of writing. Ask yourself, "Do I ever invent the spelling of a word *when* I am writing?" I'll use myself as an example. I write nearly every day, and I often write about spelling, but I am not ashamed to admit that in my early drafts I do not care whether words are spelled correctly or not. I suppose I will never give up inventing spellings for words I do not immediately know how to spell. It would slow down my writing and interfere with whatever meaning I am searching for. I suspect that most writers would say the same thing. Of course, there comes a time when I do care. I know how to fix my mistakes. I revise, edit, and proofread in a way that has come to suit my writing idiosyncrasies. (I'm having trouble spelling that last word.) As I write this chapter, I see that there are incorrectly spelled words here and there. I'll get to them later. Just now, I am concerned about the message I am trying to formulate. Many of my spelling errors are typos, but some of them are words I misspell out of pure ignorance. So what! I'm not an savant of spelling. There are lots of seldom-used words that I cannot spell; there are even a few words that I ought to know how to spell, but somehow I've managed to misspell them even to this day. Again, so what? But it is my hope that when this book appears in print, I will have corrected all of them. The ones I miss, and there will be some, I hope the copy editor will catch. And the ones we both miss will give you good readers a laugh or two at our expense, and just possibly, an opportunity to feel a tiny bit superior.

How is this different from children's use of invented spelling? It differs in quantity and quality. Mature spellers have a much larger spelling vocabulary than children, so they have less need for temporary place holders. It also differs in quality since mature spellers are likely to make better guesses about how to spell a word than children do. But the process and purpose are identical. Writers want to get their ideas down as rapidly as possible. They do not worry about spelling while they are concentrating on meaning. Later, they use a spell checker program, consult a dictionary, or ask a better speller. This is what we must teach children to do, but it takes time. First the message, then the mechanics.

Let's go back to the original question. When do we begin requiring correct spelling? We should begin formal spelling instruction in the first or second grade, and, ideally we would continue teaching it throughout high school for those who still need it—and there are plenty of high school students who do. It takes time to acquire a spelling vocabulary, concepts, and strategies.

EXPLAINING INVENTED SPELLING TO PARENTS

Spelling is a visible symbol of literacy, so when parents are told by critics that invented spelling is just another example of dumbing down the curriculum, they may be ready to believe that this is so. Looking at the issue from the standpoint of parents, it is not surprising that some are alarmed. Critics tell them that invented spelling will handicap their children with poor spelling habits from which they may never recover. On the other hand, most parents want to believe that their children's teachers are upholding excellent educational standards. It is our job as teachers to explain why invented spelling makes sense. Parents can be persuaded, but they want evidence. The most persuasive kind is always closely related to the success of their own children. Therefore, we can't just tell them; we must show them with examples drawn from children's work.

Parents also need to know that their children will be taught standard spelling. Many of them suspect that standard spelling instruction has been neglected, and in many schools that is exactly what has happened.

The following four ideas will help parents understand the purpose and importance of invented spelling.

Invented Spelling Is Temporary

Parents should be informed that invented spelling is temporary and will be replaced with correct spelling in a timely and orderly fashion. For example, when Patty spells *name* as *nm*, this is temporary, and she will soon learn to spell *name* correctly—probably in first grade. On the other hand, Patty may not learn to spell *absolutely* in first grade, unless she wants to learn it on her own. As children progress through the stages of spelling, their temporary spellings move rather quickly toward standard spelling. Haley's writing (Figures 3.3, 3.4, and 3.5) provides excellent examples of how she is beginning to move from invented spelling toward standard spelling. Look for similar examples in your children's writing and share these examples with parents.

Invented Spelling Makes Early Writing Possible

Most parents will agree that writing is important. They are charmed by their children's writings. Tell parents that the idea behind invented spelling is to enable children to write, perhaps on the first day of school. Once parents understand that correct spelling is a barrier that invented spelling can remove, they are more likely to understand its purpose. If writing is pushed into the background while spelling is acquired, children have no valid way of practicing the words they are learning to spell. Interaction between spelling and writing is crucial because children easily forget spelling words if they have little or no opportunity to use them in writing. Also, while oral vocabularies are large, spelling vocabularies are small in the beginning. Nothing interesting or sensible can be written with the few words young children can spell correctly. Patty's story "The Pet" (Figure 3.2) illustrates this point quite well.

Invented Spelling Builds Reading Knowledge

Invented spelling builds knowledge needed to read. In certain respects, spelling is the inverse of reading. The given for the reader is the visible word. The reader supplies the sounds in order to pronounce words, either orally or silently. Once words are recognized, meaning can be constructed. It works the other way around for spelling. The given for the writer are the sounds, and the writer provides the letters and words. The writer's tools are letters, sounds, known words, and the intention to create and convey meaning. The reader decodes and constructs meaning. The writer encodes and constructs meaning. Practice in one medium reinforces knowledge in the other. Most parents will understand and appreciate these issues, but you must help them by providing explanation and examples.

Invented Spelling Is Not a Substitute for Standard Spelling

One of the biggest mistakes educators have made over the past decade or so was to abandon consistent spelling instruction. Poor spelling achievement is bound to attract critics, and invented spelling is an inviting target to take the hit. But invented spelling cannot account for poor spelling achievement; abandonment of effective spelling instruction is the culprit. Thus, it is important to assure parents that along with invented spelling, adopted because it has important implications for learning to read and write, you are teaching standard spelling.

Perhaps it is also worth reminding parents that invented spelling is not to blame for whatever spelling failures may exist in schools today. Invented spelling has not been used widely enough in schools to account for general spelling failure. Poor spellers did not suddenly appear on the scene with the advent of invented spelling. A perusal of historical manuscripts shows that many of America's best and brightest often misspelled words, sometimes egregiously. Even Thomas Jefferson's early drafts of the Declaration of Independence reveal that this man, an enormously talented intellectual, made a few spelling errors. He produced a magnificent document, even if his early drafts contained a few spelling mistakes.

Instilling Confidence

Parents need to respect you as a competent professional. But you can't demand respect; you have to earn it. Most of us would be skeptical of a physician who seemed uncertain of the diagnosis and treatment of our illness. The physician who demonstrates that he or she knows what to do instills confidence. So too with teachers. Instill confidence in parents by demonstrating that you know your job, understand the treatments you have prescribed, and are convinced that your prescription for instruction will work.

Writing a thoughtful explanatory letter to parents describing your reading, writing, and spelling goals and methods of achieving them will help in this regard. If you are using invented spelling, tell parents how it will help their children in reading and writing; let them know what signs of progress they can expect to see over the next 6 months. Explain that you are also teaching standard spelling. Invite them to come in and discuss their child's progress in writing, reading, and spelling.

PERSPECTIVE AND SUMMARY

Invented spelling is controversial. Its critics have blamed it for spelling failure, and its advocates have sometimes defended it unwisely. On its face, invented spelling must seem ludicrous to those who do not understand its place and purpose in the literacy curriculum. The sensible way to overcome the critics' skepticism is to make certain that standard spelling is well taught. High expectations and standards in teaching reading, writing, and spelling are not obsolete. There is no inherent conflict between invented spelling and standard spelling *unless* there is a failure to teach standard spelling. If standard spelling is not well taught, the critics of invented spelling will have won a victory they did not justly earn.

This chapter has presented the following main ideas:

• Invented spelling describes children's first efforts to write words they have not yet learned to spell. It enables children to write before they have acquired a substantial spelling vocabulary.

• Research has established that invented spelling has a positive influence on learning to read, write, and spell. Therefore, critics' claims that it "dumbs down" the curriculum are not credible.

• In order to invent spellings of unknown words children need to be able to write the letters of the alphabet, possess a modicum of phonemic awareness, understand letter–sound relationships, and understand the sequential nature of representing letter–sound relationships in words.

• Children's invented spellings contain specific linguistic features. Knowing what these features are and why these features consistently appear in children's invented spelling can help teachers direct children's spelling growth.

• Invented spelling supports and encourages growth in reading, writing, and spelling.

• Critics claim that invented spelling confuses children, creates transition problems, and leads to bad spelling habits. None of these charges is sustained by research evidence or classroom experience.

• Parents have an interest in knowing what invented spelling is, how it works, and how it will help their children. Teachers who use invented spelling have a responsibility to educate parents about it.

REFERENCES

Ayres, L. (1993). *The efficacy of three training conditions on phonological awareness of kindergarten children and the longitudinal effect of each on later reading acquisition.* Unpublished doctoral dissertation, Oakland University, Rochester, MI.

Ball, E. W., & Blachman, B. A. (1991). Does phoneme segmentation raining in kindergarten make a difference in early word recognition and spelling development? *Reading Research Quarterly, 26*(1), 49–66.

Bear, D. R., Invernizzi, M., Templeton, S., & Johnston, F. (1996). *Words their way: Word study for phonics, vocabulary, and spelling instruction.* Englewood Cliffs, NJ: Prentice-Hall.

Beers, J. (1980). Developmental strategies of spelling competence in primary school children. In J. Beers & E. Henderson (Eds.), *Developmental and cognitive aspects of learning to spell* (pp. 36–45). Newark, DE: International Reading Association.

Beers, J. W., & Henderson, E. H. (1977). A study of developing orthographic concepts among first grade children. *Research in the Teaching of English, 11*(2), 133–148.

Bissex, G. (1980) *GYNS AT WRK: A child learns to write and read.* Cambridge, MA: Harvard University Press.

Bradley, L., & Bryant, P. E. (1983). Categorizing sounds and learning to read—a causal connection. *Nature, 301,* 419–421.

Calkins, L. (1986). *The art of teaching writing.* Portsmouth, NH: Heinemann.

Chomsky, C. (1971). Write first, read later. *Childhood Education, 47,* 269–299.

Chomsky, C. (1979). Approaching reading through invented spelling. In L. B. Resnick & P. A. Weaver (Eds.), *Theory and practice of early reading* (Vol. 2, pp. 43–65). Hillsdale, NJ: Erlbaum.

Clarke, L. K. (1988). Encouraging invented spelling in first graders' writing: Effects on learning to spell and read. *Research in the Teaching of English, 22*(3), 281–309.

Clay, M. M. (1975). *What did I write?* Portsmouth, NH: Heinemann.

Cramer, B. B. (1985). *The effects of writing with invented spelling on general linguistic awareness and phonemic segmentation ability in kindergartners.* Unpublished doctoral dissertation, Oakland University, Rochester, MI.

Cramer, R. L. (1968). *An investigation of the spelling achievement of two groups of first-grade classes on phonologically regular and irregular words and in written compositions.* Unpublished doctoral dissertation, University of Delaware, Newark.

Cramer, R. L. (1970). An investigation of first-grade spelling achievement. *Elementary English, 47*(2), 230–237.

Ehri, L., & Wilce, L. (1987). Does learning to spell help beginners learn to read words? *Reading Research Quarterly, 12,* 47–65.

Garcia, C. A. (1997). *The effect of two types of spelling instruction on first grade reading, writing, and spelling achievement.* Unpublished doctoral dissertation, Oakland University, Rochester, MI.

Gentry, J. R. (1981, January). Learning to spell developmentally. *Reading Teacher, 34,* 378–381.

Graves, D. (1983). *Writing: Teachers and children at work.* Portsmouth, NH: Heinemann.

Healy, N. A. (1991). *First grade writing with invented or traditional spelling: Effects on the development of decoding ability and writing skill.* Unpublished doctoral dissertation, University of Minnesota, Duluth, MI.

Henderson, E. H., & Beers, J. W. (1980). *Developmental and cognitive aspects of learning to spell: A reflection of word knowledge.* Newark, DE: International Reading Association.

Housel, D. K. (1989). *The effects of the writing to read program and invented spelling in kindergarten on phonemic awareness and later reading ability.* Unpublished doctoral dissertation, Oakland University, Rochester, MI.

Mann, V. A., Tobin, P., & Wilson, R. (1988). Measuring phonological awareness through the invented spelling of kindergarten children. In K. Stanovich (Ed.), *Children's reading and the development of phonological awareness* (pp. 121–145). Detroit, MI: Wayne State University Press.

Moriarty, T. (1990). *Using children's literature: How literature-based writing influences the development of phonological awareness.* Unpublished doctoral dissertation, Oakland University, Rochester, MI.

Piaget, J. (1955). *The language and thought of the child.* New York: Meridian Books.

Read, C. (1970). *Children's perceptions of the sounds of English: Phonology from three to six.* Unpublished doctoral dissertation, Harvard University.

Read, C. (1971). Pre-school children's knowledge of English phonology. *Harvard Educational Review, 41*(1), 1–34.

Read, C. (1975). *Children's categorization of speech sounds in English* (NCTE Research Reports No. 17). Urbana, IL: National Council of Teachers of English.

Stanovich, K. E. (1988). *Children's reading and the development of phonological awareness.* Detroit, MI: Wayne State University Press.

Stauffer, R. G. (1970). *The language experience approach to the teaching of reading.* New York: Harper & Row.

Stauffer, R. G., & Hammond, W. D. (1969). The effectiveness of a language arts and basic reader approach to first grade reading instruction extended into third grade. *Reading Research Quarterly, 4,* 468–499.

Stauffer, R., Hammond, D., Oehlkers, W., & Houseman, A. (1972). *Effectiveness of a language-arts and basic-reader approach to first grade reading instruction extended into sixth grade* (Cooperative Research Project 3276). Newark, DE: University of Delaware.

Temple, C., Nathan, R., Burris, N., & Temple, F. (1988). *The beginnings of writing* (2nd ed.). Boston: Allyn & Bacon.

Templeton, S. (1980). Spelling, phonology, and the older student. In E. H. Henderson & J. W. Beers (Eds.), *Developmental and cognitive aspects of learning to spell* (pp. 85–96). Newark, DE: International Reading Association.

Chapter 4

Connections: Reading, Writing, and Spelling

Read, Read, read. Read everything—trash, classics, good
and bad, and see how they do it. Just like a carpenter who
works as an apprentice and studies the master. Read!
You'll absorb it. Then write.

—WILLIAM FAULKNER

INTRODUCTION

You cannot sensibly talk about learning to spell without acknowledging the
reading–writing–spelling connection. Reading provides the raw material
for spelling, and spelling has no purpose in the absence of writing. It is
unwise to teach spelling in a context isolated from reading and writing.
Reading influences writing; writing influences reading; reading and writing together influence spelling. These three statements provide an outline
for this chapter, and I believe absolutely in their importance. However, I
also acknowledge that these are theoretical statements; they have no
practical value as long as they remain statements of our intentions and
philosophy and do not enter into our day-to-day classroom practices. This
chapter discusses the theoretical issues and presents some ideas and
activities that connect reading, writing, and spelling to the mutual benefit
of all three components of the language arts curriculum.

WRITING INFLUENCES READING

A friend told me about her earliest memory of the writing–reading
connection. At age 3, she recalls watching her dad reading a book with a

pencil in his hand. Now and then the pencil swooped down and Dad underlined a passage or wrote a note in the margin. This obvious connection between writing and reading struck Sue's fancy: Readers wrote in books with pencils. Sue loved her dad, so she accorded him the ultimate flattery; she imitated him. Unfortunately, imitating Dad was not well received. Sue learned that writing in a book was a punishable offense. Sue couldn't understand how her dad got away with connecting reading and writing right in front of Mom, and he never seemed to get caught. Dad's behavior remained a mystery. Years later, she would discover the nuances about writing in books: Ownership makes a difference, purpose likewise.

Writing influences reading in many ways, and we shall examine three of these influences. First, writing helps children understand authorship. It gives them an insiders view of the reading–writing connection. Second, writing improves reading comprehension, the ultimate purpose of reading instruction. Third, writing improves the technical skills needed for fluent reading, writing, and spelling.

Writing and Authorship

Writing makes children insiders in the world of print. Insider information is coveted knowledge. In the business world, insider information is considered so valuable that those with access to it are forbidden by law to use it for personal gain. Fortunately, in the world of literacy, there is no such taboo. Readers who are also writers are the true insiders, because writers have inside information on how authors use language to create meaning. This knowledge gives the reader–writer a unique advantage in understanding the written messages of others. The reader who is a writer knows written language from both sides—as consumer and creator.

Reading programs that lack significant writing experiences and writing programs that lack significant reading experiences fail children because they offer a one-dimensional view of the world of literacy. Those who are readers only, no matter how skilled, cannot fully compensate for the missing experience that writing alone bestows. Readers who do not write are limited partners in the world of literacy.

Young writers who publish books learn what authoring means. It starts in small ways and gradually builds into more mature understanding. Joie, a fourth grader, had written a 12-page book. She showed it to me, boasting proudly, "It has 10 chapters. That's two more than the book I just read!" Andrea, a third grader, had just published a book that has a dedication page, table of contents, six chapters, and an index. She showed it to her teacher, saying, "It's a real book, isn't it, Mrs. Mallory?" Mrs. Mallory,

Children, like professional writers, experience the thrill of authorship. These students discuss their stories, which will soon be incorporated into the books they are writing.

without hesitation, replied, "Andrea, it's as real as any book I've ever seen." Eddie, a sixth grader, had written a mystery with a pretty good plot, some false leads, and two detectives suspiciously similar to Sherlock Holmes and Dr. Watson. Eddie's book is one of many children's books cataloged in the school library. His proud comment to a visitor was "It's one of the most popular books in our library." Joie, Andrea, and Eddie write books. They know about authors, authoring, and publishing. They are insiders.

A humorous story tells of a first grader who became an insider sooner than expected. Returning home from his first day in school he shouted, "I can write! I can write!" His surprised mother asked, "What did you write?" Shrugging off the question as irrelevant, the first grader replied, "How should I know? I can't read." This story has an important point. Many children write before they read. Surveys taken on the first day of school consistently show that most first graders believe they can write, whereas few believe they can read. Of course, their writing may be at the prephonetic stage or the invented spelling stage. But this is a promising beginning, and it is exactly the right preparation for reading. Nurture the enthusiasm for writing that young children possess. It is a precious gift, the seed that grows into the tree of knowledge.

Writers like Joie, Andrea, and Eddie need to experience authorship early and often. They need to know about the authors of the books they read; they need to know what authors do and how they think; they need to ask the questions that authors pose; they need to experience the problems that authors solve; they need to write every day. "Never a day without a line," was Pliny's motto, a good one for any writing program.

Calkin (1986) quotes a 7-year-old writer, Greg, who describes how writing led him to an understanding of authorship.

> Before I ever wrote a book, I used to think there was a big machine and they typed a title and then the machine went until the book was done. Now I look

at a book and know a guy wrote it and it's been his project for a long time. After the guy writes it, he probably thinks of questions people will ask him and revises it like I do, and copies it to read to about six editors. Then he fixes it up, like how they say. (p. 224)

How can it be said more eloquently? You have to write to understand authorship, how things work in the world of written language, and that reading and writing are connected.

Writing and Comprehension

Shanahan (1980) found that writing improves reading comprehension. His data suggest that the major effect of writing on reading comprehension occurs at the intermediate grade levels. Petrosky (1982) found that writing essay responses to stories improved reading ability. Taylor and Beach (1984) have shown that writing expository text improves students' comprehension of such text. This is an especially important study because it demonstrates that writing a specific kind of discourse makes it easier to comprehend the same kind of discourse in reading. In the future, we may find this idea gaining an increasingly important role in comprehension instruction. For instance, we may supplement instruction in comprehension of explanatory text by doing explanatory writing; we may supplement instruction in propaganda analysis by writing persuasive text, and so on.

Using interview techniques, Tierney and Leys (1984) discovered numerous instances in which third graders consciously used strategies they had learned in writing to solve reading problems. Children applied to reading what they learned in writing almost without deliberate effort. Turbill (1982), Squires (1983), and Atwell (1984) have discussed similar instances in which children applied writing knowledge to solve reading problems.

Writing also has a beneficial effect on the constituent components of comprehension. Vocabulary knowledge, for instance, is an important component of comprehension, as Davis (1944) demonstrated in his classic study. Wolfe (1975) compared the effects of two methods of teaching vocabulary in a remedial class and found that writing improves vocabulary knowledge. However, if writing opportunities are restricted, as is often the case, vocabulary growth will likewise be restricted.

Taylor and Berkowitz (1980) found that sixth graders who wrote brief summaries of social studies passages comprehended the passages better than students who used the more traditional question–answer method. Writing summaries may require students to organize and reorganize information, thus helping them make the information their own in a way that answering questions does not. Collins (1985) found that 10 minutes of daily expressive writing improved reading comprehension and attitude toward learning. Stotsky (1983) concluded her review of reading–writing research with this remark: "Almost all studies that used writing activities or exercises specifically to improve reading comprehension or retention of information in instructional material found significant gains" (p. 636).

We do not know exactly how or why writing improves comprehension. It may be that writing adds a unique perspective to a reader's experience with written language. Writer's goals and reader's goals have much in common. Writers construct written texts; readers construct and reconstruct the texts they are reading. Experienced writers have the advantage of understanding the organization and structure of written text. They have built texts from scratch; they know how the task is done; they recognize features of written text that those who lack writing experience might miss; they have learned the author's craft. Writers are aware of their audience, their readers. They want their readers to comprehend, and so they learn to make their writing readable. This constant practice teaches writers how to give meaning to text and how to get meaning from it.

Writing and Technical Fluency

Writing helps children acquire skills related to reading fluency, such as word recognition, spelling, and the conventions of written language.

Word Recognition

Writing is among the most beneficial word recognition activities for young readers, providing excellent practice in learning such essential concepts as phonemic awareness and auditory discrimination (Bradley & Bryant, 1983; Ayres, 1993). Writing also helps children recognize words at sight, a skill prerequisite to fluent reading. Unlike isolated phonic exercises, writing provides a highly meaningful context for learning word recognition.

Shanahan (1980) correlated word recognition, reading, comprehension, and vocabulary knowledge with several writing variables. He found that, for second graders, the relationship between reading and writing was based on word recognition and spelling. This suggests that writing has a particularly useful effect on word recognition and spelling for younger children. Other evidence supports this idea. Stauffer and Hammond (1969, 1970) found that word recognition improved when instruction stressed integrated reading and writing. The language experience approach used in these studies emphasized dictated experience stories, independent writing with invented spelling, comprehension conducted with Directed-Reading–Thinking-Activities, individualized reading of trade books, and auditory discrimination. After 1, 3, and 6 years, the children in this integrated reading and writing program were significantly better in comprehension, word recognition, writing, and spelling than children in a nonintegrated, traditional reading program.

Word recognition is one of the major goals of primary grade reading. The finding that writing facilitates the acquisition of word recognition is especially important since it enables teachers to confidently substitute writing for some of the traditional phonics instruction given during this stage of reading development. In addition, writing enables children to acquire word recognition skills in a more meaningful context than traditional phonics drills. Writing is a challenging intellectual activity, engaging children in problem solving and creative endeavor. At the same time, written products are created that are highly motivating and meaningful to children. No phonics drill ever invented can claim as much.

Spelling

Children possess a wealth of linguistic knowledge—phonetic, semantic, and grammatical. Children can begin writing, using invented spelling, as soon as they can write some letters of the alphabet and associate sounds with these letters. Simply knowing the names of the alphabet letters provides sufficient knowledge to invent the spelling of some words. Some preschoolers and kindergarten children and most first graders are capable of inventing their own spellings if they are encouraged to write.

Chris, a first grader, wrote the dinosaurs piece shown in Figure 4.1. Notice how many words are spelled correctly and how phonetic the misspellings of these words are: *dinusors, ones, Brotusoris, bak, tale, Tranusoris.* She had been in first grade for 5 months when this story was written. Invented spelling gave Chris practice in segmenting sounds, connecting letters to sounds, and exploring spelling patterns in unknown words. Even more importantly, Chris communicates her ideas in an orderly, thoughtful way and shares them with her classmates. Her ideas are received with respect and appreciation by her teacher and peers.

Conventions of Writing

Writing develops an awareness of the conventions of written language. For instance, English is written left to right and top to bottom. Spatial orientations for writing must be learned, and writing develops these spatial orientations quickly and easily. Children must also learn to write the letters of the alphabet, a skill requiring substantial eye–hand–muscle coordina-

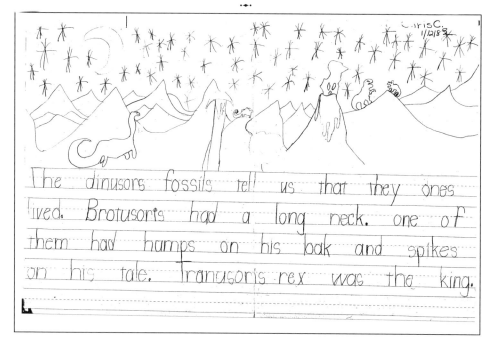

FIGURE 4.1. Chris's story: "Dinusors."

tion. Writing genuine messages provides the right motivation for tackling this difficult chore (Newman, 1984). In addition, children must learn a system of punctuation, capitalization, and other writing conventions. Young children, even prephonetic writers, soon grasp basic writing conventions. Writing is superior to reading in helping children learn these conventions, perhaps because writing requires the physical manipulation of print, whereas reading does not.

READING INFLUENCES WRITING

Faulkner's advice about connecting reading and writing (see chapter-opening page) is a bit subversive. In that spirit, therefore, I offer this imaginary conversation between William Faulkner, Nobel Prize-winning novelist, and your prototypical ivory tower university professor:

PROFESSOR: What do you think, Bill, should we teach less and read more?

FAULKNER: Read, read, read.

PROFESSOR: Could you elaborate? For instance, what literature would you recommend?

FAULKNER: Read everything—trash, classics, good and bad, and see how they do it.

PROFESSOR: But you're killing the sacred cow of literature. Shouldn't we insist that our children read only the finest literature?

FAULKNER: So, kill a few sacred cows, Professor; you might enjoy the ceremony.

PROFESSOR: I'll have to think about that, Bill. But what did you mean a moment ago when you said, "see how they do it?" I say writers are born, not made. We artists are of a higher sort, you know.

FAULKNER: They do it just like the carpenter who works as an apprentice.

PROFESSOR: That's rather cryptic, Bill. Are you comparing learning to write with learning to pound nails? Surely appreciating *les mots justes* is worlds removed from the seamless joining of two boards! I'm assuming, of course, that your carpenter analogy is just a figure of speech. And your assertion, "Just write and you'll absorb it?" Why, that's so simple-minded.

FAULKNER: *Les mots justes,* Professor? How erudite. I don't recall using French in my books. My characters spoke English—tobacco road dialect, but fitting to convey genuine feeling. Don't you agree? You have to remember, Professor, we're not talking brain surgery here. My advice is simple: "Read. You'll absorb it. Then write."

Professional writers tell us that reading has a fundamental influence on writing. Wide reading establishes the knowledge base necessary for good writing, while reading selected authors deeply can influence writing style and substance. Of course, the advice of writers is anecdotal, but intuitively it makes sense that reading should influence writing. Art influences art: Musicians listen to music; artists view works of art; writers read.

Reading like a writer involves conscious and unconscious absorption of information and ideas. Reflective readers establish a dialogue with authors: They make educated guesses about what is coming; they dispute a premise; they agree with an argument; they appreciate a delicious sentence; they celebrate a perfectly selected word; they puzzle over an unknown word; they notice an unfamiliar spelling. They do all this in an instant, consciously or unconsciously. They see how the writer has done it, and this "seeing" is reading like a writer.

If reading is crucial to learning to write, how does it exercise this influence? Are there reading experiences especially conducive to writing? Can children be taught to read like a writer? The evidence suggests that they can certainly be encouraged or discouraged. In the realm of discouragement, Dixon (1978) and Eckhoff (1983) have shown that the stilted language found in some early readers may have a negative influence on writing. They found that first- and second-grade children who read stilted language tended to produce stilted writing. These studies were limited in scope and duration, so conclusions must be drawn carefully. For instance, there is no evidence of long-term harmful effects from reading stilted language. On the other hand, we know that oral language patterns remain static over long periods of time unless effective intervention occurs (Loban, 1976). It seems possible, therefore, that long-term negative reading influences could damage writing potential.

Geva and Tierney (1984) found that the format of the text read by students influenced the format of their writing. Light (1991) found that children whose parents read to them developed better attitudes toward reading than children who had not had a similar exposure to literature. Birnbaum (1982) found that the quality of writing children produced was related to the quality of their reading. Effective reading influenced how well children wrote. Tierney and Leys (1984) found that third graders were influenced by what they read. For example, third graders reported using words in writing acquired from reading, models from reading for story ideas and topics, and dialogue from reading to enrich writing.

Other influences of reading on writing were reported. Tierney and Leys's (1984) data show that young writers use reading in an integrated fashion, as the following comments illustrate.

1. Sometimes I imagine that I am the one who is going to read it, and I think about what other people would think.
2. I read my work as another person, I like to have a hint of what other people may say about it.
3. If something doesn't make sense [I can always tell] because . . . this little person in my head tells me.
4. I wrote it down and then I read it over, and the parts that I didn't think were right or where I needed more information, I crossed it out and put it on the other side: this is a second draft and first draft put together.
5. Well, some people don't know what elliptical means, so [on my second draft] I just decided to put that there [a definition] so that they wouldn't get mixed up.
6. Interviewer: How did you think of the ideas [for your book, *Natasha's Run Away Imagination*]? Child: Well, I read this other book, and it was about this girls' imagination but I just thought about that book and I thought it would be a good title for Natasha Koren to have a runaway imagination . . . it [the other book] wasn't the same . . . she looks at pictures and stuff and she imagines they are moving and stuff like that.

7. Journal Entry: Today I was doing my health book. I'm doing blood. Can I go to the library on Monday to get some more information on blood?
8. I did a report on owls, and this chapter right here [in his detective novel] is based on owls and [the mystery] is a question about owls. (pp. 19–20)

You can read like a writer only if you write. Teachers, of course, must become writers, too. Not professional writers, but individuals who enjoy the occasional writing of a poem or story. As you write, you begin to read like a writer. The more you write, the more you discover new meaning in the poems and stories of others and find yourself making observations about writers or asking questions about writing. As you begin to think of yourself as a writer, you communicate a positive feeling about writing to children. Even a modest amount of personal writing will put you in a position to talk about writing in a more authoritative way.

Strategies for Connecting Reading and Writing

Suppose someone asked you, "How are reading and writing alike? How are they different?" Ms. Deierlein asked her second graders this question. Jenny took a pragmatic view: "When you read your hand does not get tired. When you write your hand does get tired." Aaron had a sound theoretical perspective: "If you can read, you can write, too." Billy put it cleverly, if cryptically: "You can read riteing and rite reading. It's esay." In this section, I present practical strategies for connecting reading and writing.

The best way to teach writing is to teach writing; the best way to teach reading is to teach reading. However, help children to understand that reading and writing are two sides of the same coin. Show them how to think about reading like a writer might, and to think about writing like a reader might.

There are signs of success along the road to integration that may help you recognize how you are doing. You know, for instance, that you are succeeding in integrating reading and writing when you hear one of your children say something similar to what Misha's (a second grader) comments about a book she had written: "Well, I read a book about the Black Stallion, and so when I wrote my book, I wanted it to be about a black stallion, too. But I didn't want it to be the same. I wanted it to be my own ideas. So I changed the story." Misha has the right idea. She sees clearly that *The Black Stallion* can serve as a model for her own story, and has thereby discovered a legitimate strategy for connecting reading to writing. The following strategies will help children see the practical connections between reading and writing.

Getting Started

Where and how do teachers start to build real connections between reading and writing? The task can seem like an unscalable mountain if you have no colleagues to share the adventure, but you have to start somewhere. This is how one classroom teacher, Ms. Blackburn (1985), describes how she started:

> When I started building connections between reading and writing in my first-grade classroom, I did not foresee how those connections would occur. I merely tried to narrow the gap between the children's own writing and the writing of the adult authors they read. I encouraged them to guess how professional writers found ideas for topics and how they made decisions about details, beginnings and endings. Together we speculated how a story might be changed or even how two stories could be combined. "What if . . . " I would say, "What if Hansel and Gretel met up with *The Three Robbers* in Tomi Ungerer's story?" (p. 4)

Ms. Blackburn had the courage to leap into the unknown, as her comments demonstrate. She started with modeling, an excellent way to begin, but not the only one. Shanahan (1988), for instance, recommends seven instructional techniques to guide the reading–writing connection:

1. Reading and writing both need to be taught.
2. Reading and writing should be taught from the earliest grade levels.
3. The reading–writing relationship should be emphasized in different ways at different developmental levels.
4. Knowledge and process relations need to be emphasized.
5. The connections between reading and writing should be made explicit.
6. The communications aspects of reading and writing should be emphasized.
7. Reading and writing should be taught in meaningful contexts. (p. 636)

Learning Centers and Classroom Atmosphere

A learning center is a defined space or place within the classroom devoted to a specific topic, theme, or skill. Centers can be designed to meet specific instructional needs, such as providing follow-up activities for group work or enrichment experiences. They can include opportunities for listening, viewing, reading, writing, oral language, and artistic expression. A center should be planned so that individuals or small groups can work independently, without requiring frequent teacher involvement. Guidelines for using centers should be established cooperatively by the teacher and students. Reading and writing centers can be extremely useful, and they need not require elaborate preparation. A simple writing center, for instance, can be started with a few good reference books, a variety of writing materials, and a table and chairs. It should be located slightly apart from the central focus of the classroom. Find an old rug, a selection of books, and a few pillows, and you have the makings of a comfortable reading center.

Children spend a lot of time in classrooms, and a homey atmosphere is highly desirable. An active, productive classroom atmosphere makes learning pleasant and profitable. The ambiance of a classroom should be community oriented, like a family working together. At the same time, independent learning should also be encouraged. Desks are best arranged in small groups to encourage communication; straight rows are less conducive to building a community of interactive learners. Plan space for small group conferences. Large group instruction should have an established focal point.

Revision and Rereading

To connect reading and writing, emphasize revision. Why? Because to revise well you must become an exquisitely sensitive reader. Revision is the workshop of reading and writing; its importance can hardly be overstated. William Gass, an American writer, described his own writing habits this way: "I work not by writing but rewriting. Each sentence has many drafts. Eventually there is a paragraph. This gets many drafts. Eventually there is a page. This gets many drafts. And so on" (cited in Murray, 1990).

Revision is the beginning of seriously addressing the reading–writing issue. Children are not professional writers, and Gass's method is not directly applicable to young children. Yet his remarks make an important point. Revision is the lifeblood of writing, its sustaining force. But few have realized that revision is nourished through sensitive and thoughtful reading.

When children write, a cycle of reciprocal connections is established between writing and reading. The chain of events goes something like this: write–read–revise–conference–reread–revise. This chain of events repeats itself; it recurs, with modifications, over and over again. How often the process recurs depends on the nature of the writing, the author's purpose, the writer's maturity, and the conditions of instruction. The more mature the writer, the more extended the chain of events.

Revision can be emphasized in the writing conference. Over time, writing conferences should focus on content, organization, style, composing skills, and mechanics. In addition to individual writing conferences, direct revision instruction is needed, which may be done in small groups or whole-class sessions. Revision establishes a crucial connection between the writer as writer and the writer as reader. As writers develop greater skill at critically reading their own writing, they simultaneously become more skillful readers of other people's writing.

Literary Gossip

Literary gossip is book talk between teachers and children. It is simply talking about books and stories: characters, themes, ideas, thoughts, and feelings derived from reading literature and responding to literature orally or in writing. Atwell (1987) describes how she engages her students in literary gossip in her excellent book, *In the Middle: Writing, Reading, and Learning with Adolescents*. Few experiences are more important to integrated reading and writing instruction than sharing literature and ideas about literature with children. Literature is the springboard to writing and reading (Palmer & Coon, 1985), supplying the models so essential for writing, enriching language at all levels and for all uses. It stimulates ideas and imagination and furnishes many of the topics for writing. It provides vicarious experience and expands the knowledge base that readers and writers cannot do without.

Read literature aloud every day, choosing literature appropriate to the intellectual and emotional interests of your children. The purposes of sharing literature aloud with children vary. Often, it is simply for pleasure, but sometimes more specific purposes motivate this sharing. For instance, children need to understand the decisions authors make and the techniques they use when they write. If this is your purpose, it is appropriate to ask questions directing attention to specific issues: Did you think this was a good story? What did the author do to get your interest? Did you notice how the author started this story? Why do you think the author started it that way? If you were writing this story, how would you have started it? Of course, trivial questions must be avoided. Facts are important, but primarily in the context of making inferences and judgments.

In addition to asking questions, it is important to comment and seek children's comments on literary issues. Overreliance on questions can lead to teaching by interrogation. Good teachers ask good questions, but they are more than question-asking machines. Let children know that you, too, have ideas and opinions. For instance, you might say:

> "Did you know that Shel Silverstein writes plays and songs and also
> draws cartoons? Like other authors, he can do many things well. But

to us, he's best known for his poems. When Mr. Silverstein wrote 'Lester,' the poem I just read to you, I felt sad that Lester never learned how to use his wishes well. Authors bring their characters to life by having their characters say and do specific things. For example, a character may throw rocks at dogs, spit on his little brother, and call his best friend names. This might make some readers feel angry and disappointed in the character. When you write, you can do things with your characters just the way other writers, like Shel Silverstein, did."

We want children to know about authors and their craft. We want them to know who authors are, what they do, how they think, and why they write. "Gossiping" about books and authors helps accomplish this goal.

Reciprocal Questioning

Reciprocal questioning means to move back and forth alternately from one question perspective to its counterpart. First, ask a question from the point of view of the reader, then ask the same question from the point of view of the writer. In this fashion, children learn to think about reading and writing from the different points of view that writers and readers bring to composing and comprehending. Some examples of reciprocal questioning are given below.

Main Idea

READER: What is this story [article] mainly about? What is the most important idea here? What is the author saying?

WRITER: What do I have to say that's most important? How can I get across my most important idea? What will my readers think this is mostly about?

Setting

READER: Where does this story take place? How is the setting related to the plot?

WRITER: What setting would be best for this story? Will my story idea work in this setting?

Character

READER: Who is this story about? Does the author make them seem real? How?

WRITER: Is this story about me or someone else? Who are the main characters? What can I have them say and do to make them seem real?

Sequence

READER: How does the author sequence ideas and events? Are the ideas in time order, logical order, climactic order? Is it easy to follow, or do I get lost?

WRITER: What order would work best with my topic? Will this make sense to others? What choices do I have? How can I make the order smooth and easy to follow?

READING AND WRITING INFLUENCE SPELLING

Reading and Spelling

Spelling drill dominated as a means for teaching reading for centuries, perhaps because it worked. Researchers are again asking: Is there a reciprocal relationship between learning to read and learning to spell? Gates (1936) examined the issue and concluded that a strong reciprocal relationship existed between reading and spelling. Research stretching from the 1930s to the present (Garcia, 1997) supports the idea of such a reciprocal relationship.

Learning to spell elaborates and reinforces the knowledge necessary for processing the phonology and orthography of written language, and, since reading and spelling are in certain respects reciprocal, this process works in reverse. In other words, spelling knowledge enables children to read unknown words, and reading knowledge enables children to spell unknown words. Research also supports the idea that reading and spelling are reciprocal language processes. Chomsky (1971) states that "children are well equipped to organize linguistic knowledge on the basis of rich and varied inputs, to seek regularities, and to construct tacit rule systems. What they need in reading beyond the requisite background, is adequate input of understood text" (p. 54). Henderson (1989) states:

> Children's first major source of information about correctly spelled words is the sight vocabulary of their beginning reading material, dictated stories, poems, trade books, and basal texts. As was noted earlier, children's manner of reading in the beginning stages does provide them with a reasonably detailed examination of words and their letter sequence. Beginning readers tend to spell correctly most of the words they have learned to recognize at sight. (p. 91)

While reading and spelling share common components, they are not mirror images of one another. Spelling requires more precision and control over letter–sound relationships than reading, but the tendency to separate spelling from reading, as though the two were separate domains of learning, is unfortunate. Background information about letters, sounds, meaning, and word structure can be efficiently obtained from reading. When this base of information is rich, the likelihood of developing spelling power is increased. Having many opportunities to study words in varied contexts makes an important contribution to spelling growth. While reading and spelling require instruction appropriate to their unique components and purposes it is, nevertheless, possible to integrate elements of spelling and reading instruction so that there is a mutually enriching outcome.

Research on phoneme segmentation and phonological awareness training shows an overlapping knowledge base between reading and spelling. Ball and Blackman (1991), for instance, investigated the effects of training in phonemic segmentation and instruction in letter names and letter sounds on kindergarten children's reading and spelling skills. Results indicated that phoneme awareness instruction, combined with instruction connecting the phonemic segments to alphabet letters, significantly improved the early reading and spelling skills of the children in the phoneme awareness group. The reciprocal relationship between learning to read and learning to spell is particularly pronounced among children in the primary grades, as numerous studies have shown (Blachman, 1984; Stanovich, Cunningham, & Cramer, 1984; Bradley & Bryant, 1983; Juel, Griffith, & Gough, 1986; Mann & Liberman, 1984; Cramer, 1985).

It is known that vocabulary knowledge is closely associated with success in spelling and reading. For example, Dale, O'Rourke, and Bamman (1982) state that "the most effective spelling program works simultaneously with vocabulary study" (p. 167). An emphasis on word study is an important adjunct to effective spelling instruction (Henderson & Templeton, 1986). The purpose of word study is not merely to learn rules and patterns that determine spelling, but to instill a habit of examining words that is useful for a more complete understanding of English orthography.

Word study activities should focus on sound, structure, and meaning. In early spelling development, gaining familiarity with letter–sound correspondences and spelling patterns is essential. Particular emphasis should be given to structure and meaning at the upper elementary and secondary levels. Knowledge of Latin and Greek roots and their derived forms, for example, may enable children to make more effective use of the crucial connection between meaning and spelling. Word structure rules determine how vowel and consonant patterns are spelled and how prefixes and suffixes are affixed to words. Consequently, the more children know about the logic of word structure, the more able and adaptive their interaction with written language.

There are many ways to engage children in word study and vocabulary activities. Word categorization activities are especially valuable, for example, in helping children recognize common spelling patterns and thereby predict the spelling of related but as-yet unknown words. Even words that do not fit patterns become more memorable as exceptions if the normal patterns are well established.

Research and teaching experience demonstrate that spelling provides information about words that facilitates reading, and that the sharing of information among the language-learning processes is clearly reciprocal. It is important, therefore, to ask: What are the implications of the relationship between reading and spelling? The following implications are warranted.

1. Reading promotes spelling growth by providing background knowledge about words that is crucial in learning to spell words correctly. Similarly, spelling promotes reading growth.

2. Enriching children's specific knowledge of word meaning and broadening their general awareness of word morphology has a positive effect on spelling success. An effective spelling program should emphasize the development of vocabulary and word knowledge. Vocabulary and word study emphasis can take several forms: (a) studying word meanings, (b) studying word structure, including prefixes, suffixes, syllables, roots, derived and inflected forms, and (c) studying Latin and Greek word forms and other borrowed words.

3. Phonics and word analysis instruction supports spelling achievement. Phonology has a particular influence on children in the primary grades, whereas learning about the structure of words is a useful spelling strategy for intermediate and upper-level grades. Therefore, spelling instruction ought to incorporate activities and strategies that focus on phonetic analysis and structural analysis, stressing each of these components at their appropriate developmental levels.

4. Seeing words in print may be a more effective means of learning to spell than hearing them, according to Ehri and Wilce (1987). Their research suggests that activities and strategies that emphasize close examination of the visual features of words may be a more effective spelling strategy than listening to words for cues to spelling.

Writing and Spelling

Chomsky (1979) argues, "For maximum effectiveness, school instruction should begin with writing and progress to reading, as an outgrowth of abilities developed through experience with inventing one's own spellings" (p. 43). Chomsky asks and answers the question, "How can children best learn the written language?" Chomsky believes that the traditional approach–teaching reading first and later writing and spelling–is inadequate, since it does not provide enough opportunity to produce language for personal and meaningful purposes. Writing is crucial to an integrated approach to literacy, she argues. An early writing emphasis adds enormous power to beginning reading, writing, and spelling instruction. Emphasizing writing, it is argued, gives teachers an opportunity to create a more natural learning environment for learning to spell.

The major obstacle to approaching literacy through writing is the English spelling system. It is complex, and it requires years to master, although it has more regularities than is commonly believed. However, evidence from research and teacher experience does show that an integrated reading–writing approach can help surmount the spelling obstacle (Cramer, 1968, 1970; Read, 1971; Chomsky, 1971, 1979; Clay, 1975; Clarke, 1989; Garcia, 1997). Any approach to spelling that does not make use of the natural connections between these closely related skills sacrifices the mutually reinforcing properties that learning these skills in tandem provides. The following five points illustrate how writing can contribute to spelling knowledge.

First, writing should focus primarily on the construction of meaning. Expressing ideas in writing is more important than the mechanics of writing. First draft writing should emphasize the fluent expression of ideas while *temporarily* deemphasizing spelling, grammar, and mechanics, because the amount of attention available for performing any task is limited. During the early stages of learning to spell, young writers often find themselves overwhelmed by the problem of matching letters to sounds. Two strategies help children focus their attention on the message rather than on the mechanics of writing. The first is a short-term solution, the second is long term.

1. Invented spelling relieves the immediate pressure for correct spelling while drafting.
2. The acquisition of a strong spelling vocabulary provides the automaticity needed for more fluent writing.

Second, spelling comes into primary focus during the editing–proofreading stage of writing which is the right time for emphasizing the detailed knowledge required to check for correct spelling mechanics. It is crucial, of course, to teach the strategies and skills needed to succeed at the difficult task of checking spelling and mechanical accuracy.

Third, the classroom environment should provide a rich and varied writing program. Spelling develops best in a classroom environment where there is wide exposure to words through reading, significant opportunities for personal and academic writing, and systematic spelling instruction. Spelling instruction should concentrate on developing specific spelling knowledge by teaching a basic spelling vocabulary, and also add to children's general knowledge of English through vocabulary and word study. As children develop, a new spelling vocabulary must be learned at each stage of spelling growth. If this spelling vocabulary is not established, children will not have a sufficient base upon which to build new spelling knowledge. Children need instruction in spelling starting in first or second grade and continuing through high school. Spelling cannot be left to chance in the hope that incidental exposure to reading and writing alone will suffice. Effective instruction requires specific instructional time, perhaps as much as 60–90 minutes per week. There must be meaningful activities for learning words, along with the inculcation of spelling awareness. Finally, an appropriate set of words must be studied in a context that establishes a connection between reading, writing, and learning to spell.

Fourth, writing is a concrete and physically active experience, more so than reading. Writing encourages children to invent the spelling of unknown words, a concrete, graphic experience requiring the production of language. Reading, on the other hand, starts with the more abstract task of decoding words. Children thrive on activities that require movement. Writing requires the manipulation of the tools of writing as well as an active physical engagement of the body in the act of writing. Writing and spelling by approximation give children fundamental concepts about print, its meaning function, and the spelling patterns inherent in the alphabetic system.

Fifth, writing stimulates thinking. Writers send messages, create ideas, manipulate their own knowledge. Learning about the English spelling system in the process of writing is also a cognitive activity. Young writers must constantly seek new information from a variety of sources. Thus, early writing is one of the best ways to stimulate children's naturally creative and curious minds and provide a forum for practicing spelling knowledge. Writing puts spelling to practical use.

PERSPECTIVE AND SUMMARY

Research demonstrates and anecdotal testimony from teachers and professional writers supports the conclusion that reading, writing, and spelling are closely linked. Rather than continuing to debate that issue, we should explore ways of helping teachers and children develop instructional strategies for making the connection. Fortunately, we are progressing toward this goal. There is greater emphasis on literature and the writing process; the Whole Language and Language Experience movements have empowered teachers and strengthened language arts instruction throughout the country.

Writing engages the individual in the task of producing meaning, while reading engages the reader in the process of sharing, interpreting, and reacting to the ideas and experiences of the writer. Reading and writing form the foundation of literacy, and spelling competence is essential to both. Given the right sort of instructional experiences, children not only manage the task of learning to spell, they can become adept at it.

The following major points have been made in this chapter:

- Reading, writing, and spelling are closely related; they influence each other in powerful ways.
- Writing influences reading. Three ways of strengthening the connection between reading and writing were discussed: (1) Writing makes children insiders in the world of print, helping them understanding the purpose and function of written language. (2) Writing has a positive influence on reading comprehension, particularly at the intermediate grade levels. (3) Writing helps children acquire skills related to reading and writing fluency, such as word recognition, spelling, and the conventions of written language.
- Reading influences writing. Research supports this conclusion, which is also supported, anecdotally, by professional writers. Several strategies for developing the reading–writing connection were discussed, including (1) getting started, (2) learning centers and classroom atmosphere, (3) revision and rereading, (4) literary gossip, and (5) reciprocal questioning.
- Reading and writing influence spelling. Reading provides much of the raw material needed to spell, including information about sounds, letters, words, and text. Writing provides the forum for practicing and the opportunity to explore the way in which written language system works.

REFERENCES

Atwell, N. (1984). Writing and reading literature from the inside out. *Language Arts, 61,* 240–252.

Atwell, N. (1987). *In the middle: Writing, reading, and learning with adolescents.* Portsmouth, NH: Boynton/Cook.

Ayres, L. (1993). *The efficacy of three training conditions on phonological awareness of kindergarten children and the longitudinal effect of each on later reading acquisition.* Unpublished doctoral dissertation, Oakland University, Rochester, MI.

Birnbaum, J. C. (1982). The reading and composing behavior of selected fourth and seventh grade students. *Research in the Teaching of English, 16,* 241–260.

Blachman, B. A. (1984). Language analysis skills and early reading acquisition. In G. Wallach & K. Butler (Eds.), *Language learning disabilities in school age children* (pp. 271–287). Baltimore: Williams & Wilkins.

Blackburn, E. (1985). Stories never end. In J. Hansen, T. Newkirk, & D. Graves (Eds.), *Breaking ground: Teachers related reading and writing in the elementary school* (pp. 3–13). Portsmouth, NH: Heinemann.

Bradley, L., & Bryant, P. E. (1983). Categorizing sounds and learning to read: A causal connection. *Nature, 30,* 419–421.

Calkins, L. (1986). *The art of teaching writing.* Portsmouth, NH: Heinemann.

Chomsky, C. (1971). Write first, read later. *Childhood Education, 47,* 269–299.

Chomsky, C. (1979). Approaching reading through invented spelling. In L. B. Resnick & P. Weaver (Eds.), *Theory and practice of early reading* (Vol. 2, pp. 43–65). Hillsdale, NJ: Erlbaum.

Clarke, L. K. (1989). Encouraging invented spelling in first graders' writing: Effects on learning to spell and read. *Research in the Teaching of English, 22*(3), 281–309.

Clay, M. M. (1975). *What did I write?* Portsmouth, NH: Heinemann.

Collins, C. (1985). The power of expressive writing in reading comprehension. *Language Arts, 62,* 48–54.

Cramer, B. B. (1985). *The effects of writing with invented spelling on general linguistic awareness and phonemic segmentation ability in kindergartners.* Unpublished doctoral dissertation, Oakland University, Rochester, MI.

Cramer, R. L. (1968). *An investigation of the spelling achievement of two groups of first-grade classes on phonologically regular and irregular words and in written composition.* Unpublished doctoral dissertation, University of Delaware, Newark.

Cramer, R. L. (1970). An investigation of first-grade spelling achievement. *Elementary English, 47*(2), 230–237.

Dale, E., O'Rourke, J., & Bamman, H. (1982). Pronunciation and spelling. In W. Barbe, F. Azalia, & L. Braun (Eds.), *Spelling* (pp. 162–194). Columbus, OH: Zaner-Bloser.

Davis, F. B. (1944). Fundamental factors of comprehension in reading. *Psychometrika, 9,* 185–197.

Dixon, C. N. (1978, December). *Inferences about a basis for comprehension: Beginning reader.* Paper presented at the National Reading Conference, St. Petersburg, FL.

Eckhoff, B. (1983). How reading affects children's writing. *Language Arts, 60,* 607–616.

Ehri, L., & Wilce, L. (1987). Cipher versus cue reading: An experiment in decoding acquisition. *Journal of Educational Psychology, 79,* 3–13.

Garcia, C. A. (1997). *The effect of two types of spelling instruction on first grade reading, writing, and spelling achievement.* Unpublished doctoral dissertation, Oakland University, Rochester, MI.

Gates, A. I. (1936). *Generalization and transfer in spelling.* New York: Teachers College, Columbia University.

Geva, E., & Tierney, R. J. (1984). *Text engineering: The influence of manipulated compare–contrast selections.* Paper presented at the annual meeting of the American Educational Research Association, New Orleans.

Henderson, E. H. (1989). *Teaching spelling,* Boston: Houghton Mifflin.

Henderson, E. H., & Templeton, S. (1986). A developmental perspective of formal spelling instruction through alphabet, pattern, and meaning. *Elementary School Journal, 86*(3), 305–316.

Juel, C., Griffith, P., & Gough, P. B. (1986). Acquisition of literacy: A longitudinal study of children in first and second grade. *Journal of Educational Psychology, 87,* 243–255.

Light, S. J. (1991). *Parents reading aloud to their third grade children and its influence on vocabulary, comprehension, and attitudes.* Unpublished doctoral dissertation, Oakland University, Rochester, MI.

Loban, W. (1976). *Language development: Kindergarten through grade twelve.* Urbana, IL: National Council of Teachers of English.

Mann, V. A., & Liberman, I. Y. (1984). Phonological awareness and verbal short-term memory: Can they presage early reading problems? *Journal of Learning Disabilities, 17,* 592–599.

Murray, D. M. (1990). *Shoptalk: Learning to write with writers.* Portsmouth, NH: Boynton/Cook.

Palmer, G., & Coon, G. (1985). Kids write right away. *Early Years, 14*(9), 61–63.

Petrosky, A. R. (1982). From story to essay: Reading and writing. *College Composition and Communication, 23,* 19–36.

Read, C. (1971). Pre-school children's knowledge of English phonology. *Harvard Educational Review, 41*(1), 1–34.

Shanahan, T. (1980). *A canonical correlational analysis of learning to read and learning to write: An exploratory analysis.* Unpublished doctoral dissertation, University of Delaware, Newark.

Shanahan, T. (1988). The reading–writing relationship: Seven instructional principles. *The Reading Teacher, 41,* 636–647.

Smith, F. (1983). Reading like a writer. *Language Arts, 60,* 558–567.

Squires, J. A. (1983). Composing and comprehending: Two sides of the same basic process. *Language Arts, 60,* 581–589.

Stanovich, K. E., Cunningham, A. E., & Cramer, B. B. (1984). Assessing phonological awareness in kindergarten children: Issues of task comparability. *Journal of Experimental Child Psychology, 38,* 175–190.

Stauffer, R. G., & Hammond, W. D. (1969). The effectiveness of a language arts and basic reader approach to first grade reading instruction extended into third grade. *The Reading Research Quarterly, 4,* 468–499.

Stauffer, R., & Hammond W. D. (1970). *The effectiveness of language arts and basic reader approaches to first grade reading instruction: Extended into third grade.* Unpublished manuscript, University of Delaware, Newark.

Stotsky, S. (1983). Research on reading/writing relationships: A synthesis and suggested directions. *Language Arts, 60,* 637–642.

Taylor, B. M., & Beach, R. W. (1984). The effects of text structure instruction on middle-grade students' comprehension and production of expository text. *Reading Research Quarterly, 19,* 134–146.

Taylor, B., & Berkowitz, S. (1980). Facilitating children's comprehension of content material. In M. Kamil & A. Moe (Eds.), *Perspectives on reading research and instruction.* Washington, DC: National Reading Conference.

Tierney R., & Leys, M. (1984). *What is the value of connecting reading and writing?* (Reading Education Report No. 55). Urbana-Champaign, IL: Center for the Study of Reading, University of Illinois.

Turbill, J. (1982). *No better way to teach writing. Australia:* Rozelle, NSW, Australia: Australian Primary English Teaching Association.

Wolfe, R. F. (1975). *An examination of the effects of teaching a reading vocabulary upon writing vocabulary in students compositions.* Unpublished doctoral dissertation, University of Maryland.

Chapter 5

•◆•

Systematic Spelling Instruction

> Fortunately, both my wife and my mother-in-law seem to
> love digging up mistakes in spelling, punctuation, etc. I
> can hear them in the next room laughing at me.
>
> —SHERWOOD ANDERSON

INTRODUCTION

Spelling should be systematically taught, not left to chance or incidental learning. Systematic spelling instruction means teaching a core spelling vocabulary and basic spelling concepts; it means integrating spelling with reading and writing; it means teaching spelling strategies and providing meaningful spelling activities; it means regularly scheduled instruction; it means reviewing spelling words and concepts within and across levels; it means assessing spelling achievement regularly. When these things are done well, and when spelling is integrated with writing and reading, competent spelling will result.

Systematic spelling instruction should begin in first or second grade and continue until mastery of a core spelling vocabulary and basic spelling concepts have been acquired. For many children, competent spelling can be achieved by the end of eighth grade, and some children will reach competence even earlier. Unfortunately, however, too many children exit eighth grade still lacking spelling competence. The typical high school curriculum does not include spelling, although the evidence suggests that for many children spelling instruction has ceased before a core spelling vocabulary and basic spelling concepts have been acquired. While this problem is beyond the scope of this book, much of what I have to say can be adapted to a high school spelling curriculum.

In recent years, there has been a tendency among educators to assume

that sufficient spelling growth is a natural outcome of effective engagement in reading and writing, but there is little evidence to support this
assumption that has shaped curricula across the country for the past
decade or so. While there is little hard data to make a thorough assessment
of the result, anecdotal evidence from teachers and parents strongly
suggests that spelling achievement has taken a nose dive. True, some
children learn to spell competently in the absence of systematic instruction, perhaps due, in part, to effective engagement in reading and writing,
or perhaps as a result of children's natural learning capacity. But far too
many children do not learn to spell competently because they receive little
or no systematic spelling instruction.

I most emphatically am not underestimating the importance of reading and writing in learning to spell. On the contrary, reading and writing
can make a substantial contribution to spelling achievement, as described
in the previous chapter. The language arts program should, therefore, be
rich and diverse, with a balance maintained between explicit spelling
instruction and reading and writing instruction.

THREE APPROACHES TO SPELLING INSTRUCTION

Choosing an approach to spelling instruction requires an understanding
of the strengths and weaknesses inherent in whichever one is chosen. The
choice should fit the needs of students and teachers, and be consistent
with the philosophical bent and programmatic goals of the school or
district. Finally, both teachers and administrators must understand the
principles and conventions necessary for effective spelling instruction.

There are various ways to organize spelling instruction. I have identified three approaches that can work in most school settings, as follows:

1. *Personalized spelling*: Spelling words are drawn from students' writing and reading experiences. Spelling activities are developed
   around each child's personally selected spelling words.
2. *Cooperative spelling*: Spelling words are drawn from student writing
   and reading experiences and are supplemented with teacher-selected words or words chosen at the school or district level. Spelling
   activities are developed around the personal and supplemental
   lists.
3. *Spelling textbooks*: Spelling words are drawn from research-based
   sources, and, in some instances, supplemented by student- or
   teacher-selected words. Spelling activities center around lessons
   and activities that are integrated with reading and writing.

The three approaches are not mutually exclusive. Features of any of these approaches can be blended together to create a spelling program most compatible with teachers' and students' needs. The following descriptions of each approach highlight their distinctive features, which are not necessarily exclusive to any one approach.

Personalized Spelling Approach

In the personalized spelling approach, instruction centers around writing and reading. Children select misspelled words from their writing and choose words that they want to learn to spell from their reading. Words are kept in a writing journal or on a separate form. Thus, in a class of 30 children, there will be 30 different spelling lists, although undoubtedly there will be substantial overlap due to the natural redundancy of oral and written language. One thousand of the most frequently used words in the English language will suffice to provide as much as 95% of the words ordinarily used in writing. While a spelling vocabulary of this size is a good beginning, it is by no means sufficient. A spelling vocabulary of 1,000 words would suffice for basic literacy, but would be insufficient for a well-educated individual. Adolescents or adults who misspell 5% of the words in a job application would not land a job in many business establishments. A well-educated individual should spell all of the words in a job application or résumé correctly.

The spelling activities in a personalized spelling approach assure that children learn the words they have chosen. The instructional methods associated with Personalized Spelling are similar in some instances to ones used in the other two approaches, although they are not necessarily implemented in exactly the same way. A strategy that works well in the personalized approach is to have children maintain spelling lists drawn from writing and from reading. Examples of how spelling lists may be created are shown in the following sections.

Words Drawn from Writing

As children progress through the stages of writing there are many opportunities to edit and proofread their own work. As they do so, have them underline words they are either certain they have misspelled or suspect they may have misspelled. These words are recorded in columns that look like the setup in Figure 5.1. If you are using spelling journals, the list may be kept there. If not, the lists may be kept on forms prepared for this purpose.

Words in the first column of Figure 5.1 come directly from the words children have underlined in their writing. The raw material for this column is derived from writing, particularly editing and proofreading experiences. Have children make their best guess at the correct spelling of each of these words in the second column of the list. Sometimes a misspelled word in first draft writing is one that the child can spell correctly, given an opportunity to reflect upon it. Even then there may be uncertainty about the correct spelling. Thus, words in this column may be correct or incorrect, but a "best guess" has been made. The third column becomes the child's personal spelling list. The teacher or a designated helper checks the second column and writes the words correctly if they are misspelled. The third column list can be cut off and used in spelling activities.

Words Drawn from Reading and Cross-Curricular Sources

A second set of words may be derived not directly from words misspelled in writing but from reading and cross-curricular activities associated with the daily classroom routine. This list may be kept in the same writing journal or on forms prepared for this purpose. The setup is shown in Figure 5.2.

Encourage children to look for words they want to learn from their reading and other school subjects and have them write the words in the first column. Suggest possible sources and give guidelines for word selection. Choosing a challenging word is fun and should be encouraged, but only within sensible limits. Discourage the selection of words notable only for length and semantic complexity, and encourage selecting words that are needed for writing. In this second column, children record the correct spelling of the word from the source in which it was found. Young children sometimes have difficulty copying words accurately. Still, it is useful for them to practice doing so. Before children study their list of words drawn from reading, check to make sure their words have been

How I spelled it	My best guess	Correct spelling

FIGURE 5.1. Words I chose from my writing.

Where I found it	How it is spelled	Teacher's check

FIGURE 5.2. Words drawn from reading and cross-curricular sources.

copied correctly and add any corrections to the third column. This is also an opportunity to negotiate the appropriateness of the words selected.

Cooperative Spelling Approach

Teachers and children work together to establish spelling lists in the cooperative spelling approach. Children select words misspelled in their writing or found in their reading, and the teacher supplements the student-selected words. The words shared by all students may be selected by the teacher, the school, or even the district. The idea behind cooperative word selection is to ensure that an essential core spelling vocabulary is not neglected, and also to give students the responsibility for learning words they have misspelled in their daily writing.

Supplemental spelling lists should be coordinated across grade levels, using appropriate selection criteria. The cooperative spelling approach works best in situations where management issues are dealt with effectively. For example, this approach requires cooperative efforts not only between students and teachers, but also among teachers within a given school or district.

Cooperative spelling operates on the premise that children's spelling needs can best be served by sharing the responsibility for choosing words.

Writing is a major resource for learning to spell. These students use their writing to find and record words they need to learn how to spell.

Several tasks face the teacher or school administrator in implementing this approach. Three ideas help make this approach work well:

1. An excellent reading and writing program is in place. Develop such programs, since personally selected words are an essential component of the spelling curriculum. Of course, the reading and writing programs are crucial to other approaches to spelling as well.

2. Procedures for selecting personal and supplemental spelling lists have been established. Prepare spelling lists to supplement the personally selected words. Developing lists is a major task. Criteria for word selection must be determined and will require consulting a substantial body of research on words. An especially important challenge is coordinating spelling lists across grade levels. If every teacher selects his or her own words without consulting teachers at other grade levels, there will be little coordination of spelling lists from one grade to the next. Failure to coordinate word selection across grade levels will result in a weakened spelling curriculum.

3. Activities and procedures for studying spelling words have been established. Develop instructional activities that will help children learn their words. Systematic review of spelling words and concepts must be included in the instructional program, and this review must extend across the school year and across grade levels.

Practical problems arise in the management of all approaches to spelling. For example, teachers face decisions regarding the number of words each student ought to tackle in a week's work. They also know that learning a given word or set of words may be difficult for some students and not for others. How should spelling words be practiced? There are many answers to this question, but in addition to the larger set of spelling-related activities, one basic study procedure should be taught. These two issues, discussed next, can be applied to all three approaches to spelling instruction.

Number of Words Assigned

How many words should each child work on over the course of 1 or 2 weeks? This decision is best made by the classroom teacher who knows how much work his or her children are able to handle. The teacher can begin by assigning lists of varying size to each child or group. Children who are progressing well in spelling can handle more words than children who are progressing slowly. The guidelines offered in Table 5.1 may be useful as a starting point, but should not be considered the final word. Adjustments may involve some trial and error. Determining the right

TABLE 5.1. Number of Spelling Words Assigned per Week			
Grade	Slower	Average	Rapid
1	4	8	12
2	6	12	18
3	8	16	22
4	10	20	25
5	10	20	25
6	10	20	25
7	12	20	30
8	12	20	30

number is aided by monitoring progress over the course of 5 or 6 weeks. Four ideas to guide decision making follow:

1. Have the child read his or her spelling list aloud. If the child cannot read it fluently, the list must be adjusted. Spelling and word recognition are closely related. A child is not likely to retain spelling words that he or she cannot fluently decode.

2. Spot check to see if the child knows the meanings of the spelling words. Unknown words can be learned by rote, but there is a high likelihood that they will soon be forgotten, since they are unlikely to be used in writing.

3. Monitor the level of spelling achievement. Children who are progressing satisfactorily should get 70–85% or higher on a spelling test at the end of a study period, usually a week. If a child consistently falls below this level of achievement over a 5- or 6-week period, reduce the number of words assigned.

4. Adjust the level of word complexity (see Chapter 1). A child may not be developmentally ready to handle complex spelling patterns until simpler patterns have been learned.

While there is no magic formula for making instructional decisions, the guidelines listed in Table 5.1 may help you make an initial best guess in determining the right number of spelling words for your children, but keep in mind that these are guidelines, not laws carved in stone. Trust your own best judgment as an experienced teacher if these guidelines seem not to fit a child or group in your classroom.

Studying Difficult Words

When a word is especially difficult, a procedure for learning that word is needed. The traditional practice of writing a word over and over does not

TABLE 5.2. Steps for Practicing Words	
Step 1:	Fold a piece of paper into three columns.
Step 2:	Study a correct copy of your word. Try to picture the word. Say the letters softly to yourself.
Step 3:	Write the word in the first column. Check it. If correct, go to Step 4. If not, start over.
Step 4:	Fold under the first column and write the word in the second column. Check it. If correct, go to Step 5. If not, start over.
Step 5:	Fold under the second column and write the word in the third column. Check it. If correct, stop for now. If not, start over.
Step 6:	Practice again another time.

work well because it has no method and it is boring. Errors often creep into repetitious copying. Still, a procedure that relies on a moderate amount of self-monitored repetition works well. It has method, it is brief, and it works when practiced properly.

Duplicate the procedures described in Table 5.2, give each child a copy, and post the procedures on a class chart. Take the time to teach children how to follow the procedures precisely.

Spelling Textbook Approach

Ever since Noah Webster published his *Blue Back Speller* in 1783, which sold 60 million copies by 1890, spelling textbooks have been used in American schools. They are still an appropriate option. The advantage of spelling textbooks is that they do the job reasonably well and free the teacher to spend her time on curricular matters that are, in the larger scheme of things, more important than spelling. While learning to spell is important and does indeed count, one could not reasonably argue that it is more important than learning to read with comprehension or learning to write well. After all, some of the world's best writers were dependent upon their editors to correct their spelling errors—Hemingway comes to mind.

Spelling textbooks usually cover Grades 1–8. They have ready made word lists and lessons keyed to list words. They are usually organized into 36 spelling lessons across a school year. Normally, 30 new lessons are introduced, along with 6 review lessons. Each lesson contains a basic spelling list, and may contain optional challenge words, content words, and personally chosen words.

Word lists are drawn from word frequency research, spelling error research, cross-curricular content words, and linguistically patterned words. Any given list word will be included because it meets two or more selection criteria: For example, it may be a high-frequency word, a frequently misspelled word, or a content word, or it may fit a linguistic pattern or a developmental spelling sequence. Some words fit two or three of these characteristics, some words fit all of them.

Modern spelling programs tend to have three features in common, which are found in a majority of spelling textbooks, although not in all of them:

1. *Student textbook*: Typically contains 30 weekly lesson and 6 review lessons. It may also contain cross-curricular spelling lessons, special features, handbooks, glossaries, dictionaries, spelling strategy lessons, and spelling study guides.

2. *Teacher's edition*: Contains plans for conducting weekly lessons, handbooks, enrichment suggestions, program philosophy, research information, testing materials, scope and sequence, and program word lists.

3. *Ancillary materials:* Additional materials coordinated with the basic spelling text. These materials include, but are not limited to, writing activities, bilingual materials, practice materials, testing materials, diagnostic and placement tests, and computer software.

Superficially, spelling textbooks may seem much alike, yet on close examination you will find significant differences. When choosing a spelling textbook, evaluation should be based on criteria relevant to the quality of the materials themselves as well as criteria specifically relevant to the children and teachers who will use the books. What are the special needs of the students? What are the needs of the teachers? Do the materials fit within the school's or district's language arts curriculum, instructional goals, and philosophical orientation? Following are guidelines for evaluating spelling textbooks.

Research-Based Spelling Lists

A good spelling program starts with an appropriate set of words. Not only must the right words be taught, but they must be organized and presented in a sequence appropriate to the stages of spelling growth (Beers & Henderson, 1977; Beers, 1980; Henderson, 1990; Bear, Invernizzi, Templeton, & Johnston, 1996). Spelling lists should be built on the following criteria: frequency of usage, linguistic pattern, developmental appropriateness, frequency of misspelling, special spelling difficulties, usefulness at specific grade levels, and usefulness in content subjects. The weekly spelling list is the most crucial, but other spelling lists should be available, including challenge words, content words, review lists and procedures, and room for personally chosen student words.

Student Edition: Lesson Structure and Content

Lesson content and structure are especially important. Criteria for evaluating lesson content and structure of spelling textbooks include the following:

> Pretest procedures are taught.
> Test–study–test format is used.
> Lesson content is well organized, readable, and user friendly.
> Spelling lists and activities are useful for a wide range of spelling abilities.
> Basic spelling lists conform to selection criteria: frequency, error patterns, developmental principles, and linguistic features.
> Challenge, content, and personal word options are available Words are grouped by key linguistic patterns.
> Spelling words are defined.
> Spelling, concepts and generalizations, and activities stress meaning, structure, and sound.
> Spelling strategies are taught.
> Vocabulary–spelling connection is stressed.
> Art meshes with content.
> Layout of lessons is visually appealing.
> Words and spelling concepts are reviewed within and across grades.
> Spelling-related dictionary skills are taught.
> Proofreading for spelling is taught.
> Reading–writing connection is made.
> Assessment is flexible and provides options.

Teacher's Edition

The teacher's edition should contain weekly lesson plans, options for implementing lesson plans, instructional ideas and activities, provision for special-needs children, assessment procedures, enrichment activities, placement and diagnostic tests, and professional articles and information. Above all it should be efficient and user friendly.

Ancillary Features

Ancillary features refer to materials or instructional aids that go beyond what is available in the student and teacher's editions. Ancillary materials may include extra practice materials, word cards, writing journals, testing materials, bilingual materials, electronic games, Internet access to spelling concepts, and so on. Computer software may be available for basic and enrichment activities. Ancillary materials provide options for teachers and students that can be useful, but they are rarely essential. In most cases, teachers can do without them.

SPELLING PRINCIPLES AND CONVENTIONS ESSENTIAL FOR STUDENTS

Expert spellers possess a large spelling vocabulary that they can produce fluently and without hesitation. They do not, however, come by this substantial body of spelling knowledge merely through rote memorization, although memory undoubtedly plays an important role in acquiring it. Expert spellers can often correctly spell words they have not previously studied because they have an implicit understanding of the rules that govern the English spelling system. How they come by this knowledge is not well known, but that it is there is indisputable. Three hypotheses have been advanced:

1. *Indirect acquisition*: Expert spelling knowledge comes about through an implicit knowledge of the rules and principles of English spelling. This knowledge is thought to be acquired by implicit means rather than direct instruction.

2. *Direct acquisition*: Expert spelling knowledge comes about through direct study and instruction. Spelling knowledge, in this theory, derives from systematic study of words and the rules and principles that govern English spelling.

3. *Indirect and direct acquisition*: Expert spelling knowledge comes about through a combination of direct study of words and spelling principles combined with implicit knowledge gained through reading and writing. In this formulation, reading provides background knowledge, writing provides the forum for applying word knowledge, and direct study is the catalyst.

Research does not tell us which theory is correct, but my experience with children in classrooms and clinics, my study of the issues involved, and years of discussion of these issues with teachers and parents, leads me to believe that the third theory—a combination of direct and indirect learning—is likely the most accurate. We must each decide for ourselves, having examined the evidence available and considered our experience with children. It is useful, therefore, to review the principles and conventions of the English spelling system and to consider ways we may help children incorporate them into their own body of spelling knowledge.

A spelling principle refers to a basic fact about the English spelling system. A convention is a commonly agreed-upon practice that comes about by custom and consent. Understanding the principles and conventions of spelling is fundamental to effective teaching of spelling. The English spelling system is far from perfect, yet it is not nearly the irrational, impossibly complex system of hoary myth. It has its principles and conventions that, if known and understood, improve spelling accuracy. Some spelling conventions are arbitrary; they may change over time as custom dictates. Although arbitrary, they exist and must be learned. The apostrophe is one such example. Spelling principles are inherent in the structure of the English language; they are stable and do not readily yield to change, although over centuries they may do so. The spelling–meaning connection is an example of a fundamental spelling principle. A working knowledge of spelling conventions and principles inevitably results in more accurate spelling.

How do spelling principles and conventions become part of a child's spelling knowledge base? There are three likely possibilities: (1) Children acquire them on their own as a by-product of reading and writing; (2) children acquire them through direct instruction; or (3) children acquire them through direct and indirect means, a combination of one and two. The third way seems most likely: direct instruction when and where needed, reading to increase the language knowledge base, and writing to provide the application.

Alphabetic Principle

The alphabetic nature of a language is identified by the extent to which each speech sound is represented by a specific letter. In a perfectly consistent alphabetic system, each letter would stand for only one and consistently the same sound. English letters and combinations of letters represent more than one sound, and one sound can be represented by more than one letter. English has 44 sounds but only 26 letters; consequently, a perfect match is not possible. Theoretically, a perfect match between letters and sounds should make a perfectly regular spelling system. Practically speaking, however, this doesn't occur in a language as dynamic and changing as American English.

Irregularities in letter–sound relationships contribute to spelling problems. For example, irregularity is higher among the 200 or 300 most common English words, which often follow Old English spelling patterns, accounting for their proportionately higher irregularity. Spelling reform movements have historically been based on the false assumption that the English spelling system is absurdly irregular. But when other spelling principles, which account for much of the regularity of English, are considered, it turns out that English is surprising consistent. Hanna and his colleagues (Hanna, Hanna, Hodges, & Rudorf, 1966) examined the consistency of American-English spelling and concluded that, when all relevant principles governing spelling are considered, it is 80–85% regular.

Position-within-Word Principle

Years ago, George Bernard Shaw (Tauber, 1963), an advocate of spelling reform, dreamed up a clever illustration that he thought demonstrated the utter inconsistency of English spelling. He claimed that the word *fish* could just as well be spelled *ghoti*. His argument went like this:

> /f/ sound in *fish* can be spelled *gh* as in *cough*.
> /i/ sound in *fish* can be spelled *o* as in *women*.
> /sh/ sound in *fish* can be spelled *ti* as in *nation*.

Shaw used this illustration to demonstrate that the spelling system of English was hopelessly irregular. At first glance, Shaw's logic may seem sound, but in reality his illustration merely demonstrates that he did not understand, or chose to ignore, the position-within-words principle. This principle constrains what is an allowable spelling in English. The position-within-words principle precludes spelling *fish* as *ghoti*. How a sound is spelled is constrained by the letters that surround it and by its position within a word. Let's look more closely at Shaw's *ghoti* example.

> English never spells the /f/ sound *gh* at the beginning of a word.
> English never spells /sh/ sound *ti* in the ending position of a word.
> English only once, in hundreds of thousands of words, spells /i/ with an *o*.

Two related principles constrain within-word spelling patterns. First, letters within words can influence the sound of another letter within a word. Long vowel sounds are often signaled by the presence of a silent letter. For instance, the long /a/ in *make* is signaled by the silent *e*. Many words display this same vowel–consonant–silent *e* pattern. Vowel digraphs often perform the same function. The second vowel in *boat* is silent and signals that the first vowel has a long sound.

Second, the position of a given sound within a word influences how that sound is spelled. The consonant digraph *gh* exemplifies this principle. While the consonant digraph *gh* can begin a word such as *ghost,* it never has the /f/ sound in the initial position. The consonant digraph *gh* does have an /f/ sound in a few words, but only in an ending or medial position, as in *rough* and *roughing.*

The English language, with its long history of evolution and its extensive borrowing from other languages, has its anomalies. It would be quite amazing if it did not. Even so, there is sense and structure in how it works. The English spelling system is by no means perfect, but it has a logic and structure that is quite remarkable.

Spelling–Meaning Principle

Spelling and meaning are joined at the hip, but many children are unaware of this facet of the English spelling system. Teach children how the spelling–meaning connection works. Once they understand, they will know how to spell words they have previously only guessed at. The spelling–meaning connection can be taught early, but it becomes increasingly useful in the latter stages of spelling growth because it applies most frequently to more complex word structures. With each succeeding grade level, the words used to illustrate the spelling–meaning connection should fit the spelling achievement level of the students.

The spelling-meaning connection is not complex: It consists of the fact that words that are related in meaning are often closely related in the way they are spelled. Thus, if you know the meaning and spelling of *heal* you have a good shot at spelling *health*. Notice that the sound of *heal* by itself and the sound of *heal* in *health* are quite different. *Heal* has a long /e/ sound; *heal* in *health* has a short /e/ sound. So why are they spelled the same? Because spelling them the same way preserves the spelling–meaning connection between the two words. If this were not so, the English spelling system would be more arbitrary and more complex.

While we're on the topic of spelling and meaning, it should be noted that the reason homophones have different spellings is to visually highlight the fact that they are not related in meaning, even though they sound alike. *Two is spelled differently than too,* and their visual distinctness signals their distinct meanings. It is easy to understand why homophones cause problems for spellers. Their spelling is often straightforward, but choosing the homophone that conveys the correct meaning is difficult. *There* and *their* cause problems not because of difficult spelling but because the distinction in their meanings is difficult to grasp. Sometimes a little humor helps. The poem "Homophones," written by my colleague George Coon (1976), puts the problem of homophones in an interesting context.

·•·

Homophones

Wood you believe that I didn't no
About homophones until too daze ago?
That day in hour class in groups of for,
We had to come up with won or more.

Mary new six; enough to pass
But my ate homophones lead the class.
Then a thought ran threw my head.
"Urn a living from homophones," it said.

I guess I just sat and staired into space.
My hole life seamed to fall into place.
Our school's principle happened to come buy,
And asked about the look in my I.

"Sir," said I as bowled as could bee,
"My future rode I clearly sea."
"Sun," said he, "move write ahead.
Set sale on your coarse. Don't be misled."

I herd that gnus with grate delight.
I will study homophones both day and knight.
For weaks and months, through thick oar thin.
I'll pursue my goal. Eye no aisle win.

                             —George E. Coon*

Table 5.3 shows examples of words that have a spelling–meaning connection. There are thousands of such words in the language, yet many children as well as adults seldom think of this relationship as a spelling clue. Teach children to recognize the spelling–meaning connection by using such examples. The chart is set up in terms of two categories: (1) the target word, the word you don't know how to spell, and (2) a meaning helper, a meaning-related word whose spelling is simpler and may be known; knowing the helping word increases the chances of correctly spelling the target word.

Apostrophe Conventions

The apostrophe (') has three uses in spelling English words. First, it is used to show the omission of one or more letters in contractions, as in *don't* for *do not* and *won't* for *will not.* Second, it is used to show possessive forms of nouns or indefinite pronouns, as in *Joan's house, students' desks,* and

---

*From Coon (1976, p. 652). Copyright 1976 by International Reading Association. Reprinted by permission.

TABLE 5.3. Spelling–Meaning Connection

Meaning helper	Target word
Word you can spell	Word you want to spell
major	majority
ever	every
family	familiar
author	authority
secret	secretary
inspire	inspiration
human	humane
nation	national
act	action

everybody's ideas. Third, it is used to form plurals of letters and numbers, as in three *b*'s in *bubbles,* and two *9*'s in *991.*

Spelling errors due to a misplaced or omitted apostrophe are common. When contractions are misspelled, it is often due to a misplaced or omitted apostrophe. At early or immature levels, a comma may be used instead of the apostrophe. This is a hopeful sign, indicating progress toward the convention. The error suggests that the child knows something about the convention, but does not yet know what punctuation mark is appropriate.

The following words rank among the most frequently misspelled contractions in Grades 1–8: *didn't, don't, we're, there's, you're, they're, let's, it's* (Cramer & Cipielewski, 1995). The use of apostrophes in possessive nouns is also a significant spelling problem. The rules for using apostrophes may seem simple, but they are troublesome for many students. The following rules need to be taught and retaught until they are understood:

1. *Contractions:* Apostrophes replace omitted letters: *let's* = *let us.*
2. *Possessive Nouns:* Apostrophes show ownership.
   a. Add *'s* to singular nouns: The head *coach's* new rule.
   b. Add *s'* to plural nouns that end in *s:* The *coaches'* busy schedules.
   c. Add *'s* to plural nouns that do not end in *s:* The *men's* store.

One-Word or Two-Word Conventions

When was the last time you had to ask yourself, "Is *tonight* one word or two?" "Is *away* one word or two?" "Is *awhile* one word or two?" Immature spellers ask this type of question all the time, and often they come up the

TABLE 5.4. Common Confusions about Using One Word or Two	
Word	Correct and incorrect usage
a way	he ran a way from home
away	he ran away from home
a little	had a little fun
alittle	had alittle fun
a lot	ate a lot of food
alot	alot of food
awhile	wait awhile and I'll go too
a while	wait a while and I'll go too
all ways	considered all ways of doing it
allways	considered allways of doing it
again	it's that time again
a gain	it's that time a gain
around	hang around with me
a round	hang a round with me
tonight	we'll work tonight
to night	we'll work to night
together	we'll go together
to gether	we'll go to gether
tomorrow	tomorrow is another day
to morrow	to morrow is another day
forever	you can't live forever
for ever	you can't live for ever
forget	don't forget me
for get	don't for get me
because	because it is true
be cause	be cause it is true
became	she became my best friend
be came	she be came my best friend
below	he lives one floor below me
be low	he lives one floor be low me
going to	she's going to try harder
gonna	she's gonna try harder

wrong answer. Many of the "one-word or two words" confusion problems show up in words that begin with the letter *a*—confusion related to the article *a* versus the letter *a*, most likely. Other confusions are induced by two- or three-letter words such as *to* and *be*, which are words in themselves and are also the first two letters in longer words: *because, become, tonight, tomorrow*. Table 5.4 list words that are most commonly confused (Cramer & Cipielewski, 1995). Many of these confusions are related to meaning and usage and are not confusions about the letters or order of the letters, although they are spelling errors, nonetheless.

Compound Word Conventions

A compound word consists of a combination of two or more words that function as a single unit of meaning. Compound words are written three ways: (1) as a single word or closed compound: *thunderstorm, basketball*; (2) as separate words, or open compounds: *ice cream, no one*; and (3) as hyphenated words: *seventy-five, well-known*. Notice that the three ways of writing compounds have an arbitrary quality. For instance, the term *vice-president* was hyphenated until recently, when some newspapers and magazines began writing the term *vice president* without the hyphen. If this practice prevails, we may, by gradual consensus, change the spelling convention for this frequently used word. Such changes are not uncommon, although they may take time to evolve.

When compounds are misspelled, they exhibit the full range of errors that other words exhibit: misspelled vowels and consonants; omitted, reversed, or added letters; and so on. However, compound words have an additional source of error that most words don't have: spacing errors. Words like *no one* may be joined as one word; closed compounds like *football* are written open, as *foot ball*. Another feature of compound words is that they do not usually change their spelling when joined to form a new meaning unit. This makes spelling compounds fairly simple once the issue of spacing is solved.

Capitalization and Abbreviation Conventions

It is a convention of spelling that a proper noun, naming a particular person, place, or thing, starts with a capital letter. Thus, holidays, days, months, states, cities, and so on are proper nouns and should be capitalized. Of course, there are additional capitalization conventions, but failure to capitalize proper nouns ranks among the most common capitalization problems (Cramer & Cipielewski, 1995.)

Abbreviations, like capitals, are also a convention of spelling. A period follows an abbreviated word, and is considered part of the spelling of that word, as in *Mr., Dr.,* or *Sept.* (*Mister, Doctor, September*). It may be that children may not always regard capitals and abbreviations as part of the spelling of a word, but it should be pointed out to them that they are an integral part of the correct spelling of a word.

CHOOSING SPELLING WORDS

American English is an amazing language. It is impossible to know precisely how many words are contained in our language, but estimates range as high as one million. Fortunately, there is no need to learn to spell anywhere near that many words. Learning to spell the 1,000 most common words in the English language will provide a vocabulary sufficient for correctly spelling about 95% of the words one would ordinarily use in writing. After that, however, making progress toward 100% becomes increasingly difficult. For example, to get to 96% would require the addition of several thousand words, getting to 97% even more thousands of words, and so on.

The goal of an effective spelling curriculum is to teach 8,000–10,000 words and a set of basic spelling concepts and strategies. Once these are in place, thousands upon thousands of derived and analogous words *not* directly taught can now be spelled correctly. The additional thousands of words that will inevitably be needed can be dealt with at the point of need. For instance, suppose a child wishes to use words such as *plinth* or *usury* in his or her writing. There is no point in teaching these words in the spelling curriculum because their usefulness is specialized and they will rarely be needed for writing, although they might be appropriately taught in art or economics, respectively. Furthermore, there are hundreds of thousands of words just like them, and there is no way to predict which of these relatively rare words ought to be learned in the Grades 1–8 spelling curriculum. Inevitably, however, situations arise where an unusual word is needed and its spelling is unknown. Children will have an enormous advantage if they have acquired a basic spelling vocabulary, spelling consciousness, skill in locating the correct spellings of words, and strategies for incorporating new words into their set of known words. Systematic spelling instruction seeks to endow children with a well-chosen core of known spelling words, basic spelling concepts and strategies, and spelling consciousness. When these items are in place, children will possess the tools needed to independently seek out the correct spelling of words they do not know and, when appropriate, to add these words to their core of known spelling words.

The first step in constructing a systematic spelling curriculum is to select a core of spelling words that children should learn over the course of Grades 1–8. Selecting these words requires criteria. But what criteria will enable teachers and curriculum committees to select a core spelling vocabulary that will provide a foundation upon which other words can be learned? What criteria will produce spelling lists from which basic spelling concepts can be illustrated and practiced? While the task is complex, it is manageable. Six criteria should be considered when constructing spelling lists: (1) high-frequency words, (2) frequently misspelled words, (3) linguistically patterned words, (4) content-related words, (5) developmentally appropriate words, and (6) personally chosen words.

·•·

High-Frequency Words

Word counts, particularly the frequency with which words are used in writing, are an important resource in selecting a core spelling vocabulary. Frequency lists are constructed for different purposes, drawn from different sources, and conducted across decades of educational history. No single list will suffice. Word frequency lists are most useful when they are checked against one another and when words are drawn from them with careful consideration. Fortunately, there are many excellent sources of word frequency counts, a sampling of which follow.

Carroll, J., Davies, P., & Richman, B. (1971). *The American Heritage word frequency book*. Boston: Houghton Mifflin.—Contains 86,741 different words sampled from textbooks, novels, encyclopedias, magazines, and other Grade 3–9 sources.

Dale, Edgar, & O'Rourke, Joseph. (1981). *The living word vocabulary* (rev. ed.). Chicago: World Book.—Contains 44,000 words taken from the Gates, Thorndike, and Dolch word lists. Words were tested with students in Grades 4, 6, 8, 10, 12, and 13 to determine familiarly with meanings. Each word is assigned a grade level based on a criterion of approximately two-thirds of children in a grade knowing a word's meaning.

Dolch, Edward. (1936). A basic sight vocabulary. *Elementary School Journal.*—Contains 220 high-frequency words.

Dolch, Edward. (1942). "The 2,000 commonest words for spelling." In *Better spelling*. Champaign, IL: Garrard Press.

Fitzgerald, James. (1951). *A basic life spelling vocabulary,* Milwaukee: Bruce Publishing.—Contains 2,650 words selected from lists developed by Horn, Rinsland, McKee-Fitzgerald, and Dolch. List purports to make up about 95% of the writing vocabulary of children and adults.

Fitzgerald, James. (1951). "350 most useful spelling words" and "450 very useful spelling words." In *Teaching spelling*. Milwaukee: Bruce Publishing.—The 350 words are considered most essential and the 450 second-most essential words for spelling.

Harris, Albert, & Jacobson, Milton. (1982). *Basic reading vocabularies*. New York: Macmillan.—Contains 10,000 high-frequency words from running text in eight basal reading series.

Rinsland, Henry. (1995). *A basic vocabulary of elementary school children*. New York: Macmillan.—Contains 14,571 words from running text drawn from 100,000 samples of children's writing and the oral vocabularies of first-grade children.

Thorndike, Edward, & Lorge, Irving. (1944). *The teacher's word book of 30,000 words*. New York: Columbia University.—Contains 30,000 words arranged alphabetically. Frequency of occurrence for the word in general is given, as well as its frequency in four different sets of reading matter.

High-frequency words are extremely important in any spelling curriculum. The major issue that arises is when to teach any given word. Since there are several thousand words that young writers need to know, this is not an easy decision to make. Perhaps the best decision is to make sure that the 1,000 most frequent words are taught early. While it is challenging, it is possible to take into account criteria such as linguistic pattern, frequency of misspelling, and developmental appropriateness, and still teach the most frequent words early in the spelling curriculum.

Frequently Misspelled Words

From a practical perspective, it is clear that children should learn to spell words that are most commonly used in spoken and written language. Up to a certain point, frequency in oral and written language gives important direction in selecting spelling words. But frequency alone cannot give guidance on all matters that are relevant to learning to spell; this is where spelling error analysis research comes in handy. Some words are difficult to learn and remain troublesome spelling words across many grade levels (Cramer & Cipielewski, 1995; Farr, 1989). Teachers know that words such as *because, a lot, you're, probably, believe, friends, their, there, too,* and many more are frequently misspelled at every grade level. Therefore, in constructing spelling lists, consideration must be given to features of words that are especially troublesome, because this information has important implications for when to first teach a word and how often to reteach it. The notion that a word or spelling concept should be taught only once or twice over the course of Grades 1–8 is unwise. It ignores a body of research that clearly demonstrates that certain words and spelling concepts are unlikely to be learned permanently in one or two exposures. The following studies that focus on spelling errors are useful in establishing well-balanced spelling lists.

Cramer, Ronald; Beers, James; Hammond, Dorsey; & Cipielewski, James. (1995). *The Scott, Foresman research in action project: A study of spelling errors in 18,599 written compositions of children in grades 1–8.* Unpublished study.—Screens 1,584,758 words to determine most frequently misspelled words across and within grade levels 1–8 and categorizes 55 different types of spelling error patterns across eight grade levels.

Farr, Roger. (1989). *An analysis of the spelling patterns of children in grades two through eight.* Center for Reading and Language Studies. Unpublished study, Indiana State University, Bloomington.—Identifies words children often misspell and reports patterns of spelling errors.

Gates, Arthur. (1937). *A list of spelling difficulties in 3876 words showing the "hard spots," common misspellings, average spelling grade placement, and comprehension grade ratings of each word.* New York: Teachers College, Columbia University.— Early study of spelling difficulties that locates the features within words that are most likely to generate spelling errors.

Greene, Harry. (1955). *The new Iowa Spelling Scale.* Iowa City: State University of Iowa.—Contains 5,507 high-utility words used by adults and children in written communication. Words were selected from earlier lists developed by Horn and by Thorndike and Lorge. Percentage of spelling accuracy for each word at each grade level was determined through testing of a large, nationwide sample of children.

Linguistically Patterned Words

Spelling lists should, in most instances, be organized by linguistic patterns and features such as meaning, sound, structure, etymology, and error patterns. Linguistic patterns and features are crucial because research has shown that they influence success or failure in learning to spell (Gates, 1937; Farr, 1989; Cramer & Cipielewski, 1995) and provide insight into how words are spelled (for example, the link between spelling and meaning discussed in the previous chapter). A spelling curriculum that ignores the linguistic features of words in organizing spelling lists and spelling instruction does so at a high cost in efficiency and effectiveness. Of course, other criteria may be taken into consideration as well.

Certain features of English spelling are more complex than others. Vowels are more variable than consonants and present more problems for the beginning speller than do consonant spellings. Homophones, word structure features, and usage features play varying roles in generating spelling errors. Table 5.5 shows the percentage of spelling errors that can be attributed to specific linguistic features across grade levels (Cramer & Cipielewski, 1995).

Information of the sort indicated in Table 5.5 can help teachers and administrators formulate plans for developing or evaluating spelling lists. While generally these data show that students' spelling achievement improves over time, certain features remain troublesome spelling problems across grade levels. Partly this is due to the inherent difficulty of certain spelling concepts, homophones, double letters, and word endings, for example. The proportional increase in certain error categories may also reflect children's increasingly sophisticated oral language and writing fluency, which may not have commensurate orthographic knowledge to support it.

Content-Related Words

Content words are associated with specific subjects: mathematics, health, science, social studies, reading, English, writing, and so on. Every day children encounter content words, and they have to deal with these words

TABLE 5.5. Proportion of Major Error Types by Grade Level

Error type	Grade level							
	1	2	3	4	5	6	7	8
Vowel	.488	.438	.402	.361	.434	.307	.318	.290
Consonant	.177	.183	.185	.168	.165	.149	.156	.148
Structure	.041	.044	.043	.051	.049	.056	.056	.056
Inflected	.051	.053	.057	.058	.060	.056	.053	.054
Compound	.034	.056	.060	.081	.083	.110	.096	.110
Usage	.058	.091	.104	.122	.140	.165	.176	.188
Twilight zone	.151	.136	.148	.159	.161	.158	.146	.154

as listeners, speakers, readers, and writers. Every content subject has a key vocabulary, and this vocabulary changes as children progress up the grades. There is, therefore, good reason for including high-utility content words in the spelling curriculum. Content words can be incorporated into the weekly spelling list; they can be dealt with separately; or they can be dealt with both ways. When incorporated into weekly spelling lessons, content words can be selected to fit a linguistic pattern since content words have the same range of linguistic features as do other words. The problem is timing. Will the content word fit into a linguistically patterned list at a time when you need to teach it? Perhaps not. Therefore, an alternative is to teach some content words in separate lessons without regard to linguistic patterns. Teachers can, in this case, prepare specific lists of content words covering curricular subjects. Such lists should deal with meaning as well as spelling.

Unlike word frequency research and spelling error research, there are few studies available to guide the selection of content words. Still, there are ways in which content word lists can be established and sources that can provide guidance in the selection of content words. Three suggestions follow.

1. *General curricular texts and materials*: Many content-oriented textbooks include lists of key words in the teacher's or student edition. Content words can be selected from these lists. If no list is available, then it will be necessary to peruse the materials and select key words that fit the needs of the children who will be using the lists.

2. *Spelling textbooks*: Spelling textbooks sometimes provide separate cross-curricular spelling lists and lessons. These word lists and lessons are usually based on careful research covering the content subjects and key vocabulary children encounter in widely used textbooks and other content-oriented instructional materials. When spelling textbooks provide separate content list and lessons, teachers can use them when and as needed.

3. *Frequency lists*: Frequency lists, of course, include content words in whatever place they fall in a frequency count. Thus, content words can be identified in these lists in the same manner as other words are identified—on the basis of frequency. Some frequency lists will tell you the grade level at which a given word is most widely used in written or oral language.

Developmentally Appropriate Words

Spelling growth occurs in stages across a span of years. It is obvious, for example, that young children should not encounter spelling words that are unlikely to be in their oral language vocabulary. The word *egregious* is not likely, therefore, to appear on a spelling list for children because few, if any, will know its meaning and they would not use it in their writing. It is perhaps less obvious that children need to encounter words that are appropriate to their growth in spelling knowledge. There is a sequence of spelling growth that children pass through, and that sequence is related to orthographical principles inherent in written English. Researchers, principally under the leadership of Edmund Henderson, have identified five stages of spelling development: prephonetic, phonetic, patterns within words, syllable juncture, and meaning derivation, described in Chapter 1. Each stage implicitly suggests the need for the introduction of certain orthographic patterns and principles and the avoidance of others. The development of word lists, therefore, is constrained by the boundaries of knowledge children have acquired as they proceed through the stages of spelling growth. Issues relevant to spelling stages and their implications for the development of word lists are discussed in Chapter 1 of this book.

Personally Chosen Words

Personal words are words chosen by individual students to supplement an already established spelling list, or they may constitute the entire spelling list, as they do, for example, in the personalized spelling approach. Personal words are drawn from words misspelled in writing and selected from reading material. It is important to monitor children's word choices. The following criteria should be met when children choose their own words:

- The words should be ones misspelled or inconsistently spelled in writing.
- They should be in a child's meaning vocabulary.
- They should be in the child's word recognition vocabulary.

When left without guidance, children may select words because they are exotic rather than functional. An occasional exotic word is fun and can be an acceptable choice, but if left unmonitored, such choices can get out of hand. The challenge is to create the best possible spelling lists. It is a formidable challenge.

SYSTEMATIC REVIEW OF WORDS AND SPELLING CONCEPTS

The "Look, Jane, look. Look, look, look" basal readers of not-so-fond memory started out with an important learning principle—repetition—but excessive repetition diminished the quality of the narrative and sacrificed meaning to word learning. However, let's not throw Dick and Jane out with the bath water. Repetition remains an important learning principle, but it matters what kind of repetition. In spelling, the moral equivalent of old fashioned basal repetition is, "Write your spelling words 10 times." It's repetitious all right, but its quality stinks. It doesn't work, and it is highly inefficient. Nevertheless, planned, properly spaced repetition is essential. Systematic review provides the necessary repetition. Three types of review are needed: (1) Review within grade levels, (2) review across grade levels, and (3) review spelling principles, conventions, and strategies.

Review within Grade Levels

Spelling words must be recycled within grade levels. Choose a period of time, say, 3 to 5 weeks, and spend a week reviewing words previously taught. Continue this pattern throughout the year. Three review procedures are especially useful for within-grade review.

1. Review words on a regular basis, normally every 3–5 weeks. Administer a pretest of the review words. Follow pretest procedures recommended later in this book. After students have checked their pretest, have them study the words they have missed. Suggest follow-up activities and use the word study procedure outlined earlier in this chapter.

2. Monitor daily writing, looking for misspellings of recently studied words. Make a list of these words and put them on a wall chart. Have children refer to this chart when proofreading their final drafts. It is inevitable that in daily writing children will misspell a few words they have recently studied. It would be quite surprising if this were not the case. This is not necessarily a sign that your spelling program is failing, but it tells you that review is necessary.

3. Make a top 10 list of your children's most frequently misspelled words. Do this once every 5 weeks. Put these words on a wanted poster: "Ten Bad Words Wanted for Robbing Writing." Have your children suggest ways to capture these misbehaving words. If you give these words special attention, you will find that children will accept the challenge of learning to spell them.

Review across Grade Levels

Research has shown that the most frequently misspelled words at early grade levels continue to plague students at later grade levels: *too, a lot, there, their, can't,* and *probably,* come to mind (Cramer & Cipielewski, 1995). Often the most troublesome words are among the most common words in the language. They do not "look" difficult to the mature speller, but they are a challenge to the immature speller. For example, research on the 100 most frequently misspelled words at the eighth-grade level (see Appendix H) shows that about half of the words have six letters or fewer. These words are difficult not because of length or orthographic complexity, but for reasons having to do with usage, reversible letters, and uncertainty about how to apply certain spelling conventions. Regardless of the reason, review across grade levels is needed. If frequently misspelled words are taught only once, say at grade 3, there will be a significant number of students who will not learn these troublesome words at that time. Words that are known to be difficult for a subpopulation of students ought to appear and reappear on spelling lists to assure that all students have learned them, not just the more capable spellers.

Review of Spelling Principles, Conventions, and Strategies

There are spelling principles, conventions, and strategies that all children need to know, but that cannot be learned in one or two instructional episodes. A spelling concept, such as the conventions for using apostrophes or the manner in which compounds are spaced, dictates how a word appears in print. Failure to understand and apply spelling concepts of this sort is a major source of spelling errors (Cramer & Cipielewski, 1995). Spelling principles and conventions must be taught and retaught within and across grade levels.

Spelling strategies must also be reviewed. Unlike principles and conventions, a spelling strategy is a plan for learning. A strategy can be applied to a single word or to a class of words; strategies are tools for tackling spelling problems. Even good spellers are not likely to learn strategies in a few exposures. Poor spellers especially need patience and time to develop their repertoire of spelling strategies. Strategies must be applied at different levels, within different contexts, using different example words. When students have many ways of approaching spelling challenges, the chances are increased that they will succeed.

TIME ON TASK

Time on task is an important variable in learning. Spelling is no exception to this general rule of learning. A classroom teacher has the challenging task of prioritizing the time available. Like any busy executive, he or she must decide what's most important, how to distribute his or her time, and how to use time efficiently. Spelling is important, and therefore deserves some teaching time. Clearly, however, there are other tasks that are more important—reading, writing, and arithmetic, for instance. Where does spelling fit into this jigsaw puzzle of allotting instructional time?

How much time should you to devote to formal spelling instruction? Ninety minutes a week is typically needed. It could be slightly more or less, depending on the spelling approach you have decided to use and the activities you have incorporated into your spelling program.

How often should you schedule formal spelling instruction? Three to five times a week will likely be necessary, but again this will depend on the instructional approach and the activities you choose to pursue. I have used the term "formal" spelling instruction to denote time devoted exclusively to spelling as distinct from incidental time in which students are working on their writing, for instance, and may spend time proofreading it for spelling errors. Spelling instruction is less likely to succeed if the time devoted to its pursuit arises solely out of incidental opportunities. Table 5.6 presents three plans for devoting time to formal spelling instruction. These plans can be modified to fit your own schedule of time devoted to spelling.

TABLE 5.6. Time Allotted for Spelling Instruction				
	Day 1	Day 2	Day 3	Day 4	Day 5
5-day plan	20	15	20	15	20
4-day plan	25	0	25	20	20
3-day plan	35	0	35	0	20

SPELLING STRATEGIES

All children, whether good or poor spellers, need strategies to learn unknown words. Words that are already in one's spelling vocabulary are spelled fluently by memory. Getting new words into the long-term memory bank is the purpose of a spelling strategy. Research indicates that good spellers have a broader repertoire of spelling strategies than poor spellers, and good spellers are more likely to use the more efficient and effective strategies. Good spellers, for example, are more likely to cite visualization or meaning as a spelling strategy than poor spellers.

In the earliest stages of spelling, children tend to rely on sound, and in the beginning sound cues are the major strategy used to spell unknown words. This strategy has limitations, but it does enable children to write at a time when they have a modest set of known spelling words (Cramer, 1968; Read, 1970, 1971; Beers & Henderson, 1977). As children move through the stages of spelling growth, they acquire additional, and more sophisticated, spelling strategies. For instance, by the time children have moved into the latter stages of spelling growth they have added meaning, analogy, and word structure to their strategy pool. Unfortunately, it is the good spellers who are most likely to add spelling strategies to their spelling knowledge base; poor spellers remain stuck with a small strategy pool.

While we do not know for certain, it appears that some good spellers learn many strategies on their own, since there is little evidence that spelling strategies are widely taught. Poor spellers are less likely to learn strategies on their own, yet they are the ones who are most in need of effective spelling strategies. It behooves teachers, therefore, to teach spelling strategies to all of their children, especially those students whose spelling knowledge is weakest. The following six strategies are ones that students need to know.

Pronunciation Strategy

Analysis of spelling errors suggests that there is a category of words that are misspelled because they are mispronounced or not fully articulated (Cramer & Cipielewski, 1995). For example, failure to pronounce the *r* in *February* is not so much a mispronunciation as it is an alternative pronunciation. The /r/ sound is not fully articulated in the alternative pronunciation. Consequently, when *February* is misspelled, the *r* is often omitted. Many words fall into this category. In addition, doubled letters in words such as *mirror* and *middle* are, by convention, pronounced only once. Omitting one of the pair of doubled letters in words is a major cause of

TABLE 5.7. Applying Pronunciation Strategy

Target spot	Fully articulated
lit*tl*e	lit-tle
Feb*ru*ary	Feb-ru-ary
fav*o*rite	fav-o-rite
pic*tu*re	pic-ture
diff*er*ent	diff-er-ent
chas*ing*	chas-ing

spelling errors (Cramer & Cipielewski, 1995). When children are taught to attend to pronunciation they have a better shot at correct spelling.

Here is an example of how to handle a word where pronunciation or enunciation may interfere with correct spelling. Assume that the word *interesting* is not yet in your children's spelling vocabulary. Say the word in the way it would normally be pronounced: *in-trest-ing*. Then say the word in a slightly exaggerated way, clearly articulating each part: *in-ter-est-ing*. The fully articulated pronunciation helps reveal the correct spelling of the second syllable—the place where a pronunciation-induced error frequently occurs. Clear articulation of the unarticulated or underarticulated troublesome part of a word will often help children correctly spell words to which this strategy applies. Table 5.7 presents some examples of words to which this strategy applies.

Visualization Strategy

Visualizing is the creation of a mental picture. This strategy is used in many learning situations and can be applied to spelling as well. Visualization in spelling has two dimensions reported by research subjects: (1) visualizing the target word or a related word in its written form, and (2)

Spelling knowledge is acquired in a variety of ways. These students exchange ideas and information about their writing, including suggestions for improving spelling.

visualizing a setting in which images are pictured to help spell the target word.

Visualizing Written Forms of Words

When children are asked how they spelled a word, they sometimes report visualizing a written form of the target word or a related known word. For example, they might report that they had seen the word *eagle* on a poster and are visualizing what it looked like in its written form, or they might report that they visualized the word *day,* which they knew, giving them an idea of how to spell *hay,* which they didn't know. Visualizing may come naturally to some children; others need to be coached on how to visualize for spelling.

Visualizing a Setting

Visualizing may involve creating a mental picture in which images of people, animals, objects, and actions play a role in remembering or imagining the spelling of a word. For example, a child might report visualizing a *knight* in shining armor with a big *k* on his chest as a way of remembering or recalling how to spell the word *knight.* This sort of visualizing is an extension of a mnemonic device into the visualization realm.

Radebaugh (1985) reported that good spellers used visualization far more often than poor spellers. In fact, poor spellers did not report using visualization at all in this study. Their overwhelming strategy was "sounding out" words—a useful but limited strategy. All children need a broad repertoire of spelling strategies, and poor spellers especially need a broad range of strategies. Below are ideas for teaching visualization as a spelling strategy.

1. *Ask questions.*

   What part of the word gives you trouble?
   What part is hardest for you to remember?
   Can you picture the troubling part?
   What pictures can help you remember?
   Have you seen your word in print before?
   How did the word look in print? When? Where?

2. *Make suggestions.*

   Imagine or picture the word in your mind's eye.
   Your picture can be silly, which might even be easier to remember.

Your idea doesn't have to make sense, it just has to help.
Your picture may apply to the whole word or part of the word.
Think of your picture when you write the word.
Your mental picture should help you remember or recall the word.

3. *Give examples.*

Picture a *mosquito* who has *quit* biting.
Picture a *diamond* who shouts "*i am*" bright.
Picture an explosion and a telephone ringing to recall *boom e rang*.
Picture a *page* being carried by an *ant*: *pageant*.

Mnemonic Strategy

For most of us, certain words are demonic; for such words a mnemonic may aid recall. A mnemonic is a memory strategy designed to help recall an especially troublesome word or word part. For most of my lifetime, I couldn't remember whether the *e* in *weird* came before *i* or whether *i* came before *e*. Then I came up with a mnemonic. Here it is (don't laugh): *we bird*. I drop the *b* in *bird* and put the two pieces together: *we* and *ird*—weird. I haven't misspelled that word since I invented the mnemonic. I can't misspell it because the mnemonic won't go away. But that's what makes it effective.

Mnemonics are useful for a few special words that are tricky for a particular person. It is not a broadly useful strategy, such as meaning and visualization. But the more arrows in the quiver, the more likely one is to hit the target. Encourage children to develop their own mnemonic for a particular word they find difficult. Table 5.8 lists a few sample mnemonics.

Divide-and-Conquer Strategy

Long words present more opportunities for misspelling than short ones. A strategy for studying long words is to divide them into structurally appropriate parts and conquer the parts piecemeal. There are several ways to divide words that do not violate their structural integrity. Three such

TABLE 5.8. Applying the Mnemonic Strategy	
Target spelling problem	Mnemonic
three *b*'s in *bubbkes*	*big, beautiful, bubbles*
you in *you*ng	*you* are *young*
dance in abun*dance*	food in *abundance* at the *dance*
hide in *hide*ous	*hide* from the *hideous* monster

TABLE 5.9. Applying the Divide-and-Conquer Strategy

Compounds	Words with affixes	Syllables
Divide between meaning units	Divide between affix and base word	Divide between syllables
basket/ball	truck/er	in/spi/ra/tion/al
book/case	re/place/ment	hu/man/oid
humming/bird	un/help/ful	in/sin/u/a/tion
wall/board	thank/ful	pro/duc/tive
desk/top	root/less/ness	ge/ra/ni/um

categories are compound words, words with affixes, and syllabication. Examples of how to present this strategy are shown in Table 5.9.

Adding suffixes often changes the spelling of base words, and confusion about how this influences spelling leads to many spelling errors. On the other hand, when two base words are joined in a compound, the spelling of the base words seldom changes. It is important to discuss these issues when teaching the divide-and-conquer strategy.

Analogous Word Strategy

Analogous words share a linguistic feature that is similar or comparable. Many words have similar spelling patterns and are sometimes referred to as family words, words that share a common phonogram, usually a vowel–consonant combination, as in clown, town, brown. Rhyming words sound alike and usually have the same spelling pattern, as in *short–fort.* When children are learning spelling strategies, it is useful to have them think of rhyming helpers. Encourage children to search their universe of known words to think of a word they know that will help them spell a word they may not know. Examples are provided in Table 5.10. Make a game of this search by starting out with a few rhymes that younger children might find humorous, as in this silly ditty:

> There was a *clown,*
> Whose eyes were *brown.*
> He lived in *town,*
> And wore a *frown.*
> We laughed and laughed,
> When his pants fell *down.*

When working with rhyming helpers, inevitably children suggest words that rhyme but do not fit the spelling pattern. For instance, if you were

·•·

TABLE 5.10. Selected Spelling Patterns	
ab	cab, crab, dab, jab, scab
ace	ace, face, place, race, space
ack	back, black, pack, sack, track
ad	bad, dad, had, mad, sad
ade	fade, made, shade, trade, wade
ag	bag, flag, rag, snag, tag
ail	fail, jail, mail, sail, snail
ain	brain, drain, main, pain, plain
ake	bake, cake, lake, snake, take
all	ball, call, fall, tall, wall
ap	clap, map, nap, scrap, snap
are	care, dare, mare, scare, share
art	art, cart, dart, smart, start,
ash	cash, crash, flash, smash, trash
at	bat, chat, flat, rat, that
ave	brave, cave, grave, save, shave
aw	claw, draw, law, raw, saw
ay	clay, gray, play, stay, way
each	beach, each, peach, reach, teach
eal	deal, meal, real, seal, steal
eam	beam, dream, scream, stream, team
ear	dear, fear, hear, near, spear
eat	beat, cheat, meat, seat, wheat
eed	bleed, feed, need, seed, weed
eel	feel, heel, kneel, peel, steel,
eep	deep, keep, sheep, sleep, weep
ell	bell, fell, sell, shell, smell
end	bend, end, lend, send, spend
ess	bless, dress, guess, less, press
est	best, chest, nest, rest, test
ew	dew, few, chew, grew, knew
ice	ice, mice, nice, price, rice
ick	brick, kick, pick, quick, sick
ide	hide, pride, ride, side, slide
ig	big, dig, pig, twig, wig
ight	bright, might, light, night, right
ike	bike, hike, like, spike, alike
ile	file, pile, smile, tile, while
ill	chill, drill, hill, fill, spill
ime	chime, crime, dime, lime, time
in	chin, grin, skin, spin, thin
ind	blind, find, kind, mind, wind
ine	dine, nine, shine, vine, whine
ing	bring, king, ring, sing, wing
ink	drink, link, shrink, sink, stink
ip	clip, flip, hip, ship, whip

(continued)

·•·

TABLE 5.10. *(continued)*

it	hit, mit, quit, sit, spit
ite	bite, kite, site, white, write
ive	dive, five, hive, live, strive
oat	boat, coat, float, goat, throat
ob	job, knob, mob, rob, sob
ock	block, clock, knock, lock, rock
od	cod, nod, pod, rod, sod
og	cog, dog, fog, frog, hog
oil	boil, broil, oil, soil, spoil
oke	broke, choke, joke, smoke, spoke
old	bold, cold, gold, hold, sold
ole	hole, mole, pole, stole, whole
one	bone, lone, stone, throne, alone
ong	along, long, song, strong, wrong
ook	book, crook, hook, look, took
ool	cool, fool, pool, school, tool
oom	bloom, boom, broom, loom, room
oop	hoop, loop, scoop, stoop, troop
op	chop, drop, hop, mop, stop
ore	more, score, shore, store, tore
ot	got, knot, pot, shot, spot
ound	found, ground, hound, pound, sound
out	about, out, scout, spout, trout
ove	above, dove, glove, love, shove
ow ($\bar{o}$)	crow, grow, know, show, snow
ow (ou)	cow, how, now, plow, allow
owl	fowl, growl, owl, prowl, scowl
own (ou)	brown, clown, down, drown, town
own ($\bar{o}$)	blown, flown, known, shown
ub	club, cub, rub, scrub, tub
uck	duck, luck, stuck, struck, truck
ug	bug, drug, jug, plug, rug
um	drum, gum, plum, slum, sum
umble	fumble, humble, jumble, rumble, stumble
ump	bump, dump, jump, stump, thump
un	fun, gun, run, spun, sun
unch	bunch, crunch, lunch, munch, punch
ung	lung, rung, sprung, stung, sung
unk	bunk, drunk, junk, skunk, sunk
unt	blunt, grunt, hunt, punt, runt
urn	burn, churn, turn, urn, return
ush	blush, brush, crush, hush, mush
ust	bust, crust, dust, just, must
ut	but, cut, hut, nut, shut

working with the *-ail* phonogram, it would not be surprising if children suggested this set of rhyming helpers: *bail, fail, jail, mail, pail, rail, sail, tail, tale*. Write *tail* and *tale* on the board. Now you have the opportunity to make the point that spelling patterns are not always consistent. There is a challenge they have to confront. Awareness of the inconsistencies is just as important as awareness of the consistencies. This is also a good time to explain why homophones are spelled differently—different spellings of *tail* and *tale* signal different meanings.

In addition to rhyming patterns, words also share other common features: *think–thin* share the same consonant digraph; *mortal, mortuary, mortality* share the same base word; *nation, station, situation* share the same suffix. There are a host of similarities among words. Many children figure these similarities out for themselves through reading and writing experiences, but not all. Even those who have discovered similarities benefit from activities that heighten awareness of common spelling patterns and the inevitable exceptions to these patterns. Word sorts, described earlier in this book, are an example of a major source of discovering analogies between and among words. The use of word walls as described by Cunningham (1995) is also an excellent way to develop the awareness and curiosity about words that helps develop knowledge of the many analogies between and among words in the English language. Word walls are lists of words and sentences written on poster board or other suitable material. They are placed in strategic places in the room, usually on walls, hence the name. The lists of words are organized around categories such as frequency, rhyming, spelling, meaning, and structural and phonetic components of words. Cunningham (1995) popularized this concept in her book, *Phonics They Use: Words for Reading and Writing,* 2nd edition.

Spelling Consciousness Strategy

Spelling consciousness is a heightened awareness of spelling. Good spellers are aware of their spelling knowledge, whereas poor spellers seem not to possess this awareness, at least not to the same degree. The challenge, therefore, is to help children develop spelling consciousness, a stance of self-monitoring that will help them recognize when a word may or may not be spelled correctly. It is a difficult challenge, but one that must be accepted if we are to succeed in helping children become better spellers. Here are a few ideas that will help you meet this challenge.

Strategy Awareness

Teach a wide range of spelling strategies, such as the ones previously discussed. Do not be discouraged when you discover, as you certainly will, that teaching spelling strategies and getting children to apply them is a long-term task. It can't be done in a semester or two. More likely it will occur over years rather than months.

Editing and Proofreading

The best exercise for developing spelling consciousness is to have children engage in writing, particularly bringing their own writing to a final stage of development. Selected pieces of writing should be taken to the final stage of the writing process, in which the final product must have correctly spelled words. There need be no compromise on this stand. Here are some ideas that have worked for teachers who have had success in teaching editing and proofreading.

• Ownership of writing is paramount. Thus, most editing and proof-reading should be conducted on one's own writing.

• Stress the importance of audience. We write not only for ourselves but for an audience. Audience is the motive for improving writing and for presenting writing in its best form.

• Now and then, pair students for editing and proofreading so that good spellers can help weaker spellers.

• Model editing and proofreading techniques, using your own writing. Students need to see that even teachers make mistakes.

• Teach editing and proofreading techniques and attitudes. Editing and proofreading are not merely a relentless search for errors; rather, they are a relentless search for ways to make writing better. There is a world of difference in these two ways of looking at writing tasks.

• Organize classroom editing and proofreading tasks. For instance, write a short note on the board or a list of words commonly misspelled by your students. Have children look for spelling errors you have deliberately made. Children love it when teachers make mistakes that they can correct.

• Teach children to edit and proofread works that they have not produced themselves. While one's own writing is the primary place for editing and proofreading, valuable experience can be gained from working with the writing of other authors.

• Work in cooperative groups or pairs should be part of the editing and proofreading experience.

• Editors sometimes read backwards, from the end to the beginning, in order to concentrate solely on technical matters such as spelling. This may confuse younger readers, but older children can manage this proce-dure satisfactorily.

• Experiment with editor-of-the-week assignments. The idea is to pass around the task of helping edit and proofread other children's work. This strategy works best after children have had sufficient experience in editing and proofreading.

Looking for Misspelled Words on Signs

Give homework assignments in which children look for signs that have misspelled words. Advertisers sometimes deliberately misspell words, and sometimes they do it inadvertently. Have children bring in examples of misspellings they have found on signs or in print and discuss their examples in class.

Word Awareness

Talk about words with your children. Show, by example, your own curiosity and interest in words. Many writers date their interest in words to a teacher who first roused their interest. When teachers show an interest in words, it is not long before students get the idea, and begin sharing their word discoveries. Once this happens the game is on, as Sherlock Holmes would say.

PERSPECTIVE AND SUMMARY

The past decade has seen a turning away from systematic spelling instruction in many schools. The reason for this abandonment was sometimes motivated by a laudable desire to emphasize meaningful reading and writing. More often this abandonment had more to do with an educational ideology that rejected word study as meaningless and insufficiently whole. In some venues, spelling textbooks and spelling lists were cast aside in favor of drawing words from "literature." Thus was born the idea of "literature-based spelling," as though drawing words from *Catcher in the Rye* or *The Red Pony* somehow elevated everyday words into a meaning-rich category merely because they were drawn from an excellent piece of literature. The fact is that any well-organized spelling curriculum will inevitably include precisely the kind of words that appear in good literature because of the naturally occurring redundancy of the English language and because good writers tend to use the common language.

Nevertheless, the educational ideology that drove out systematic spelling instruction rightly placed the reading of good literature and writing at the head of the line, the most positive educational reform of the past decade. Those who emphasized the role of meaning and wholeness deserve much credit. But systematic spelling instruction is not incompatible with these sensible ideals. Systematic spelling instruction flourishes in an environment where children read widely and write frequently. Consequently, it is imperative that we recognize three basic premises of systematic spelling instruction: (1) Reading provides the background knowledge that enhances learning to spell; (2) writing provides the practice field on which spelling knowledge is most meaningfully applied; and (3) systematic spelling instruction provides the organization and discipline required to make this trinity work.

The following main ideas have been presented in this chapter.

• Three approaches to spelling instruction have been described: (1) personalized spelling, in which students draw words from their reading and writing, (2) cooperative spelling, in which students and teachers cooperatively create spelling lists, and (3) spelling textbook, where words are typically drawn from research- based sources. All three approaches may use similar activities and procedures for learning, reviewing, and assessing spelling achievement. No spelling activity or procedure need be considered the exclusive province of any one approach, as teachers may, and indeed should, adapt and adopt instructional concepts to fit the students' needs.

• Seven principles and conventions of spelling have been described: (1) alphabetic principle, (2) position within-word principle, (3) spelling–meaning principle, (4) apostrophe conventions, (5) one-word or two-word convention, (6) compound-word conventions, and (7) capitalization and abbreviation conventions.

• Choosing spelling words is an important and challenging task. All three spelling approaches are largely defined by their method of word selection. Criteria for word selection not only determine what words are chosen, but influence how lists are organized into coherent instructional units. There are six criteria to consider when constructing spelling lists: words that are (1) high frequency, (2) frequently misspelled, (3) linguistically patterned, (4) content related, (5) developmentally appropriate, and (6) personally chosen.

• Learning requires meaningful repetition. Thus, systematic review has been stressed. Review should be carried out within grade levels as well as across grade levels. While it is important to review words, especially words that are frequently misspelled, there must also be review of spelling concepts, strategies, and conventions.

• Time on task is an important variable in learning. It is necessary, therefore, to have regularly scheduled time for teaching spelling. While the amount of time devoted to spelling may vary, 60–90 minutes a week usually will be required.

• Spelling strategies are plans or methods designed to achieve a particular outcome or goal. Six strategies were described: (1) pronunciation, (2) visualization, (3) mnemonic, (4) divide-and-conquer, (5) analogous word, and (6) spelling consciousness.

REFERENCES

Bear, D. R., Invernizzi, M., Templeton, S., & Johnston, F. (1996). *Words their way: Word study for phonics, vocabulary, and spelling instruction.* Englewood Cliffs, NJ: Prentice-Hall.

Beers, J. (1980). Developmental strategies of spelling competence in primary school children. In J. Beers & E. Henderson (Eds.), *Developmental and cognitive aspects of learning to spell* (pp. 36–45). Newark, DE: International Reading Association.

Beers, J. W., & Henderson, E. H. (1977). A study of developing orthographic concepts among first grade children. *Research in the Teaching of English, 11*(2), 133–148.

Coon, G. (1976). Homophones. *The Reading Teacher, 29*(7), 652.

Cramer, R. L. (1968). *An investigation of the spelling achievement of two groups of first-grade classes on phonologically regular and irregular words and in written compositions.* Unpublished doctoral dissertation, University of Delaware: Newark.

Cramer, R. L., & Cipielewski, J. F. (1995). Research in action: A study of spelling errors in 18,599 written compositions of children in grades 1–8. In *Spelling research and information: An overview of current research and practices* (pp. 11–52). Glenview, IL: Scott, Foresman.

Cunningham, P. M. (1995). *Phonics they use: Words for reading and writing* (2nd ed.). New York: HarperCollins.

Farr, R. (1989). *An analysis of the spelling patterns of children in grades two through eight.* Center for Reading and Language Studies. Unpublished manuscript, Indiana State University, Bloomington.

Gates, A. (1937). *A list of spelling difficulties in 3876 words showing the "hard-spots," common misspellings, average spelling-grade placement, and comprehension grade ratings of each word.* New York: Teachers College, Columbia University.

Hanna P. R., Hanna, J. S., Hodges, R. E., & Rudorf, E. H. (1966). *Phoneme–grapheme correspondences as cues to spelling improvement.* Washington, DC: U.S. Department of Health, Education and Welfare, Office of Education.

Henderson, E. H. (1990). *Teaching spelling* (2nd ed.). Boston: Houghton Mifflin.

Radebaugh, M. R. (1985). Good spellers use more visual imagery than poor spellers. *The Reading Teacher, 38*(6), 532–536.

Read, C. (1970). *Children's perceptions of the sounds of English: Phonology from three to six.* Unpublished doctoral dissertation, Harvard University, Cambridge, MA.

Read, C. (1971). Pre-school children's knowledge of English phonology. *Harvard Educational Review, 41*(1), 1–34.

Tauber, A. (Ed.). (1963). *George Bernard Shaw, on language.* New York: Philosophical Library.

Chapter 6

•─•─•

Assessing Spelling Growth
and Achievement

The most creative theories are often imaginative visions
imposed upon facts.

—Stephen Jay Gould

INTRODUCTION

How do we help children attain good spelling amidst the daily imperatives
of teaching? We start with sensible assessment that can be easily managed
in the classroom. Spelling achievement must be assessed so that children
can be placed at their instructional levels and so that appropriate spelling
words, activities, concepts, and strategies can be provided in a timely
fashion. First, procedures for analyzing early spelling growth are presented
in this chapter. Next, procedures for determining spelling levels are
discussed.

ASSESSING EARLY SPELLING GROWTH

An effective way to determine how children are progressing in their early
spelling knowledge is to administer a spelling assessment test at regular
intervals. A school or district may wish to assess spelling growth across a
1-, 2-, or 3-year span. On the other hand, a classroom teacher may only
want to know how her children are progressing across a single school year.
Examples of progress in spelling across time are discussed in the following
case studies, using data for two students, Laurie and Toni.

Case Study: Laurie

Table 6.1 presents the results of administering the Morris Spelling Test to a first-grade child, Laurie, four times during the school year.

The purpose of administering the Morris Spelling Test is to obtain a consistent, analyzable sample of spelling knowledge across a span of time to see how spelling growth is progressing. Laurie's responses indicate consistent developmental spelling growth. An analysis of her spelling development is outlined for each time period in which assessment took place: October, January, and June.

October

The October testing took place just 1 month after the school year began. Analysis indicates the following signs of spelling growth:

1. Laurie attempted to spell one sound in seven of the list words (*back sink, mail, dress, side, letter, stick*), two sounds in six of the words (*table, feet, stamp, bike, seed, monster*), and three sounds in *elevator*.

2. Every sound–letter connection she attempts is represented with two letters—lowercase and uppercase. Attempting to spell sounds with both lowercase and uppercase letters is fairly common among first-grade children. This strategy probably stems from the manner in which the alphabet is typically presented in schools. Lowercase and uppercase letters are often written side by side, usually on charts over the chalkboard. This "double-

TABLE 6.1. Laurie's Spelling Performance across 1 School Year

Test words	October	January	June
back	Bb	bac	back
sink	Cc	sece	secek
mail	Mm	mal	mail
dress	Gg	tes	drees
table	Tt Bb	tabule	table
side	Cc	sode	side
feet	Ff vV	feet	feet
stamp	CcBb	stamp	stamp
letter	Rr	letre	lettre
stick	Cc	stike	stik
bike	Bb Kk	buce	bike
seed	Cc Dd	sede	sede
monster	Mm Dd	mostre	monttr
elevator	Ll tt vv	eavatr	elvattr

letter" strategy is quickly abandoned by children, as was the case when Laurie was retested in January.

   3. Most of the time Laurie's guesses were correct, and they were, in all instances, linguistically reasonable guesses. For instance, *table* is spelled *Tt Bb*—the beginning sound of each syllable in *table.*

   4. *Elevator (littvv)* is spelled with three doubled letters, *ll, tt, vv,* although not in correct sequence.

   5. She spelled the /s/ sound with the letters *Cc* in *sink, slide, stamp, stick,* and *seed,* an excellent example of her use of the letter-name strategy.

   6. Laurie's educated guesses reveal above-average knowledge of beginning consonant spellings, given only 1 month's experience in first grade.

   7. Laurie demonstrated no attempts to spell vowel sounds, a wholly predictable circumstance at this stage of spelling growth.

   Laurie's overall October performance indicates that she is at the earliest level of the phonetic stage of spelling growth. Judging from this sample, the prognosis for continued growth in spelling knowledge is good.

January

Testing in January demonstrates that Laurie has made progress, particularly in her knowledge of vowel spellings—rather remarkable progress actually. These items should be noted:

   1. Every word has a vowel letter included in its spelling, 10 of which are correct vowel spellings. She has learned the function of the marking vowel (see Chapter 1) in certain long vowel spellings: *side, feet, bike, seed, table.* However, the only one she spells correctly is the *ee* in *feet.*

   2. Every word now has two or more consonant sounds represented, usually the first and last consonant sounds.

   3. The /s/ sound in *sink, slide, stamp, stick,* and *seed* is no longer represented with the letter *c* but is now correctly spelled.

   4. Two words are now spelled correctly, *feet* and *stamp.*

   Laurie's performance in January shows steady progress. She is beginning to understand certain vowel spelling principles, has learned the correct spelling of a few words, and is now spelling many consonant sounds correctly. Her progress is quite dramatic and the prognosis is excellent. From this January sample, one would predict a good spelling performance at the end of the year.

June

Analysis of Laurie's performance in June reveals that her spelling development has progressed rapidly over the past year. The evidence can be summed up with five conclusions:

1. Laurie correctly spells half of the words on the Morris list.
2. She correctly spells most beginning, middle, and ending consonant spellings.
3. She correctly spells many long and short vowel patterns: long—*mail, table, side, bike, feet*; short—*stamp, back.*
4. The error patterns in the seven words still incorrectly spelled (*secek, drees, lettre, stik, sede, monttr,* and *elvattr*) reveal consistent developmental progress toward correct spelling.
5. There is no evidence of any spelling pathology.

Interestingly, most of Laurie's misspelled words in the June assessment are the first or second alternative spelling on my computer spell-checker program. Her spelling of *monster* is not yet close enough for the computer to predict *monttr* as a likely misspelling. An educated guess is that Laurie will spell 13 or 14 of these words correctly by the end of second grade, if not sooner. With appropriate spelling instruction and frequent opportunities to read and write, Laurie will become a good-to-excellent speller.

Case Study: Toni

The Morris Spelling Test is an excellent way to assess progress over time. The more samples you examine of how spelling knowledge develops, the more you are able to learn about the individual variance you can expect from student to student. Toni's performance in October is especially instructive because her performance reveals a strategy that may be easily misjudged unless you have looked at many examples of early spelling development. Examine Table 6.2 closely.

October

Toni's performance in October may appear strange at first glance, but a closer look reveals significant knowledge. Note the following items:

1. Toni represents the first letter–sound relationship correctly on 10 words (*back, sink, mail, table, side, feet, stamp, stick, bike, monster*). She probably represented the first and last consonant sounds correctly on these words:

TABLE 6.2. Toni's Spelling Performance across 1 School Year

Test words	October	January	June
back	bil	bak	back
sink	shkvel	cokt	cenk
mail	mavel	malk	male
dress	kvetb	drsi	drast
table	tbakb	tab	table
side	sdbk	cod	side
feet	ftvel	fent	feet
stamp	sthvbmi	satp	stape
letter	mtwet	late	latr
stick	stvetkbk	stkc	stik
bike	bvetukyeeth	bik	bike
seed	cdvetvetc	cedi	sede
monster	mtdkkwe	mock	mustr
elevator	mvetkekyelve	lavt	lavtr

mail, side, feet, table, stamp, stick, although it is difficult to distinguish correct representations from random guesses represented by the unnecessary letters that most of her attempts contain. In any case, it is clear that there is much more going on here than the long letter strings might seem to suggest.

2. Toni knows that most of the words on this test require more letters than she knows how to correctly spell. She resorts, therefore, to a strategy sometimes used by children at this stage of spelling development: When in doubt add additional letters from your inventory of known letters. This results in some impressively long spellings. *Bike* is represented by 11 letters (*bvetukyeeth*), *seed* by 9 letters (*cdvetvetc*) and *elevator,* the longest word in the list, by 12 letters (*mvetkekyelve*). There is an important lesson here. Things are not always what they seem with children's written performance. When you talk to children about their performance, you often find they are able to articulate a thoughtful, though mistaken, strategy behind what on the surface looks bizarre.

January

Clearly, Toni has made progress in her spelling knowledge over the past 3 months. These items are worth noting:

1. Every word begins with a correct or nearly correct initial letter-sound relationship. The exceptions are *sink* (*cokt*), *side* (*cod*)*seed* (*ced*) and *elevator* (*lavt*). Note, however, that each exception represents the use of an appropriate letter name strategy (see Chapter 1).

2. Vowel spellings begin to appear (*bak, malk, tlab, fent, satp, late, bik, cedi, mock, lavtl*). Although seldom correct, these vowel spellings show progress toward understanding that vowel sounds must be accounted for in words.

3. None of the 14 words is spelled correctly, but this is neither distressing nor surprising. Why? Because her educated guesses suggest that some six or seven or these words will soon be spelled correctly. Her spelling of *bak* for *back, malk* for mail, *tab* for *table, cod* for *side, fent* for *feet, bik* for *bike, cedi* for *sede* are close to the point of correct spelling.

Toni's long strings of letters produced in October might lead you to guess that something was seriously wrong. This would have been an incorrect analysis, for you can see that Toni's January performance is much like Laurie's. There were strengths in Toni's October performance that were difficult to detect.

June

By June solid progress is evident.

1. Five words are spelled correctly (*back, table, side, feet, bike*). Many near misses also appear (*cenk* for *sink, male* for *mail, stape* for *stamp, latr* for *letter, sede* for *seed*). Each of these near-misses reveals a significant spelling strength.

2. The two most challenging words show progress toward correct spelling (*mustr* for *monster* and *lavtr* for *elevator*).

Toni is on her way toward spelling success, assuming appropriate spelling instruction, wide reading, and opportunities to write frequently. There is reason to expect that she can become a competent, perhaps excellent, speller.

These two case studies, Laurie and Toni, provide a framework for analyzing children's spelling performance as they move from the early phonetic stage, a beginner's start, to the beginning of the third stage, patterns within words. Diagnosis ought always to look for strengths as well as weaknesses, correct spellings as well as incorrect. Keep in mind that corrective instruction proceeds best when it builds on strengths while looking for opportunities to correct weaknesses. Often building on strengths eliminates or ameliorates weaknesses without any special concentration upon them.

·◆·
PLACEMENT FOR INSTRUCTION

Placing children at their correct spelling level is crucial. The best way to place children correctly at their instructional level is to administer a spelling placement inventory, which consists of randomly selected words, usually 20, for each grade level, 1–8 (Table 6.3). Many spelling textbooks provide a spelling inventory. If not, one can be easily built by randomly selecting words from the complete list of all words at a given grade level. Spelling textbooks usually include a list of all words for a given level at the back of each book.

The inventory shown in Table 6.3 was drawn from the textbook series *Scott Foresman: Spelling, Words and Skills,* levels 1–8. Although placement inventories are reasonably accurate, mistaken assessment can occur. It is essential, therefore, to continue monitoring progress after initial placement

TABLE 6.3. The Scott, Foresman Spelling Placement Test

Grade 1	Grade 2	Grade 3	Grade 4
at	all	anything	asleep
bed	before	barefoot	beat
boy	both	bite	circle
cat	car	candy	count
deep	coat	coach	drift
end	dream	dollar	fern
five	fish	friends	helpful
go	gave	grew	idea
her	has	highway	ladder
jump	keep	house	melt
mother	long	learn	ocean
old	much	meat	plow
play	part	noise	ready
red	reading	pencil	recess
sister	running	rope	snap
star	sheep	scrub	suddenly
time	singer	slipped	trailer
us	team	tennis	unknown
yellow	track	trash	worm
you	white	words	zebra
No. correct	No. correct	No. correct	No. correct
% score	% score	% score	% score

Note. Formula: No. correct × 5 = % score; example: 15 correct × 5 = 75%.

(continued)

TABLE 6.3. (*continued*)

Grade 5	Grade 6	Grade 7	Grade 8
apartment	ancient	advantage	advertisement
castle	chalk	business	believed
coupon	delay	chatter	cashier
eleven	double	courageous	comedian
fasten	example	difficult	detective
given	ghost	endanger	evidence
horseback	horizon	everybody	foreign
leaves	independence	freedom	guilty
matches	junior	immigrants	librarian
nickel	milk	kidnap	magnetic
paper	nearby	nonsense	movable
prefix	ownership	organization	opportunity
review	popular	peaceful	pressure
scissors	receives	population	radioactive
sharks	screaming	safety	scenery
skunk	soccer	studying	society
steal	surface	thrown	telephone
taught	upstairs	undecided	traveled
whistle	wrestled	wolves	wasted
No. correct	No. correct	No. correct	No. correct
% score	% score	% score	% score

From Cramer (1978). Copyright 1978 by Scott, Foresman and Company. Reprinted by permission of Addison-Wesley Educational Publishers, Inc.

has been made to assure that students are operating at a comfortable instructional level.

Administering a Spelling Inventory

A spelling inventory is easily administered using the following steps.

1. Divide the class into three groups according to your best estimate of their spelling ability, as based on reading ability, especially word recognition ability.

2. Start each group on a list of words where they are likely to perform at an independent level. An independent level is defined here as 85–100% correct performance. Use Table 6.4 as a guide for where to start each group.

If you unintentionally start at a level that is too difficult, move back as many levels as necessary until you have reached one at which an independent performance is more likely.

Children learn best when instruction is attuned to their growing edges. These children's teacher knows how to identify their instructional levels or zone of proximal development, as Vygotsky puts it.

3. Administer the test to all three groups at once: Say the test word; give the test word in a sentence: repeat the test word again. The procedure goes something like this:

> Group 1, your word is *ten*. The number *ten* comes after nine. *Ten*.
> Group 2, your word is *away*. The dog ran *away* with the bone. *Away*.
> Group 3, your word is *picture*. Arnold drew a *picture* of his house. *Picture*.

4. Administer one to four lists at a sitting, depending on the age of the group. Walk around, observing students' performance as you administer the inventory. If a student appears to be misspelling half or more of the words, have that student stop.

Three Levels of Performance

Traditionally, three levels of spelling performance have been identified: independent, instructional, and frustration levels. The notion of three levels of performance harks back to the work of Emmet Betts (1946) in his classic book *Foundations of Reading Instruction*. Betts applied his ideas

TABLE 6.4. Estimated Starting Point for Spelling Inventory

Grade level	Low	Average	High
1	1	1	1
2	1	1	2
3	1	2	3
4	2	3	4
5	3	4	5
6	4	5	6
7	5	6	7
8	6	7	8

to reading performance and stipulated criteria for determining levels. The criteria specified here are somewhat different from the traditional criteria originally proposed by Betts.

Independent Level

The independent level is defined as the highest level at which students can work without teacher guidance. Performance criteria for an independent level in spelling are 85–100%. Students do not always have an independent level—this is simply a fact of life. Don't look for something that may not exist for certain students.

Instructional Level

The instructional level is defined as the highest level at which a student can make progress in spelling with the help of the teacher. Performance criteria for an instructional level in spelling are 65–84%. It is important to know that some students show instructional level performance across more than one grade level. Place these students at the highest level at which they have achieved an instructional score. In other words, if they score in the instructional range at Grades 4 and 5, place them at the fifth-grade level.

Frustration Level

The frustration level is that at which students have significant spelling difficulty. A frustration level is reached when students score 64% or lower. However, testing continues until a score of 50% or less is reached. If testing stops earlier, say at 60%, there is a good chance that a score in the instructional range may be achieved on the next highest level. There is much less likelihood of scoring in the instructional range, although it is not impossible, once students have missed half or more of the words on the test.

Students should not be given spelling materials or assignments at the frustration level, or spelling growth will be impeded, even though such students may temporarily memorize a list of words and perform satisfactorily on a weekly test.

If school policy requires that all students at a given level work in the same textbook or on the same spelling list, certainly some children will be forced to work at their frustration level and others at a level that is not sufficiently challenging. Placement at the frustration level usually results in spelling failure. When teachers are forced, through no fault of their own, to make this unwise decision, the next best thing to do is adjust the pace of spelling instruction. For example, it may be possible to assign only half of the weekly spelling words and activities to students having difficulties. While this strategy is not the best solution, it may be the best a teacher can do under adverse circumstances. However, this strategy would not work for those students whose spelling level is two or more levels below grade placement. In other words, if a fifth grader is at the third-grade instructional level in spelling, adjusting the number of words in such cases will do little to adjust spelling instruction for this student. In such cases, it is essential that he or she be placed at a more developmentally appropriate spelling level. Nothing else is likely to work.

A summary of the scoring criteria used to determine independent, instructional, and frustration spelling levels is shown in Table 6.5.

Determining the Best Placement Level

Place students at their highest instructional level. If a student scores 65–84% at grade levels 4 or 5, the correct placement is Grade 5, since this is the highest instructional level. Many students achieve instructional scores spanning two or more grade levels. Placement at the lower end of this range can impair spelling growth, whereas placing students at their highest instructional level will ensure it.

Avoid placing students at their frustration level. Spelling growth will surely be hindered by placement at levels that are too difficult. Students can actually regress by prolonged placement at frustration spelling levels.

It is also inadvisable to place students at their independent spelling level (85–100%), since this would provide little challenge and may result in failure to grow at a pace commensurate with ability.

Although an effective spelling placement test will usually place students at their proper level, misplacement can occur. Look for the following signs of it:

1. Consistently scores below 65% on review tests, usually administered every 4–6 weeks.

TABLE 6.5. Criteria for Determining Independent, Instructional, and Frustration Spelling Levels

Level	Criterion score (%)	What it means
Independent	85–100	Without teacher help
Instructional	65–84	With teacher help
Frustration	64 or lower	Too hard even with teacher help

2. Consistently scores below 65% on weekly spelling tests.
3. Consistently spells poorly on final draft writing.

If any combination of these signs of misplacement occur over an extended period of time, usually 6 weeks, adjust instruction downward. This can be done by giving the student a lower-level spelling book, reducing the number of words assigned, or developing new spelling assignments if the child is working in a personalized spelling program. Spelling performance on written work is, of course, the final arbiter of spelling success. It is particularly important to monitor spelling performance on revised and final draft writing.

Case Studies Illustrating Level Placement

Table 6.6 shows the spelling scores of three fifth-grade students. Study the scores and the recommended level placements.

Adam

No independent level was achieved. Adam could be tested at the second-grade level to see if he can spell independently at Grade 2, but this is probably not necessary since it is often the case that students do not have an independent level. Adam shows a two-grade instructional range, Grades 3 and 4. Therefore, place Adam at the fourth-grade instructional level since it is the highest level at which he shows an instructional score. Adam's frustration level is fifth grade. Teaching Adam spelling at this level is highly inadvisable.

Amanda

Amanda shows an independent level at fourth grade. Do not teach her at this level since it will not challenge her current spelling knowledge. Her instructional level is Grade 5, at which level she scored 75%. It is probably best to instruct Amanda in spelling at the fifth-grade level. At sixth grade

			TABLE 6.6. Scores on Spelling Test by Grade Level					
Student	1	2	3	4	5	6	7	8
Adam			80	75	45			
Amanda				90	75	60	40	
Manuel					90	70	50	40

she scored 60%, a score that falls within the frustration range, but this is a borderline score, close to the instructional range but sufficiently low to warrant caution. One might experiment with an instructional placement at sixth-grade level, but this should be done only with caution and close monitoring to assure that misplacement has not occurred. Other factors, such as reading and writing performance, motivation, and work habits can also enter into the placement decision. Amanda's frustration level is seventh grade, indicating that she should not be placed at this level.

Manuel

Manuel's independent level is Grade 5, his instructional level Grade 6, and his frustration level Grade 7. His scores suggest that he is unlikely to succeed in spelling if taught in materials that are above the sixth-grade level. He should be taught at the sixth-grade level and monitored closely to assure that he can perform satisfactorily at this level, that is, make progress in spelling in his daily spelling assignments and in his written composition.

PERSPECTIVE AND SUMMARY

Assessment can be good or bad, helpful or destructive. It can stimulate growth, or it can be a subtle poison. Assessment works best when it is knowledgeable, gentle, and encouraging. Effective assessment not only has a positive tone, it achieves positive results. Assessment plays a crucial role in growth if it is informed and properly administered, and when data is intelligently analyzed. Children can learn and grow as a result of good assessment, accompanied by encouraging words to sustain them as they struggle toward mature learning.

This chapter has presented the following main ideas:

• An effective way to assess early spelling growth is to administer and analyze the results of a test specifically designed to represent linguistic features expected to be acquired during the early stages of spelling growth. The Morris Spelling Test is an excellent example of such a test. The case studies of Laurie and Toni indicate that one can study current perform-ance and predict future performance by analyzing the test results.
• Placing children at their appropriate instructional spelling level is crucial, since overplacement can stifle growth and underplacement can

stifle motivation to excel. A spelling placement test can be used to make placement decisions. Follow-up procedures are essential to make sure that initial placement decisions are accurate.

REFERENCES

Betts, E. A. (1946). *Foundations of reading instruction.* New York: American Book.

Cramer, R. L. (1978). *The Scott, Foresman Spelling Placement Test for Spelling: Words and skills.* Glenview, IL: Scott, Foresman.

Chapter 7

Questions Teachers Ask about Spelling

> Now, for years I have rarely asked a child a question un-
> less I really did not know the answer myself and believed
> that he could tell me.
>
> —HUGHES MEARNS

INTRODUCTION

Everywhere I go, teachers ask questions about spelling. They are curious about it, perhaps more curious than they have been for the past decade. Many teachers think spelling is on the decline, and they are right. This decline has come about because many schools have discontinued system-atic spelling instruction. A romantic notion has grown up, absent any supporting data, that spelling can be learned if children just read and write enough. For some children, this may indeed be so. But for many children this is simply not sufficient. Spelling, like math and reading, must be taught. Spelling must be taught systematically, and it must be taught in close association with reading and writing. When this happens, spelling competence will no longer be in decline.

I have found that teachers sometimes ask questions that they already have answered for themselves. They may ask a question hoping for support for their established beliefs, but more often they ask questions that have arisen out of public debate about sound instructional practices. Invented spelling is just such an issue. Teachers are concerned about sound instruc-tional practices. They want to be good teachers, and they want the best for their students.

The questions and answers in this chapter represent a sampling of the kinds of questions teachers have asked me about spelling. In answering these questions, I have occasionally alluded to research findings. More often I have not, preferring in this chapter to answer the question briefly with few excursions into research findings. Those seeking more thorough discussion of issues raised in the following questions will find that I have provided much greater detail elsewhere in this book. I have, for instance, devoted an entire chapter to invented spelling. Nevertheless, I have included a question on invented spelling in this chapter because it is the question most often asked by teachers.

DOES SPELLING COUNT?

High school and college students, when preparing a writing assignment, sometimes ask, "Does spelling count?" The answer ought to be "Yes, spelling counts." It need not count in first draft writing, of course, but when writing is presented as a finished product, spelling accuracy is important. It is important to distinguish between the final work product of writing and the process that necessarily precedes final draft writing. The reasons are obvious.

Spelling counts when one submits a résumé for employment; spelling counts when one presents a report in the normal course of business or schooling; spelling counts, in other words, in the real world. We do no favor for our students when we encourage the idea that spelling accuracy is optional. We ought to set high standards for spelling accuracy and inculcate in our students a spelling consciousness.

Nevertheless, it should also be made plain that, while spelling counts, the quality of ideas and the writing itself are even more important. Ideas are fundamental; perfect spelling cannot mask inferior ideas. Perfect spelling cannot mask inaccurate or inadequate information in a report;

Spelling counts in the social, cultural, business, and academic world. These children are fortunate. They read, write, and spell every day, increasing their chances of becoming competent spellers.

perfect spelling is no substitute for an entertaining story, a tightly argued essay, a beautifully written poem. Fortunately, it is not necessary to sacrifice ideas and good writing on the altar of spelling accuracy. It is possible to have both. We can have good writing, good ideas, and accurate spelling. Indeed, we must insist on high standards and apply these standards to all aspects of writing: ideas, writing, grammar, usage, mechanics, and spelling. Separating the technical aspects from the message conveyed is an abdication of our responsibility to teach the written language in all of its subtle power and beauty.

DOES INVENTED SPELLING DAMAGE
OR DELAY SPELLING GROWTH?

The evidence is clear, despite the critics, that invented spelling has an appropriate, even an essential place in early writing. First, invented spelling is far more likely to aid the development of spelling knowledge than it is to hinder it. Second, invented spelling makes writing possible as early as kindergarten or first grade, thus giving a head start to the development of writing skill. If children are not encouraged to invent their spellings at the beginning of writing, they will not be able to write independently until they have mastered a substantial spelling vocabulary. This would mean delaying writing until third or fourth grade—an intolerable and unnecessary delay. Even then, children would be forced to write with a restricted spelling vocabulary, since even after 3 or 4 years of schooling, only a modest spelling vocabulary is possible.

We are fully aware of these circumstances when it comes to oral language. We know that children need 5–7 years before their oral language reaches maturity, and even then, growth of vocabulary continues throughout one's lifetime. We do not delay oral language while we wait for perfectly accurate oral utterances—quite the opposite. We honor the beginners' imperfect attempts at communicating their oral messages. Young children are constantly "inventing" their way toward mature speech. Similarly, we must not delay writing until spelling reaches mature development.

Invented spelling does not harm children's spelling development; indeed, it is far more likely to enhance it. Spelling knowledge grows more rapidly when reading, writing, and spelling instruction proceed simultaneously. Reading provides much of the raw material for spelling development, while writing provides the forum in which spelling knowledge is exercised. Delaying writing until the ability to make a perfect rendering of written language is acquired is akin to delaying oral language production until a perfect rendering of pronunciation has been achieved. Of course, we wouldn't think of delaying oral language until accurate utterance of words and sentences had been learned. We know this would do far more harm than good. Delaying writing until an accurate spelling vocabulary has been acquired also does more harm than good.

WHAT WORDS DO CHILDREN MOST OFTEN MISSPELL?

Cramer and Cipielewski (1995) reported the results of one of the largest spelling studies ever conducted in the United States. Among other findings, the study identified the 100 most frequently misspelled words across eight grade levels. Additional information on frequently misspelled words by grade level is contained in Appendices A–H.

As you peruse the 100 most frequently misspelled words in Table 7.1, notice that these 100 words are virtually unavoidable in almost any type of writing. The list contains words of the highest frequency found in reading, writing, and speaking. Knowing how to spell these 100 words would substantially improve the spelling performance of the poorest speller.

WHAT TYPE OF SPELLING ERRORS WITHIN WORDS DO CHILDREN MOST OFTEN MAKE?

Cramer and Cipielewski (1995) identified and categorized 55 types of spelling errors made by children in Grades 1–8. Table 7.2 shows the order, from most to least frequent, of the 55 error types for grade levels 1–8 combined (see also Appendix I). The study also reported this information by grade level (see Appendix J).

Certain types of errors failed to decline significantly over time. Omitted letters, homophones, and scrambled letters are three notable examples. These three error categories appear among the top 10 error types at every grade level. Across all grade levels, omitted letters are the single greatest type of spelling error. Homophones are a close second. Another interesting finding, not often reported in the literature on spelling errors, is that omitted letters, scrambled letters, and added letters are significant factors in generating spelling errors. Yet another significant spelling problem is running words together that should be separated (*alot* for *a lot*) and separating word parts inappropriately (*a nother* for *another*). Not surprisingly, problems associated with vowels and consonants are also among the top 10 error types.

TABLE 7.1. 100 Most Frequently Misspelled Words across Eight Grade Levels

1. too	34. upon	67. there's
2. a lot	35. probably	68. little
3. because	36. don't	69. doesn't
4. there	37. sometimes	70. usually
5. their	38. off	71. clothes
6. that's	39. everybody	72. scared
7. they	40. heard	73. everyone
8. it's	41. always	74. have
9. when	42. I	75. swimming
10. favorite	43. something	76. about
11. went	44. would	77. first
12. Christmas	45. want	78. happened
13. were	46. and	79. Mom
14. our	47. Halloween	80. especially
15. they're	48. house	81. school
16. said	49. once	82. getting
17. know	50. to	83. started
18. you're	51. like	84. was
19. friend	52. whole	85. which
20. friends	53. another	86. stopped
21. really	54. believe	87. two
22. finally	55. I'm	88. Dad
23. where	56. thought	89. took
24. again	57. let's	90. friend's
25. then	58. before	91. presents
26. didn't	59. beautiful	92. are
27. people	60. everything	93. morning
28. until	61. very	94. could
29. with	62. into	95. around
30. different	63. caught	96. buy
31. outside	64. one	97. maybe
32. we're	65. Easter	98. family
33. through	66. what	99. pretty
		100. tried

WHAT WORDS SHOULD CHILDREN LEARN TO SPELL?

Children should study the words they need to use when they write, but this begs the question of what words children should learn to spell. Children do not know in advance which words they may want to use in their writing. Writing is discovery; topics are widely varied, rightly so. If, for example, David writes about farming equipment, he will need many common words as well as a highly specialized set of words. If Toni writes about her trip to Disney World she will also need content words that may not be fully established in her spelling vocabulary. Obviously, given the

TABLE 7.2. Top Error Categories for Combined Grade Levels 1–8

1. Omitted letters	29. Double consonant +
2. Homophones	inflected ending
3. Consonant substitution	30. Compound word spelling
4. Scrambled letters	31. Vowel: /er/
5. Schwa (other)	32. Long *o*
6. Short *e*	33. Easily confused pairs
7. Long *e*	34. Vowel: /u/
8. Schwa final syllable	35. Suffix spelling
9. Consonant blend	36. Truncated/bizarre
10. Run together/separated	37. Silent consonant
11. Consonant digraph	38. Mispronunciation
12. Added letters	39. Compound wrongly joined
13. Short *i*	40. Final *e* + inflected ending
14. Double consonant in root	41. Double consonant + suffix
15. Inflected spelling	42. Vowel: /ou/
16. Compound wrongly separated	43. *y* to *i* + inflected ending
17. Apostrophe with contraction	44. Short *o*
18. Complex consonant	45. Short *a*
19. Vowel: /o/	46. Vowel: /u/
20. Capitalization	47. Final *e* + suffix
21. Long *a*	48. Regularizing irregulars
22. Silent *e* overgeneralized	49. Vowel: /a/
23. Single consonant doubled	50. Vowel: /yu/
24. Silent *e* other	51. Repeated sequence
25. Short *u*	52. Prefix spelling
26. Apostrophe with possessive	53. Abbreviation
27. Long *i*	54. Vowel: /oi/
28. Silent *e* long vowel	55. *y* to *i* + suffix

substantial redundancy of the language, David and Toni will need high-frequency words, the words commonly used in reading, writing, and speaking.

Word-frequency studies tell us that if Toni and David could spell about 1,000 of the commonest words in the English language they would correctly spell about 95% of the words they would need for their topics. But this information, while accurate, is misleading. At first glance, it may seem to suggest that studying 1,000 words would be sufficient to make David and Toni pretty good spellers. No so! A 5% error rate in finished writing is not satisfactory in either the business world or the world of schooling.

Of course, children must learn to spell correctly the most common words in the language, but this does not anywhere near approach spelling competence. Competent spelling requires the ability to spell many thousands of words correctly, perhaps as many as 20,000. In addition, children must also have a repertoire of spelling concepts and strategies at their command so that their spelling vocabulary can continue to grow throughout their lifetime, just as their oral vocabulary does.

WHAT ARE THE COMPONENTS OF AN EFFECTIVE SPELLING CURRICULUM?

An effective spelling curriculum consists of words and skills learned in the context of a rich oral and written language environment. This language environment includes direct instruction in spelling, wide reading in books and other materials of merit, and frequent writing that includes all of the elements of the writing process. An effective spelling curriculum enables children to learn words through a variety of routes: reading provides visual data; speaking provides auditory data; writing provides haptical data. A spelling curriculum should directly teach 8,000 to 10,000 words. In addition, it should teach spelling principles and patterns that will enable children to spell correctly additional thousands of words.

Reading, writing, speaking, and spelling are best learned through integrated language arts instruction. When this happens, most children will come to know and apply the principles that govern English spelling. For instance, there are principles that govern the affixing of base words, and there are derivational-meaning principles which assure that words are spelled consistently across changes in sound that come about when base words are affixed with prefixes or suffixes (combine/combination). Rote memorization of words and principles will not work in the long run, although in the short term they sometimes appear effective. Words and spelling principles should not be learned by rote, but rather in conjunction with known learning principles. Language learning must be meaningful, and it must be seen to be useful by its practitioner. This is why spelling cannot be isolated from its context and use; spelling is useful and meaningful only when it can be used for writing, which also must be seen as meaningful and useful to its practitioner.

ARE PRETESTING AND SELF-CORRECTION EFFECTIVE SPELLING STRATEGIES?

Pretesting and self-correction are among the most effective spelling strategies, yet they are often overlooked, perhaps because they are so challenging to teach. Pretesting and self-correction are excellent metacognitive learning strategies. *Metacognition* describes an old but excellent idea involving knowledge and control of one's own understanding or lack of it. Metacognition is knowing, and *knowing* you know, or not knowing, and *knowing* you do not know. A simpler term for metacognition is self-monitoring or self-regulation. Reflection and self-regulation are central components of growth in learning to spell. As children acquire skill in monitoring their own performance, they will gradually develop a spelling consciousness. It will take some time and effort to teach children how to apply this strategy. However, once they have gained experience with it, their spelling performance will begin to improve.

Good spellers usually know if a word they have spelled is right or wrong, whereas poor spellers usually do not. A promising way to improve spelling achievement of both good and poor spellers is to teach them to monitor their own spelling performance. Self-monitoring and reflection on one's performance develops greater awareness of spelling strengths and weaknesses. For example, students can learn to identify specific trouble spots in words. Over half a century ago, Gates (1937) showed that many common words have specific trouble spots that cause spelling difficulty.

A self-monitoring strategy works like this. After taking a pretest, teach students should peruse their list and divide their words into three categories before checking for correctness—known, unknown, and unsure. The following steps should be followed:

1. Place a check mark beside words you think you have spelled correctly–*known words.*
2. Place an X beside words you are fairly sure you may have misspelled—*unknown words.*
3. Place a question mark beside words, whose correctness or incorrectness you are unsure about—*uncertain words.*
4. After you have made your best guesses, compare your pretest spellings with a correct copy of the pretest words.
5. Decide how effective you were in monitoring your spelling correctness.
6. Practice all words you missed on the pretest.

CAN GOOD READERS BE POOR SPELLERS?

Anecdotal and research evidence shows that some good readers are poor spellers, although this is not common. It is more generally true that good readers are good spellers. Why this is not universal is not known. One is tempted to attribute this circumstance to normal individual variability, although this explains nothing about why it happens. Two explanations seem plausible.

First, there may have been little or no effective spelling instruction. While some children gain from reading an implicit understanding of the principles that govern spelling, others do not. This suggests that direct instruction about spelling principles may be especially useful to good readers who are poor spellers. Spelling instruction, whether direct or indirect, is a necessary condition for acquiring spelling knowledge for most students.

Second, good readers who are poor spellers may have had little or no opportunity to write during early formative years. Writing is the forum in which spelling knowledge is applied. When there is no application of learning, what is learned is easily forgotten. Writing is the only legitimate reason for learning to spell in the first place, and it is the only "real world" opportunity to practice spelling in a meaningful setting.

HOW CAN I HELP POOR SPELLERS?

Poor spellers can be helped. A diagnostic approach is essential so that you can identify the dimensions of the problem. The following four steps will get you started:

Step 1: Administering and analyze the results of diagnostic and placement spelling inventories. Also analyze misspellings in daily writing.

Morris Spelling Test: A list of 14 key spelling words (see Chapter 6).
Spelling placement test: A graded list of spelling words used to determine the grade level at which a student is operating (see Chapter 6).
Analyze misspelling in daily writing: Check samples of daily writing to see what words and linguistic patterns are commonly misspelled and spelled correctly.

Step 2: Analyze the results of the tests and daily writing. Try to answer these questions: What key words and patterns are misspelled and spelled correctly? What strengths and weaknesses are detectable? What is the highest instructional spelling level?

Step 3: Provide spelling instruction at the instructional spelling level. Check to ensure that word recognition capability and spelling instruction are congruent.

Step 4: Make the connection between spelling, reading, and writing. Success in spelling is more likely if spelling instruction, writing, and reading are integrated.

HOW CAN SPELLING INSTRUCTION BE ORGANIZED TO ACCOUNT FOR INDIVIDUAL DIFFERENCES?

Some students learn words more readily and rapidly than others. In a typical fifth-grade classroom, for instance, there will likely be students who can spell words at a seventh- or eighth-grade level. Others may be able to spell at only a third- or fourth-grade level. When spelling textbooks are used, the best way to accommodate different achievement levels is to assign textbooks commensurate with a student's spelling instructional level. However, some teachers and administrators are uncomfortable with this solution since it requires schoolwide implementation to work effectively. Another way to adjust instruction is to assign fewer words to students who are having difficulty performing at an instructional level with a given set of words. For instance, if a student is consistently unable to spell 65% or more of a list of 20 words at the end of a given period of time (usually a week) then try adjusting the number of words to 10 or 15. Determining the right number of words for any student can only be established through trial and error. Monitor progress on weekly tests, review tests, and spelling in written composition and make adjustments as needed.

Not all teachers use spelling books either because their schools cannot afford them or because they are philosophically opposed to spelling books. In such cases, it is still possible to accommodate individual differences by having students study more or fewer words according to their ability to master assigned or self-selected spelling words within the time frame established.

Whether spelling instruction is organized through the use of spelling textbooks, student-selected lists, or student–teacher selected lists, only those words students can read are suitable words for spelling. When students are required to spell words they cannot read or whose meaning they cannot fathom, they quickly forget such words, even though they may spell them correctly on a weekly test.

PERSPECTIVE AND SUMMARY

Andrew Jackson, a rough and ready man, is reported to have said, "It's a damn poor mind that can only think of one way to spell a word." I admire the cleverness of his statement and have, from time to time, thought that Jackson had me in mind when he said it. Andrew Jackson could probably get away with inconsistent and inaccurate spelling. Given the times in which he lived, "rough and ready" applied to spelling as much as to living generally. Abraham Lincoln and Andrew Jackson were extraordinarily eloquent men, although their spelling, now and again, could be pretty "rough and ready."

But Jackson and Lincoln lived in frontier days in America. The frontiers have moved on into the information age, to computers, to space travel. Rough and ready will no longer do. Accurate spelling is a necessity for most of us; it is a sign that we have acquired literacy. And while one should not, even in this day and age, assume that poor spelling is, *ipso facto*, a sure sign of illiteracy, it is definitely an academic and economic adjunct to literacy that we cannot afford to ignore.

REFERENCES

Cramer, R. L., & Cipielewski, J. F. (1995). Research in action: A study of spelling errors in 18,599 written compositions of children in grades 1–8. In *Spelling research and information: An overview of current research and practices* (pp. 11–52). Glenview, IL: Scott, Foresman.

Gates, A. (1937). *A list of spelling difficulties in 3876 words showing the "hard-spots," common misspellings, average spelling grade placement, and comprehension grade ratings of each word.* New York: Teachers College, Columbia University.

Appendices

APPENDIX A

100 Most Commonly Misspelled Words, Grade 1

Grade 1

because	what	end	school
when	our	pretty	dinosaurs
like	their	sometimes	is
they	nice	I'm	made
went	of	one	much
too	once	other	next
said	I	saw	night
there	some	thank	out
house	that	come	played
know	little	Easter	think
with	then	everybody	wanted
have	to	party	where
very	and	sister	witch
friend	part	but	your
my	for	came	babies
was	favorite	didn't	bird
would	get	girl	funny
are	Mom	good	got
want	birthday	will	teacher
friends	going	always	them
were	her	brother	a lot
people	outside	don't	after
about	the	home	again
Christmas	could	love	around
play	Dad	scared	before

APPENDIX B

100 Most Commonly Misspelled Words, Grade 2

Grade 2

because	that's	like	have
too	house	started	knew
they	Halloween	to	nice
when	with	some	one
there	very	it's	there's
went	baseball	took	watch
their	heard	special	always
Christmas	then	they're	aunt
people	what	through	brought
favorite	everybody	caught	children
friends	I	really	everything
were	and	other	getting
said	another	presents	happily
our	little	swimming	him
a lot	first	where	second
would	night	don't	something
upon	sometimes	family	wanted
know	thought	into	world
friend	want	them	believe
outside	two	tried	cheese
Easter	about	was	down
once	every	beautiful	great
again	whole	brother	haunted
didn't	before	different	hurt
scared	could	found	I'm

APPENDIX C

100 Most Commonly Misspelled Words, Grade 3

Grade 3

too	different	would	swimming
because	they're	brother	very
there	once	could	who
their	until	pretty	back
a lot	where	caught	first
Christmas	before	whole	into
were	presents	morning	school
said	we're	took	stopped
went	and	believe	animals
they	another	his	brought
favorite	sometimes	it's	family
when	didn't	started	let's
friend	heard	beautiful	Mom
know	little	two	about
that's	through	almost	around
upon	off	clothes	bought
with	outside	cousin	friend's
our	something	everything	happily
really	thought	getting	teacher
friends	Halloween	I'm	told
then	people	scared	coming
I	everybody	was	happened
always	want	what	tried
finally	house	everyone	are
again	one	found	girl

APPENDIX D

100 Most Commonly Misspelled Words, Grade 4

Grade 4

too	where	first	before
a lot	caught	watch	doesn't
because	chocolate	people	dollars
there	friend	always	every
their	into	took	found
favorite	everybody	everyone	maybe
that's	off	morning	once
our	through	school	other
when	friends	something	stopped
really	swimming	with	there's
they're	want	would	and
were	you're	are	bought
it's	another	enough	Easter
know	beautiful	except	getting
finally	I'm	friend's	going
again	let's	probably	little
they	then	upon	no
Christmas	believe	vacation	stuff
went	cousin	brought	together
until	especially	house	turned
outside	happened	might	usually
said	heard	myself	against
we're	I	basketball	birthday
sometimes	whole	hospital	break
different	didn't	opened	buy

APPENDIX E

100 Most Commonly Misspelled Words, Grade 5

Grade 5

a lot	probably	there's	excited
too	Christmas	thought	outside
their	to	upon	piece
there	when	usually	school
because	didn't	Dad	field
favorite	heard	knew	friend's
that's	then	sometimes	myself
finally	we're	want	since
our	everybody	which	family
they're	Mom	caught	grabbed
it's	everyone	let's	once
really	one	stopped	people
different	went	TV	right
where	decided	beautiful	should
again	especially	before	vacation
until	getting	buy	weird
friend	Halloween	Dad's	what's
they	off	doesn't	already
you're	always	everything	college
friends	whole	except	exciting
through	happened	tried	first
were	I'm	and	himself
believe	into	another	surprised
know	maybe	clothes	threw
something	said	don't	aren't

APPENDIX F

100 Most Commonly Misspelled Words, Grade 6

Grade 6

a lot	again	especially	Hawa
too	clothes	field	he's
it's	didn't	Florida	heard
because	everybody	friend	house
that's	off	grabbed	I
their	TV	since	I've
there	myself	something	into
you're	basketball	swimming	license
favorite	let's	to	met
were	there's	getting	no
everything	which	guess	now
finally	themselves	I'm	planet
our	then	know	someone
probably	always	one	sometim
they're	awhile	want	started
until	Christmas	went	stopped
different	doesn't	would	than
really	except	and	together
usually	outside	bored	upstairs
beautiful	when	can't	wear
college	whole	cousin's	what's
they	beginning	environment	wouldn't
through	business	exciting	anything
where	don't	friends	anyway
we're	elementary	happened	around

APPENDIX G

100 Most Commonly Misspelled Words, Grade 7

Grade 7

there	usually	no	happened
a lot	we're	restaurant	into
too	went	Saturday	knew
their	sometimes	someone	against
that's	through	there's	awhile
it's	which	beautiful	clothes
because	doesn't	can't	field
don't	favorite	Mom's	friend's
probably	heard	outside	going to
they're	different	thought	minutes
Easter	everything	whole	morning
they	again	without	people
you're	believe	and	remember
finally	except	another	right
our	something	basketball	supposed
Christmas	were	beginning	to
off	always	couldn't	tomorrow
where	anything	Friday	trying
Halloween	especially	grabbed	upstairs
didn't	everyone	relatives	what's
until	friends	vacation	backyard
buy	everywhere	wasn't	before
let's	around	college	caught
really	everybody	Dad's	coming
then	maybe	downstairs	cousin's

APPENDIX H

100 Most Commonly Misspelled Words, Grade 8

Grade 8

a lot	going to	maybe	again
too	through	now	anyway
it's	they	wear	awhile
you're	to	business	coming
their	which	since	except
that's	different	were	happened
there	everything	couldn't	heard
they're	believe	downstairs	knew
because	Christmas	families	one
probably	clothes	friend's	separated
don't	I'm	into	thought
we're	no one	lose	tried
finally	our	restaurant	whole
there's	than	what's	about
where	especially	whether	aren't
can't	let's	without	cannot
usually	then	your	Dad's
doesn't	weird	beautiful	decided
really	favorite	definitely	every day
allowed	friends	everyone	everywhere
didn't	know	friend	experience
off	outside	grabbed	Grandma's
TV	always	hear	having
until	beginning	no	myself
something	college	people	nowhere

APPENDIX I

55 Error Categories for Classifying Misspelled Words

Following are the 55 categories that were used for classifying misspelled words in Research in Action, with examples of the types of spelling errors that were classified in each error type.

Vowel Errors

1. Long *a* (*age, braid*)
2. Long *e* (*be, complete*)
3. Long *i* (*five, sky*)
4. Long *o* (*open, oak*)
5. /ü/ (*rule, move*)
6. Short *a* (*hat, plaid*)
7. Short *e* (*let, said*)
8. Short *i* (*it, pin*)
9. Short *o* (*hot, watch*)
10. Short *u* (*cup, flood*)
11. /ä/ (*father, heart*)
12. /ô/ (*all, more, bought*)
13. /ù/ (*full, good*)
14. /oi/ (*boy, voice*)
15. /ou/ (*house, owl*)
16. /yü/ (*few, music*)
17. /èr/ (*bird, word*)
18. /ə/ final syllable (*middle, angel*)
19. /ə/ others (*favorite*)
20. Silent *e*, long vowel (*rode*)
21. Silent *e*, other (*love, have*)
22. Silent *e*, overgeneralized (*had—hade*)

Consonant Errors

23. Consonant substitution (*cat—kat*)
24. Single consonant, doubled (*city—citty*)
25. Double consonant in root (*little—litle*)
26. Consonant blend (*bump—bup*)
27. Consonant digraph (*patch—pach*)
28. Silent consonant (*wrong—rong*)
29. Complex consonant (*stomach—stomak*)

Word Structure Errors: Affixes

30. Prefix (*misspell—mispell*)
31. Suffix (*nervous—nerves*)
32. *y* to *i* + suffix (*happily—happyly*)
33. Final *e* + suffix (*argument—arguement*)
34. Doubled consonant + suffix (*finally—finaly*)

Word Structure Errors: Inflected Endings

(-ed, -ing, -er, -est, -s, -es)

35. Inflected spelling (*looked—lookd*)
36. *y* to *i* + inflected ending (*cried—cryed*)
37. Final *e* + inflected ending (*posing—poseing*)
38. Double consonant with inflected ending (*hated—hatted*)

Compound

39. Compound word spelling (*everything—everthing*)
40. Compound wrongly joined/hyphenated (*baby-sit—babysit*)
41. Compound wrongly separated (*outside—out side*)
42. Wrongly run together/separated (*because—be cause; a lot—alot*)

Usage Convention

43. Capitalization (*Iowa—iowa*)
44. Abbreviation (*Feb.—Febre*)
45. Homophone (*too—to—two*)
46. Easily confused pairs (*where—were*)
47. Regularizing irregulars (*ran—runned*)
48. Apostrophe with possessive (*mom's—moms*)
49. Apostrophe with contraction (*didn't—didnt*)

Twilight Zone Errors

50. Added letters (*athlete—athalete*)
51. Omitted letters (*probably—probly*)
52. Repeated sequence (*remember—rememeber*)
53. Scrambled letters (*only—olny*)
54. Truncated or bizarre (50% or more omitted: *because—bcz*)
55. Mispronunciation (*want to—wanna*)

APPENDIX J

Error Categories by Grade Levels and Total Sample

Primary 1–3	Intermediate 4–6	Upper 7–8	Total Sample
1. consonant substitution	omitted letters	homophones	omitted letters
2. omitted letters	homophones	omitted letters	homophones
3. short *e*	consonant substitution	schwa (other)	consonant substitution
4. consonant blend	scrambled letters	scrambled letters	scrambled letters
5. long *e*	schwa (other)	consonant substitution	schwa (other)
6. schwa (final syllable)	run together/separated	run together/separated	short *e*
7. scrambled letters	long *e*	apostrophe with contraction	long *e*
8. homophones	short *e*	compound wrongly separated	schwa (final syllable)
9. consonant digraph	schwa (final syllable)	long *e*	consonant blend
10. inflected spelling	compound wrongly separated	short *e*	run together/separated
11. complex consonant	added letters	schwa (final syllable)	consonant digraph
12. short *i*	consonant blend	double consonant in root	added letters
13. schwa (other)	apostrophe with contraction	capitalization	short *i*
14. vowel: /ô/	short *i*	short *i*	double consonant in root
15. added letters	double consonant in root	consonant digraph	inflected spelling
16. double consonant in root	consonant digraph	added letters	compound wrongly separated
17. long *a*	inflected spelling	single consonant doubled	apostrophe with contraction
18. silent *e*–overgeneralized	complex consonant	consonant blend	complex consonant
19. silent *e*–other	single consonant doubled	apostrophe with possessive	vowel: /ô/
20. short *u*	capitalization	inflected spelling	capitalization
21. silent *e*–long vowel	vowel: /ô/	complex consonant	long *a*
22. long *i*	silent *e*–overgeneralized	double consonant + inflected end	silent *e*–overgeneralized
23. run together/separated	long *a*	long *a*	single consonant doubled
24. capitalization	double consonant + inflected end	silent e–overgeneralized	silent *e*–other
25. truncated/bizarre	apostrophe with possessive	vowel: /ô/	short *u*
26. vowel: /ėr/	silent *e*–other	compound wrongly joined	apostrophe with possessive
27. single consonant doubled	compound word spelling	easily confused pairs	long *i*
28. compound wrongly separated	short *u*	suffix spelling	silent *e*–long vowel
29. apostrophe with contraction	easily confused pairs	compound word spelling	double consonant + inflected end
30. long *o*	long *i*	mispronunciation	compound word spelling
31. compound word spelling	suffix spelling	short *u*	vowel: /ėr/
32. vowel: /ou/	silent *e*–long vowel	vowel: /ü/	long *o*
33. short *o*	long *o*	double consonant + suffix	easily confused pairs
34. short *a*	compound wrongly joined	silent *e*–other	vowel: /ü/
35. silent consonant	vowel: /ėr/	*y* to *i* + inflected ending	suffix spelling
36. vowel: /ü/	mispronunciation	final *e* + suffix	truncated/bizarre
37. final *e* + inflected ending	double consonant + suffix	silent consonant	silent consonant
38. double consonant + inflected end	vowel: /ü/	long *o*	mispronunciation
39. vowel: /ů/	silent consonant	long *i*	compound wrongly joined
40. mispronunciation	final *e* + inflected ending	vowel: /ėr/	final *e* + inflected ending
41. apostrophe with possessive	*y* to *i* + inflected ending	silent *e*–long vowel	double consonant + suffix
42. easily confused pairs	truncated/bizarre	final *e* + inflected ending	vowel: /ou/
43. suffix spelling	final *e* + suffix	regularizing irregulars	*y* to *i* + inflected ending
44. vowel: /ă/	short *a*	truncated/bizarre	short *o*
45. *y* to *i* + inflected ending	vowel: /ou/	short *a*	short *a*
46. double consonant + suffix	short *o*	short *o*	vowel: /ů/
47. compound wrongly joined	regularized irregulars	vowel: /ou/	final *e* + suffix
48. regularizing irregulars	vowel: /ů/	vowel: /ă/	regularizing irregulars
49. vowel: /yü/	repeated sequence	vowel: /yü/	vowel: /ă/
50. repeated sequence	vowel: /yü/	prefix spelling	vowel: /yü/
51. vowel: /oi/	vowel: /ă/	vowel: /ů/	repeated sequence
52. final *e* + suffix	prefix spelling	repeated sequence	prefix spelling
53. *y* to *i* + suffix	abbreviation	abbreviation	abbreviation
54. prefix spelling	*y* to *i* + suffix	*y* to *i* + suffix	vowel: /oi/
55. abbreviation	vowel: /oi/	vowel: /oi/	*y* to *i* + suffix

Index